The Gulf Cooperation Council at Forty

The Gulf Cooperation Council at Forty

*Risk and Opportunity
in a Changing World*

Edited by
TARIK M. YOUSEF
ADEL ABDEL GHAFAR

BROOKINGS INSTITUTION PRESS
Washington, D.C.

Published by Brookings Institution Press
1775 Massachusetts Avenue, NW
Washington, DC 20036
www.brookings.edu/bipress

Co-published by Rowman & Littlefield
An imprint of The Rowman & Littlefield Publishing Group, Inc.
4501 Forbes Boulevard, Suite 200, Lanham, Maryland 20706
www.rowman.com

86-90 Paul Street, London EC2A 4NE

The Brookings Institution is a nonprofit organization devoted to research, education, and publication on important issues of domestic and foreign policy. Its principal purpose is to bring the highest quality independent research and analysis to bear on current and emerging policy problems.

British Library Cataloguing in Publication Information Available

Library of Congress Cataloging-in-Publication Data

ISBN: 978-0-8157-4005-6 (cloth)
ISBN: 978-0-8157-3953-1 (paperback)
ISBN: 978-0-8157-3954-8 (electronic)

♾™ The paper used in this publication meets the minimum requirements of American National Standard for Information Sciences—Permanence of Paper for Printed Library Materials, ANSI/NISO Z39.48-1992

To Layla & Laila

Contents

PART 5
GEOSTRATEGIC CONCERNS

Acknowledgments

IN MARCH 2019, the Brookings Doha Center and the Hollings Center for International Dialogue held a two-day conference in Muscat, Oman, where the idea for this volume germinated. We gratefully acknowledge the support of the Hollings Center, which helped initiate the conference that made the research and writing of this volume possible.

We are especially grateful to the authors who contributed to this volume during the COVID-19 pandemic in 2020–2021, which caused several delays to the project. We appreciate their efforts and patience as well as those of the reviewers and editors. We also appreciate the support we have received from the Brookings Doha Center's team, especially from research assistant Theodosia Rossi, who helped manage the project from the start and provided excellent editorial support. We would also like to acknowledge our BDC colleagues Nejla Ben Mimoune, Ghadeer Abu Ali, Nadine Masri, and Al Hasan Zwayne for their support. We are also indebted to our intern Hana El Shehaby who supported the final phase of the project.

This is not our first collaboration with Brookings Institution Press, and we continue to be indebted to them for their efforts supporting our research. In particular, we would like to acknowledge William Finan and Elliott Beard. We also thank production editor Angela Piliouras at Westchester Publishing Services and copyeditor Janet Mowery for all their hard work on the volume.

Most important, this volume would not have been possible without the support of our families, for whom we are forever grateful. During work on this project, Adel Abdel Ghafar was blessed with baby Laila, which is also the name of Tarik M. Yousef's daughter Layla, and thus the book is dedicated to both of them.

The Gulf Cooperation Council at Forty

ONE

Introduction

The GCC in Transition

TARIK M. YOUSEF
ADEL ABDEL GHAFAR

IN 2021, THE GULF COOPERATION Council (GCC) marked the fortieth anniversary of its founding. Its member states, the Kingdom of Saudi Arabia (KSA), the United Arab Emirates (UAE), Kuwait, Qatar, Oman, and Bahrain, are undergoing historic economic transitions. Over the past decade, they have faced enormous strains on their public finance systems due to fluctuating oil prices, demographic pressures, limited economic diversification, and an uncertain external environment. Since the collapse of oil prices in 2014, they have sustained public spending by shrinking the size of their sovereign wealth and increasing debt levels through international borrowing. These pressures have created a strong incentive for policy reform efforts aimed at stabilizing fiscal imbalances, addressing structural rigidities and rationalizing welfare programs.

The emergence of the COVID-19 pandemic in early 2020 disrupted forecasts of an economic recovery. Closely linked to early hotspots by air transit hubs, the Gulf states saw the arrival of the novel coronavirus before the World Health Organization (WHO) declared a pandemic. Despite rigorous efforts to combat the spread of COVID-19, they were not able to prevent a sharp rise in infection rates. The pandemic has come at a tremendous economic cost that exposed the vulnerabilities of the GCC to the resultant oil price shock, the disruption in global supply chains, and the complexities of hosting a large population of guest workers. Their full recovery from the pandemic recession will depend not only on the trajectory of international oil prices but also on their ability to effect reforms to a more resilient economic model.[1]

In addition, global shifts in energy supply and demand continue apace, as the international community struggles with the competing policy objectives of reducing carbon emissions, growing the developing world's access to modern energy, and enabling technological innovation in renewable sources. The ongoing global drive to combat climate change creates further uncertainty for the GCC economies. In particular, an accelerated energy transition away from fossil fuels means that over the next few decades GCC states will have to prepare their economies for a post-oil future.[2] The magnitude of policy adjustment to their redistributive systems that would be required over a short time horizon would be unprecedented, with far-reaching political economy implications for state-society relations.

Compounding these challenges, global and regional geopolitical and security uncertainties continue to mount, with significant implications for the Gulf and the wider Middle East. Perceptions of US withdrawal from the region under the Obama administration were reenforced by the hasty withdrawal of American forces from Afghanistan.[3] With growing concerns about the commitment of the US to Gulf security, member states have started diversifying their security partnerships with regional powers, including Israel (with Bahrain and the UAE)[4] and Turkey (with Qatar), as well as building up their domestic defense and security capabilities through expanded technological cooperation with China.

KSA and the UAE have responded to their security concerns over the past decade by adopting a more interventionist approach in the post–Arab Spring political transitions and civil wars in the Middle East.[5] The ensuing geopolitical competition with other regional actors—Iran, Turkey, and Qatar—destabilized other countries and pushed the GCC itself to the brink of collapse in 2017 when KSA, the UAE, and Bahrain together with Egypt imposed a blockade on Qatar. Four years later, in 2021, strategic exhaustion, reputational damage, military stalemates, a new US administration, and the COVID-19-induced economic recession created the conditions to end the blockade on Qatar and deescalate regional confrontation without resolving the underlying sources of discord.

The next decade of the twenty-first century will increasingly be defined by the US-China rivalry in the Indo-Pacific and across the globe, including in the Gulf. Meanwhile, Russia is expanding its relevance to Middle Eastern energy and security needs while Iran, Turkey, and Israel are attempting to fill the void created by the US withdrawal from the region. In the absence of stable security arrangements, GCC states will need to delicately balance relations with global powers and recalibrate engagement with aspiring regional players. After a prolonged period of divergent political views and foreign policies that bred mistrust and undermined coordination, they will also be increasingly forced to overcome national preferences if they hope to restore collective action in responding to security threats.

Taken together, this myriad of economic, political, and security challenges at the domestic, regional, and global levels will require GCC policymakers to navigate multiple sources of external uncertainty while steering domestic reforms to manage change and ensure future prosperity. In turn, they will need to adjust their policymaking institutions and tools to become more innovative, agile, and sustainable in order to develop and implement long-term solutions. How will global megatrends impact Gulf states and societies? How will countries diversify economies to deal with the consequences of the energy transition? How can labor markets accommodate growing cohorts of skilled youth and women? How will GCC relations with international and regional actors shift in the coming years? How can the GCC states achieve deeper integration and policy coordination?

To help answer these questions, in 2019 the Brookings Doha Center (BDC) and the Hollings Center convened a two-day expert roundtable in Muscat, Oman, that brought together policymakers, academics, think tank representatives, civil society actors, and private sector professionals. Participants in the workshop, as well as other experts, were invited to contribute forward-looking, policy-oriented chapters to this volume, which focuses on key socioeconomic, political, and security issues and trends shaping the GCC's future.

Structure of the Volume

This volume is divided into five parts. Following the introduction, Part 1 focuses on global trends and their consequences for the Gulf region. In chapter 2, Aidyn Bibolov, Tim Callen, and Tian Zhang consider the impact of the global economy and argue that the difficult short-term outlook and other longer-term factors reinforce the need to push ahead with domestic reforms to better enable economies to weather challenges. In chapter 3, Rory Miller focuses on US leadership and Gulf security in a multipolar world. He posits that while the United States will remain the major security provider for its Gulf allies in the foreseeable future, it will be operating in an increasingly multipolar system. In chapter 4, Steven Wright looks at the changing patterns of global energy markets, arguing that changes in the energy sector are ushering GCC states into uncharted territory, with implications for the Gulf region and global politics.

In chapter 5, Samantha Gross presents an integrated approach to climate change and economic diversification. She argues that GCC countries must participate in the global response to climate change in ways that drive economic diversification and make their economies more sustainable. In chapter 6, Adel Abdel Ghafar looks at the evolution of Sino-Gulf engagement and suggests that in order to deepen relations, Chinese and GCC policymakers will have to navigate a complex set of regional and international factors that may limit their engagement. In chapter 7, Tarik M. Yousef looks at the impact of the COVID-19 pandemic on the Gulf through an assessment of the public health and economic impact, the institutional and policy response, and the long-term development implications.

Part 2 covers the transition underway in the Gulf economies. In chapter 8, Nader Habibi assesses the level of economic cooperation among GCC countries, focusing on how economic relations have evolved in the aftermath of the Qatar crisis and how to restore the drive for deeper integration. In chapter 9, Jean-François Seznec looks at financial markets and offers policy recommendations for how Gulf financial markets can play a larger role in regional development. In chapter 10, Martin Hvidt assesses economic diversification across the GCC, arguing that present challenges make it necessary for countries to immediately enact forward-looking diversification policies in order to prevent future crises.

In chapter 11, Robert P. Beschel Jr. focuses on the governance of economic and fiscal policy in the GCC. He argues that while governments have frequently resorted to institutional reorganization in order to strengthen policy integration, they should learn from and scale regional success stories in order to address developmental challenges more holistically. In chapter 12, Sara Bazoobandi and Theodosia Rossi address the shift in sovereign wealth fund strategies in the GCC over the past decade and argue that wealth management strategies should focus on minimizing government expenditures. In chapter 13, Irfan Aleem considers challenges of transition to a post-oil future in the GCC, emphasizing the structural reforms needed to help achieve fiscal sustainability and intergenerational equity.

Part 3 focuses on Gulf labor markets. In chapter 14, Samer Kherfi discusses labor market dynamics and policy responses. He argues that the main policy challenge at present is how to reconcile private sector conditions with the career expectations and skills of job seekers. In chapter 15, Marvin Erfuth and Natasha Ridge examine the development of human capital. They underscore that if Gulf countries are to become knowledge-based economies, they must address improving education quality and students' performance and investing more in research. In chapter 16, Karen Young writes about the role of women in the workforce. She argues that the challenge facing the Gulf countries is matching the skills and aspirations of young women with opportunities for advancement in government and private sector organizations.

In chapter 17, Nader Kabbani examines the pervasiveness of youth unemployment in many Gulf countries and recommends the implementation of higher work permit fees for foreigners and limited wage subsidies with on-the-job training for nationals. In chapter 18, Imco Brouwer focuses on Gulf population dynamics, employment characteristics, and foreign workers. He recommends that systematic and periodic research be conducted among migrant workers in order to determine whether policies targeting them have been effective. In chapter 19, Noha Aboueldahab writes about social protection for migrant laborers in the GCC. She articulates three key requirements that should be implemented simultaneously to ensure that legislative labor reforms are enforced and practiced.

Part 4 tackles state-society relations in the Gulf. In chapter 20, Kristian Coates Ulrichsen considers the politics of economic reform, arguing that the social and political components of reform will need to be closely interlinked in order to change the relationship between citizen and state in eventual "post-rentier" polities. In chapter 21, Matthew Gray revisits the topic of late rentierism. He posits that, while certain genuine changes are under way in the Gulf, ultimately these are designed to maintain the existing political order, not to upset it. In chapter 22, Steffen Hertog makes the case for why the GCC's economic diversification challenges are unique. He argues that diversification will require cautious experimentation and gradual reformulation of the social contract to reduce distortions while maintaining living standards.

In chapter 23, Courtney Freer considers the relationship between representation, parliaments, and austerity programs in the Gulf. She makes the case that legislative political structures help explain the variation in compliance with proposed austerity measures across countries. In chapter 24, Sean Foley writes about art and social change in Saudi Arabia. He proposes that the country's creative class seek to express the views of the Saudi masses while proposing new ways to discuss challenges, enabling them to illuminate solutions that others cannot. In chapter 25, Geneive Abdo explores the topic of sectarian relations in the GCC. She argues that sectarianism will likely be a characteristic of the region for the foreseeable future and that space for religious contestation within Islam has perhaps never been greater.

Part 5 deals with geostrategic concerns in the Gulf. In chapter 26, Yasmina Abouzzohour examines some of the key challenges affecting the relations between GCC states, and how they can be overcome. In chapter 27, Zach Vertin explores the ramifications of the Gulf Arab crisis in the Horn of Africa. He argues that the crisis has catalyzed new geopolitical competition in the Red Sea region and that African states have both welcomed the new attention and struggled to manage the accompanying strife. In chapter 28, Ibrahim Fraihat seeks to answer the question of whether the Iran-Saudi conflict is resolvable. He posits that the escalation of the conflict is driven by security, sectarianism, and the involvement of the US administration.

In chapter 29, Rami Khouri reflects on the state of GCC-Arab relations after the Arab uprisings, highlighting the impact of GCC states' interventions in various flash points, conflicts, and transitions across the region. In chapter 30, Perla Srour-Gandon addresses the topic of relations between the GCC and the European Union (EU). She argues that while these relations were initially based on economic and trade engagement, recent developments have proved that they should become more strategic. In chapter 31, Omar Rahman examines the topic of GCC-Israel relations. He argues that relations between most Gulf states and Israel are not new or uniform, but that changes in regional dynamics have given some GCC members a new strategic imperative to draw closer to their former adversary. The concluding chapter 32 examines future challenges from the perspective of collective action among member states and makes the case for deeper integration and policy coordination, including through reform of the GCC organization.

Notes

1. International Monetary Fund, "Regional Economic Outlook: Arising from the Pandemic: Building Forward Better," (Washington, October 2021) (https://www.imf.org/en/Publications/REO/MECA/Issues/2021/04/11/regional-economic-outlook-middle-east-central-asia).

2. M. T. N. Mirzoev and others, *The Future of Oil and Fiscal Sustainability in the GCC Region* (Washington, International Monetary Fund, 2020).

3. Charles Dunne, "The Biden Administration Contemplates a New Pivot to Asia" (Washington: Arab Center, February 23, 2021) (https://arabcenterdc.org/resource/the-biden-administration-contemplates-a-new-pivot-to-asia/).

4. Omar Rahman, "The Emergence of GCC-Israel Relations in a Changing Middle East," Policy Note (Doha, Qatar: Brookings Doha Center, July 28, 2021) (https://www.brookings.edu/research/the-emergence-of-gcc-israel-relations-in-a-changing-middle-east/).

5. See, e.g., M. Darwich, "Escalation in Failed Military Interventions: Saudi and Emirati Quagmires in Yemen," *Global Policy* 11, no. 1 (2020), pp. 103–12; M. Dunne, "Fear and Learning in the Arab Uprisings" *Journal of Democracy* 31, no. 1 (2020), pp. 182–92; K. E. Young, "A New Politics of GCC Economic Statecraft: The Case of UAE Aid and Financial Intervention in Egypt," *Journal of Arabian Studies* 7, no. 1 (2017), pp. 113–36; and R. Ziadah, "The Importance of the Saudi-UAE Alliance: Notes on Military Intervention, Aid and Investment," *Conflict, Security & Development* 19, no. 3 (2019), pp. 295–300.

PART 1

GLOBAL TRENDS AND THEIR IMPACT ON THE GCC

TWO

The Global Economy and the GCC

AIDYN BIBOLOV
TIM CALLEN
TIAN ZHANG

THE COVID-19 PANDEMIC LED to an unprecedented global recession in 2020. As governments across the world implemented restrictions on activities in an attempt to contain the pandemic, the global economy contracted sharply. At the time of writing, a robust growth rebound had taken place in 2021, but there is still uncertainty and considerable risk to the outlook. This is related both to the future path of the pandemic, as well as to the scarring the crisis will leave as labor markets take time to heal, investment is held back by uncertainty and balance sheet problems, and lost schooling impairs human capital.

Transmission Channels from the Global Economy
to the GCC Countries

The global economy affects the GCC countries through trade and financial channels. GCC countries are heavily dependent on the export of oil and gas, for which both prices and export quantities are affected by global conditions.[1] A large share of domestic demand is met by the import of goods and services, while local production is heavily reliant on expatriate labor. The influence of global financial market conditions is also growing in the region. Governments and firms in most GCC countries have increased their

Figure 2-1. GCC GDP Growth, Current Account, and Fiscal Balances, 2012–2020

GCC current account and fiscal balance, 2012–2020

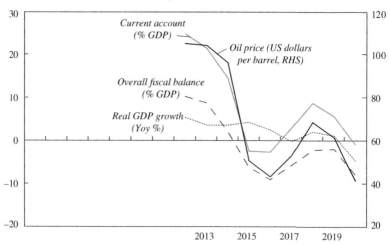

Sources: Country authorities and IMF staff calculations.
Notes: Yoy = year over year; RHS = right-hand side.

external borrowing, and there is now greater connection to global financial markets through inclusion in global bond and equity indexes (as well as, in some cases, through the GCC's role as a regional financial center). In addition, both the public and private sectors hold large foreign assets whose value moves with global financial market conditions.

The most important transmission channel is the global oil market. Oil gross domestic product (GDP) makes up about 30 percent of total GDP on average in GCC countries, while non-oil growth is heavily dependent on government spending, which is financed from oil revenues. Oil revenues constitute about 65 percent of fiscal revenues and oil exports around 52 percent of total export revenues (all figures are 2015–2019 averages). Over time, there has been a notable correlation between oil prices, GCC fiscal and external balances, and real GDP growth (see figure 2-1). From 2000 to 2013, GCC oil export revenues grew by an average of 12 percent a year and supported an average increase in government spending of 11 percent a year. In turn, real GDP growth averaged 4.9 percent (non-oil growth: 7 percent) a year during this period. As oil export revenues declined between 2014 and 2019 by an average of 8.3 percent a year, government spending declined by an average of 1.3 percent a year and real GDP growth slowed to an average of 2.1 percent (non-oil growth: 3 percent) a year. The GCC fiscal balance fell from an average surplus of 9.9 percent of GDP between 2000 and 2013 to a deficit of 5 percent of GDP between 2014 and 2019, while the current account surplus declined from an average of 16.5 percent of GDP to 3.9 percent of GDP.

In response to the spread of COVID-19, GCC countries implemented strict lockdown measures starting in March 2020, before undertaking a gradual reopening of their economies, with most activities resuming by fall 2020. To mitigate the economic impact of the pandemic, GCC countries introduced a range of supportive policy measures, including providing liquidity to banks, extending the repayment period for bank loans—particularly for small and medium-sized enterprises (SMEs)—reducing fees and deferring taxes for businesses, and extending social benefits to households. Policy interest rates were reduced following the US Federal Reserve rate cuts in line with the pegged exchange rate regimes. These policy measures helped blunt the economic impact of the pandemic, but GCC non-oil growth is still estimated to have contracted by 3.9 percent in 2020. Service-oriented sectors, such as airlines, tourism, and hospitality were particularly badly affected owing to cross-border travel restrictions.

The COVID-19 pandemic led to an abrupt decline in global oil demand. The fall in demand and initial supply increases saw Brent oil prices fall to around $20 a barrel in mid-April 2020, before recovering and subsequently surging to over $100 a barrel in early 2022. As part of the OPEC+ agreement, GCC countries reduced their oil production, resulting in a sharp decline in real oil GDP in 2020. Further, the decline in oil revenues contributed to deterioration in the GCC fiscal and current account balances. Nevertheless, as OPEC+ started returning production to the market in 2021, oil GDP began to recover.

Financial inflows into the GCC increased 2.6 times between 2013 and 2019. Since the beginning of 2019, five GCC countries have joined Oman in the J. P. Morgan Emerging Market Bond Index (EMBI), and Saudi Arabia has joined the MSCI Emerging Markets Index (together with Qatar and the United Arab Emirates) and the FTSE Russell emerging equity index (together with Kuwait, Qatar, and the UAE). Foreign ownership in the Saudi stock market increased by $29 billion between December 2018 and September 2020, almost tripling the share of foreign ownership in the market. This was also driven by the listing of shares in Saudi Aramco, the national oil company, on the domestic stock exchange. At the same time, several GCC sovereign wealth funds continued with high-profile investments abroad.

Policies to Mitigate the Effects of Global Shocks
and to Strengthen Non-Oil Growth

The volatility in global oil markets and longer-term factors such as the on-going shift toward greener sources of energy that may eventually reduce demand for oil reinforce the need to push ahead with domestic reforms to better enable the GCC economies to weather such developments. Fiscal policy needs to continue to adjust to become more resilient to volatility in global oil markets; further structural reforms are necessary to promote private sector development and reduce the dependence of economies on government spending; and consideration will need to be given to how best to manage increased financial flows into the region. GCC countries have long recognized the importance of encouraging sustained private sector growth and diversification, and all have development plans that aim to move their economies in this direction.

Governments will need to keep tight control of their spending and raise additional revenues from non-oil sources to reduce their dependency on oil while ensuring the incomes of the less well-off are protected from adverse effects of reforms. This will entail tackling high government wage bills, ensuring capital spending is targeted at essential development needs, further raising domestic energy prices where they remain below international levels, and implementing broad-based taxes such as the value-added tax (VAT) where they are still absent.[2] Medium-term fiscal frameworks need to be developed to strengthen fiscal planning, delink spending decisions from swings in oil prices, and enable the clear communication of fiscal intentions to businesses and investors. The procyclicality of government spending that has been evident in the past should be reduced; spending should be maintained at a level that is sustainable across different oil price environments. Otherwise, large adjustments in spending will be needed during times of low oil prices, which cause undue volatility in growth.

The incentives facing workers and businesses have been affected by the distribution of oil revenues in the economy. Significant wage and benefit gaps skew the supply of national labor toward the public sector and the demand for labor in the private sector toward expatriates.[3] These preferences are amplified by working conditions, including a shorter work week for government employees and the perceived stability of public sector employment. Education and skills also play a key role—nationals are often perceived as not having the skills needed by the private sector, while the desire for public sector work skews educational choices. Analysis suggests there is a considerable gap between the wages and productivity of nationals in GCC countries.[4] For businesses, it has been less risky and more profitable to use the ready supply of low-skilled and low-wage expatriate labor to produce nontradables in sectors like construction that are heavily reliant on government spending.

The public sector can no longer be the employer of first resort for nationals, and as spending adjusts, government contracts will be less easily available for private sector firms. This means that nationals will increasingly need to find jobs in the private sector and private businesses will need to become more resilient and self-sustaining in the absence of growth in government spending.

GCC countries already have in place many features that are favorable to private sector development. Infrastructure is generally very good, taxes are low, and populations are young and growing. Governments, however, can do more to support the private sector, encourage tradable production, and promote investment.[5] Growth payoffs are likely to come from market reforms that focus on business competition, regulations, and property rights. Improving the business environment and reducing trade barriers (including in the services sector) will help boost competition. Ensuring that exporters have adequate access to finance, are supported with market information, and are not hamstrung by too many restrictions will encourage businesses to look for markets overseas rather than just focusing on home. Improving financial access, particularly for young and growing companies, women, and youth, will also support growth in the non-oil sector.[6]

Labor market reforms are essential. The competitiveness of national workers in the private sector will need to increase. This will require better education and training to equip workers with the skills in demand by the private sector. Allowing more flexibility for expatriate workers to move between jobs will also begin to erode some of the advantages that businesses see in employing expatriates over nationals. This is already beginning to happen as some countries move to ease or remove restrictions imposed through the sponsorship (kafala) system. The government itself needs to clearly communicate with the population that public sector job opportunities will be more limited in the future. This will help reduce the reservation wage for nationals to take private sector jobs. Companies themselves will need to do more to offer attractive working conditions, such as on-the-job training and a greater focus on career development. In addition, despite recent important gains, female participation in the workforce remains far too low in most GCC countries. Women are as well educated as men, and continuing to bring women into the workforce will help boost productivity and growth.

Lastly, with GCC economies looking to attract more foreign investment to help finance fiscal deficits and support private sector development, they will integrate further into global financial markets. Deep and robust financial markets, together with strong financial sector regulation and supervision and liquidity management frameworks, will help reap the benefits and reduce the risks that will come with this greater financial integration.[7]

Notes

The views expressed in this chapter are those of the authors and do not necessarily represent the views of the IMF, its Executive Board, or IMF management.

1. In the chapter, the term *oil* is used to cover both oil and gas. Qatar has substantial gas output and exports.

2. See the following reports for more details on these policies: International Monetary Fund (IMF), "Diversifying Government Revenues in the GCC: Next Steps" (Washington, 2016); IMF, "Strengthening Liquidity Management Frameworks in Support of Stability and Growth in the GCC" (Washington, December 14, 2017) (www.imf.org/en/Publications/Policy-Papers/Issues/2017/12/14/pp121417gcc-liquidity -management-frameworks); IMF, "How Can Growth-Friendlier Expenditure-Based Fiscal Adjustment Be Achieved in the GCC?" (Washington, December 14, 2017) (www.imf.org/en/Publications/Policy-Papers/Issues/2017/12/14/pp121417gcc -expenditure-based-fiscal-adjustement); IMF, "How Developed and Inclusive Are Financial Systems in the GCC?" (Washington, December 6, 2018) (https://www.imf .org/en/Publications/Policy-Papers/Issues/2018/12/04/pp120618gcc-how-developed -and-inclusive-are-financial-systems-in-the-gcc#:~:text=%D8%A7%D9%84%D8%B 9%D8%B1%D8%A8%D9%8A%D8%A9-,Gulf%20Cooperation%20Council%3A%20 How%20Developed%20and%20Inclusive,Financial%20Systems%20in%20the%20 GCC%3F&text=Financial%20development%20in%20the%20GCC,to%20 equity%20markets%20is%20narrow.); IMF, "Trade and Foreign Investment— Keys to Diversification and Growth in the GCC" (Washington, December 6, 2018) (www.imf.org/en/Publications/Policy-Papers/Issues/2018/12/04/pp120618gcc-trade -and-foreign-investment).

3. London School of Economics Middle East Centre, "The Political Economy of Labour Markets and Migration in the Gulf," Workshop Proceedings, August 2016 (http://eprints.lse.ac.uk/67919/1/Labour%20and%20Migration%20Report.pdf); Steffen Hertog, ed., *National Employment, Migration, and Education in the GCC* (Berlin: Gerlach Press, 2012) (https://doi.org/10.2307/j.ctt1s474nj).

4. See Divya Kirti, "Policies to Drive Diversification for Saudi Arabia," in "Saudi Arabia—Selected Issues," IMF Country Report No. 19/291 (Washington, September 2019) (www.imf.org/~/media/Files/Publications/CR/2019/1SAUEA2019002.ashx).

5. See IMF, "How Developed and Inclusive are Financial Systems in the GCC?"; IMF, "Trade and Foreign Investment."

6. Ibid.

7. See IMF, "Strengthening Liquidity Management Frameworks in Support of Stability and Growth in the GCC"; IMF, "How Can Growth-Friendlier Expenditure-Based Fiscal Adjustment Be Achieved in the GCC?"

THREE

US Leadership and Gulf Security in a Multipolar World

RORY MILLER

THE UNITED STATES WILL remain the major supplier of security for its Gulf allies into the foreseeable future. Nevertheless, subsequent US administrations will operate in an increasingly multipolar system in which the power differential will continue to shrink, when measured in either material terms or by less tangible indicators like legitimacy and credibility. As the global COVID-19 pandemic has demonstrated, US leadership will continue to be tested in novel ways that have the potential to further undermine Washington's standing and influence. Other crises, such as the Russian invasion of Ukraine in early 2022, will offer Washington opportunities to reassert its leadership on the world stage. At the same time, domestic realities will make it harder for future administrations to justify the political and economic costs of continued leadership and security guarantees in the Gulf and elsewhere.

This is a far cry from the early 1990s, when the United States established itself as the preeminent actor in the international system following the collapse of the Soviet Union. One of the formative events of this period was the removal of the Iraqi army from Kuwait by a US-led military coalition in February 1991.[1] As US Secretary of State James Baker testified before Congress at the time, America was the "one nation that has the necessary political, military, and economic instruments at our disposal to catalyze a successful response by the international community."[2]

Over the past quarter of a century, much of the international community has acknowledged this reality by embracing US leadership and formal and informal security guarantees as key pillars of their defense and security doctrines. In the case of the Arab Gulf, this has taken the form of explicit and public de facto security commitments, though not formal security guarantees or treaty obligations that require military intervention in the case of attack.

Before the 2003 US invasion of Iraq, the heavy American military presence across the Gulf Cooperation Council (GCC) states was intended to neutralize threats posed by aspiring regional hegemons Iran and Iraq through a dual containment strategy. As part of this expansion of bilateral security cooperation, successive US administrations endeavored to co-opt the Gulf states to serve their regional security priorities.

The George W. Bush administration's "'emirates strategy" attempted to improve the fighting capabilities of local partners in the (false) hope that they would serve as the frontline in the containment of Iran.[3] Partly in response to the ongoing debacle in Iraq, President Barack Obama pursued a form of "selective multilateralism."[4] This looked to achieve a "workable balance" between traditional Arab Gulf dependence on the bilateral US security guarantee and a regionwide security architecture centered around the GCC.[5]

Unfolding events during the Obama presidency between 2009 and 2016 multiplied doubts, among friends and foes alike, over whether the United States had the political will to use its impressive hard-power capabilities in defense of their interests. In the Arab Gulf, the perception of the Obama administration as an increasingly unreliable and fatigued actor was a consequence of Washington's refusal to fully and publicly back Egyptian leader Hosni Mubarak and the Bahraini royal family during the 2011 Arab revolutions. This view was compounded by America's perceived unwillingness to stand up to Syrian president Bashar Assad's government, Russia and Iran in Syria, Shi'a militias in Iraq, or Iran on the nuclear issue.

While European policy circles responded to Donald Trump's presidential election victory with trepidation, many American allies in Asia and the Middle East approached it with an open mind. The new president was unpredictable and lacked foreign policy experience but appeared to be a pragmatist committed to revitalizing the US role on the global stage. This misunderstanding of Trump's approach to governing engendered widespread hope, especially in the Gulf, that he would move quickly after taking office to reassure his allies, where Obama had not, on the US commitment to their security.

The "Make America Great Again" narrative did little to assuage preexisting concerns. On the contrary, even before its mishandling of the external and domestic ramifications of the COVID-19 crisis, the Trump administration had pursued an arbitrary and ill-informed approach to foreign affairs. This was defined by violent rhetoric, public climb-downs, a disdain for international and multilateral institutions, and a disinclination to differentiate between traditional friends and longtime competitors and adversaries.

All of this has further empowered many of America's regional opponents (Iran, North Korea) and international competitors (Russia, China). It has also left a trail of deeply disillusioned allies, united only in their concerns over Washington's capacity to provide leadership and security in an era of extreme uncertainty and upheaval. Trump's pronouncements on Twitter and in official speeches fueled this disillusionment. In an October 2019 special address from the White House on the Middle East, he was adamant: "We're getting out. Let someone else fight over this long blood-stained sand," before adding, "Other nations must step up and do their fair share."[6] Such statements on the Middle East fed into a preexisting and vigorous political and policy debate on the merits of American withdrawal from its longtime role as a security provider for the wider international system.[7]

America's allies, including those in the Arab Gulf, are responding to this state of affairs in four interconnected ways: (1) They are becoming more outspoken in challenging Washington over suitable security strategies—defensive, offensive, or preventive—for dealing with shared regional threats. (2) They are sidelining Washington in discussions on important regional issues in a way that was unthinkable even one decade ago. (3) They are factoring in the shrinking power differential between the United States and its main international competitors, notably Russia and China, when making foreign policy decisions. (4) They are pursuing alternative security structures and arrangements, including closer relations with America's competitors, to fill the growing vacuum.

The significant erosion of confidence in the United States across the Gulf cannot be questioned. It is shared by American allies in Europe and Asia who express growing dismay at Washington's ineffectiveness in preventing Moscow and Beijing from achieving their policy goals. At least until its invasion of Ukraine in 2022, Russia, in particular, capitalized on these changing perceptions to present itself as a potential bilateral strategic partner for many US allies around the world, including the three key Gulf actors—the United Arab Emirates (UAE), Saudi Arabia, and Qatar. The Russian willingness to take calculated risks in order to achieve its foreign policy goals has made "a clear contribution towards drawing up a new map for a multipolar world," said Syria's Assad, a major beneficiary of this new proactivism, in 2014.[8]

All of this was evident in October 2019 when the Trump administration backed a Turkish offensive into territory in northern Syria controlled by America's Kurdish allies in the war against the Islamic State (IS) group. The absence of any clear and coherent strategic rationale for this decision, and the very public clash between the White House and Congress that followed, further undermined US standing. This was made worse by the administration's predictable but ineffective backtracking from its original position. As Prince Khalid bin Bandar bin Sultan Al-Saud, the understated Saudi ambassador to the United Kingdom, was forced to acknowledge, "What is happening in Syria with Turkey and the pulling out the [US] troops does not give one incredible confidence."[9]

Russia, on the other hand, moved decisively to take advantage of the situation. In coordination with the Assad government, Russian troops immediately entered areas abandoned by US forces. Notably, President Vladimir Putin hosted his Turkish counterpart Recep Tayyip Erdogan at a specially convened summit in the Russian coastal retreat of Sochi, where the two leaders proceeded to decide the fate of northern Syria without taking into account American preferences or interests. Putin also traveled to Saudi Arabia, a key regional player, to capitalize on the growing disillusionment with the United States. This trip came a few days after Putin's visit to the UAE where, in a sharp if indirect rebuke of Washington, he promised his hosts, "You will not be disappointed by your Russian partners."[10] The US withdrawal from Afghanistan in August-September 2021, further fueled global, including Russian, perceptions of American weakness. There was widespread speculation that the Biden administration's decision to leave Afghanistan influenced President Putin's thinking on US impotence in the run-up to his invasion of Ukraine.[11]

For its part, China has increased its military capabilities in recent years to reflect its global economic weight and to dislodge the United States from its position as the dominant security actor in East Asia. Beyond its home region, it has also demonstrated a new willingness to take into account the strategic and security concerns of local actors—a prerequisite for international leadership. In the Arab Gulf, this has taken the form of a series of bilateral security and counterterrorism agreements with GCC member states that complement wide-ranging trade and energy deals. As Chinese President Xi Jinping explained as far back as 2014 on a visit to Kuwait, his country "stands ready to work with countries in the region to promote political solutions of regional issues and safeguard local peace and stability."[12]

Even in these altered circumstances, the United States will remain the major security supplier for most local allies into the foreseeable future. Decades of (over)reliance mean that many of Washington's international partners, including those in the Arab Gulf, are woefully unprepared to provide for their own security needs. Nor are there obvious alternative regional security mechanisms that can provide a substitute for the US security guarantee. There has been a proliferation of regional organizations across the globe in recent decades. Yet only a small number have ever considered using force proactively, and then almost only to restore peace rather than to promote specific strategic or security goals.

In the case of the Arab Gulf states, the "explicit" US commitment to provide protection on a bilateral basis diminished the incentive for security integration inside the GCC.[13] The embargo of Qatar in 2017—led by Saudi Arabia, the UAE, and Bahrain—has further reduced the likelihood that the GCC will provide an effective framework for security cooperation in the future.

Until recently, another by-product of dependence on the United States was a lack of sustained local diplomatic and political investment in building substantive security relations with other external partners. China is becoming more involved in Gulf affairs but, outside its home region, soft power in the service of economic priorities is still far more important for it than military power.[14] As long as its economic interests are not impeded, Beijing has no desire to provide an alternative to the US security guarantee or assume the burdensome role of strategic balancer in the region.[15]

Unlike China, Russia has consistently demonstrated the political will required to build partnerships on the regional level in ways that challenge American primacy in security affairs. In doing so, it has been adept at using its full range of available instruments of power—informational and energy, as well as diplomatic, economic, and military—in ways that assert its influence in multiple regions, including the Gulf and wider Middle East. The reluctance of the majority of Gulf actors (as well as most other states across the Middle East) to openly oppose the Russian invasion of Ukraine in early 2022 underscored this reality. The UAE abstained on a US-sponsored UN Security Council resolution condemning Russian military action, and only Kuwait was prepared to condemn Moscow publicly.[16] At the same time, even before Russia's intervention in Ukraine threatened to undermine its influence and legitimacy, the country lacked the surplus economic capabilities, as well as the overlapping interests and shared hierarchy of threats with many current American allies, that could turn its recent achievements into lasting partnerships of the type that Washington has developed over a generation.[17]

Local actors are well aware that the United States retains a significant advantage over all competitors in most areas of military technology and is the world's preeminent arms supplier. Having deployed troops to an estimated 150 countries in recent decades, including all of the GCC states, the United States has access to and control of 800 overseas military bases in eighty-nine countries and territories. This accounts for between 90 and 95 percent of the world's total foreign military bases.[18]

The US military and intelligence services have also developed unprecedented links over many decades with their counterparts in allied nations across the world, again including the GCC states. These institutional links are resilient and, even if they start to wane, they cannot be replicated to the same degree by any other international actor.

In practical terms, the United States will continue to offer the best way for local allies in the Gulf and elsewhere to gain access to intelligence, training, and the transfer of preferred military technologies. It also provides the best option for local actors who desire strategic depth and freedom of movement and flexibility in their "near abroad." Such considerations influenced the moves by Bahrain and the UAE to normalize relations with Israel since 2020. They also explain the willingness of Gulf allies to pay heed to the Trump administration's call for the establishment of an "Arab NATO" or some other form of Sunni Arab security alliance with the United States at the center.[19]

Preserving bilateral and multilateral security relations with the United States is also smart politics as it gives local actors some hope of having, albeit limited, influence over US policies in their home region. This is an important consideration for those with memories of the US invasion of Iraq, who understand how the unilateral decisions of a superpower, even a diminished one, can undermine regional stability and security.

All of this means that even in the wake of the Trump administration's response to the COVID-19 pandemic, and the Biden administration's withdrawal from Afghanistan, local Gulf partners will continue to view the United States as the ally of last resort, if not the "grand balancer of power" of previous eras. Yet in order to take advantage of this perception, the current Biden administration and indeed future US administrations must take into account the changing strategic circumstances in the formulation of foreign policy. In doing so, they should look to demonstrate to a wary and watching world that the United States is committed to reintroducing stability into the international system.

These efforts should prioritize confidence building in ways that help Washington to regain the trust of local partners. Security policies should also contribute to "regional resilience," by improving the autonomous capabilities of local allies and encouraging them to take more responsibility for their own stability and security.[20]

One way the United States could do this is to take advantage of its considered but effective leadership during the early days of the Ukraine crisis, to harness its still significant hard- and soft-power resources to support the development, in consultation with local actors, of inclusive, multilateral, and collective frameworks that can facilitate the arbitration of disputes and enhance attempts at conflict management and mediation on the regional level. Such efforts would be of great value in the Gulf and wider Middle East, a region with a woeful shortage of mechanisms that can bring together actors with common goals, never mind sectarian and strategic foes. Such a move would also be a fitting and ambitious way for the United States to renew and reimagine its global role in a greatly changed international environment.

Notes

1. Andrew Fenton Cooper, Richard A. Higgot, and Kim Richard Nossal, "Bound to Follow? Leadership and Followership in the Gulf Conflict," *Political Science Quarterly* 106, no. 3 (Autumn 1991), pp. 391–410 (https://doi.org/10.2307/2151739).

2. Andrew Bennett, Joseph Lepgold, and Danny Unger, "Burden-Sharing in the Persian Gulf War," *International Organization* 48, no. 1 (Winter 1994), p. 50 (www.jstor.org/stable/2706914).

3. Marc J. O'Reilly, "The Crusader: George W. Bush and the American Empire in the Persian Gulf," in *Perspectives on the Legacy of George W. Bush,* edited by Michael Orlov Grossman and Ronald Eric Matthews Jr. (Newcastle: Cambridge Scholars Publishing, 2009), p. 155; Michael Abramowitz and Ellen Knickmeyer, "As Bush Heads to Mideast, Renewed Questions on Iran," *Washington Post,* January 7, 2008.

4. Michael Kraig, "Assessing Alternative Security Frameworks for the Persian Gulf," *Middle East Policy* 11, no. 3 (Fall 2004), p. 151 (https://mepc.org/journal/assessing-alternative-security-frameworks-persian-gulf).

5. Kristian Coates Ulrichsen, "Internal and External Security in the Arab Gulf States," *Middle East Policy* 16, no. 2 (Summer 2009), p. 53 (https://mepc.org/internal-and-external-security-arab-gulf-states); The White House, "Presidential Determination—Gulf Cooperation Council," December 16, 2013 (https://obamawhitehouse.archives.gov/the-press-office/2013/12/16/presidential-determination-gulf-cooperation-council).

6. "Donald Trump Vows to Get out of 'Blood-Stained' Middle East," *Al Jazeera*, October 24, 2019 (www.aljazeera.com/news/2019/10/donald-trump-vows-blood-stained-middle-east-191024074507902.html).

7. Andrew J. Bacevich, "Ending Endless War: A Pragmatic Military Strategy," *Foreign Affairs*, September/October 2016 (www.foreignaffairs.com/articles/united-states/2016-08-03/ending-endless-war); Bernie Sanders, "Ending America's Endless War: We Must Stop Giving Terrorists Exactly What They Want," *Foreign Affairs*, June 24, 2019 (www.foreignaffairs.com/articles/2019-06-24/ending-americas-endless-war).

8. "Assad: Russia Is 'Re-establishing Multipolar World,'" *Al Arabiya*, April 2, 2014 (https://english.alarabiya.net/en/News/middle-east/2014/04/02/Syria-s-Assad-says-Russia-is-re-establishing-multipolar-world.html).

9. Patrick Wintour, "Saudi Ambassador Accuses Turkey of Causing Chaos in Syria," *The Guardian*, October 15, 2019 (www.theguardian.com/world/2019/oct/15/saudi-ambassador-accuses-turkey-of-causing-chaos-in-syria).

10. "Russia's Putin Signs Deals Worth $1.3bn during UAE Visit," *Al Jazeera*, October 15, 2019 (www.aljazeera.com/news/2019/10/russia-putin-signs-deals-worth-13bn-uae-visit-191015194158423.html).

11. Jen Kirby and Jonathan Guy, "The Increasingly Complicated Russia-Ukraine Crisis, Explained," *Vox*, February 23, 2022 (https://www.vox.com/22917719/russia-ukraine-invasion-border-crisis-nato-explained).

12. Xinhua, "Xi Meets Kuwait Prime Minister," *China Daily*, June 4, 2014 (www.chinadaily.com.cn/china/2014-06/04/content_17563183.htm).

13. Jon B. Alterman and Kathleen H. Hicks, "Federated Defense in the Middle East" Report of the Federated Defense Project (Washington: Center for Strategic and International Studies, September 2015), p. 45 (www.csis.org/analysis/federated-defense-middle-east).

14. Robert Mogielnicki, "How China Is Quietly Expanding Its Economic Influence in the Gulf," *World Politics Review*, July 21, 2020 (https://www.worldpoliticsreview.com/articles/28924/how-china-is-quietly-expanding-its-economic-influence-in-the-gulf).

15. Phillip C. Saunders and Julia G. Bowie, "US-China Military Relations: Competition and Cooperation," *Journal of Strategic Studies* 39, nos. 5–6 (2016), pp. 662–84 (https://doi.org/10.1080/01402390.2016.1221818); Wu Xinbo, "The China Challenge: Competitor or Order Transformer?," *Washington Quarterly* 43, no. 3 (2020), pp. 99–114 (https://doi.org/10.1080/0163660X.2020.1813402).

16. Simeon Kerr, Samer Al-Atrush and Andrew England, "Gulf States' Neutrality on Ukraine Reflects Deeper Russian Ties," *Financial Times*, February 28, 2022 (https://www.ft.com/content/5e3b0998-705f-46c4-8010-9972b3c8a847).

17. Becca Wasser, "The Limits of Russian Strategy in the Middle East," *Perspectives* (Washington: Rand Corporation, November 2019), pp. 1–27 (www.rand.org/pubs/perspectives/PE340.html).

18. David Vine, "Where in the World Is the US Military?," *Politico Magazine*, July/August 2015 (www.politico.com/magazine/story/2015/06/us-military-bases-around-the-world-119321).

19. For two contrasting perspectives on this issue, see Muhammad Mansour, "US Withdrawal, Arab NATO, and How America Can Be a 'Force for Good,'" *Fikra Forum* (Washington Institute, February 11, 2019) (www.washingtoninstitute.org/fikraforum /view/u.s.-withdrawal-arab-nato-and-how-america-can-be-a-force-for-good1); and Doug Bandow, "Why America Should Say No to an Arab NATO," *National Interest*, November 26, 2018 (https://nationalinterest.org/blog/skeptics/why-america-should-say -no-arab-nato-37162).

20. Craig Snyder, "Emerging Regional Security Co-operation in Europe and the Asia Pacific," *Pacific Review* 9, no. 4 (1996), p. 556 (https://doi.org/10.1080/095127 49608719203).

FOUR

Changing Patterns of Global Energy Markets

STEVEN WRIGHT

TRANSFORMATIONAL CHANGES IN THE energy sector are steering the Gulf Cooperation Council (GCC) states into uncharted territory. The changes have implications for the Gulf region, as well as broader repercussions for global politics. It is vital to appreciate the Gulf region in its international context in order to understand how the states will need to respond to the new international landscape.

The Impact of Energy Dynamics on US Engagement in the Gulf

Energy supply and consumption dynamics have wide implications for the global energy market, which one can argue has entered a new era. Devising policies to manage the emerging trends will be challenging. The biggest change in the global landscape was the United States regaining its title as the world's largest producer of oil in 2018.[1] For much of the twentieth century, the United States was the world's largest producer of oil; its dominance lasted until 1974 when it was overtaken by the Soviet Union at the height of the Cold War. After 1976, Saudi Arabia dominated the oil market for the following four decades.[2] The manner in which the United States overtook Saudi Arabia's position in 2018 necessitates a broader consideration of geopolitical change in global energy markets—and what this means for US engagement with the Middle East and supply to global markets.

The emergence of the United States as the world's largest producer of oil, as well as an exporter of natural gas, heralds a new era in which it perceives itself to be energy-independent (even though it continues to import both crude oil and natural gas).[3] With the election of Donald Trump to the presidency, whose global foreign policy perspective had an isolationist character and was more "nationalist" than "internationalist," the context changed. Indeed, the US's position as the world's largest producer of oil, in addition to its perceived energy independence, will require changes in its strategic calculations toward the Middle East, and in particular the Gulf region, leading to a new dynamic in US foreign policy.

The implications of this newfound self-perception are significant, signaling a shift in how the United States calculates its national security and economic interests. It is likely that the security of natural resources, which has been a central feature of US engagement with the Middle East since the end of World War II, will play a less important role in foreign policy designs. The emergence of the United States as a major player in the global energy market also heralds greater supply and competition, driven by the exploitation of shale, and has had a dampening effect on global oil prices.[4] The key beneficiaries of this strategy have been major energy-importing countries such as China, as cheaper oil has fueled economic growth and dulled inflation.

A Gulf That Looks Eastward: Energy and Capital Investment

While the changing fortunes of the United States have certainly had a global impact, there has likewise been a shift in global energy demand, most dramatically from Organization for Economic Cooperation and Development (OECD) to non-OECD nations, especially China and India. This shift began in the 1990s, driven by the rising economic prosperity enjoyed by billions of people in developing countries.[5] Indeed, China's demand for oil has almost tripled since the turn of the twenty-first century.[6] Between 2007 and 2017, China and India accounted for the largest increases in global demand.[7] China has also been the largest driver of demand for natural gas over the past decade, and this trend is projected to continue.[8] Yet, at a geopolitical level, it is important to recognize that southern and northern East

Asia constitute the majority of global demand for natural gas, with China, Japan, South Korea, and India accounting for more than 60 percent of global consumption.[9] Because these countries are the "Big 4" in the liquefied natural gas (LNG) sector, their markets will hold special importance for Qatar and other leading LNG suppliers in meeting current and future market demand.

As both oil consumption patterns and supply sources shift, a key issue will be oversupply. Historically, it is possible to identify at least four similar market cycles: (1) for twelve years, from 1973 to 1985, the price of crude oil was in a high-price cycle; (2) this was followed by a fourteen-year low-price cycle, from 1986 to 2000; (3) then by thirteen years of high oil prices from 2001 to 2014; finally, (4) the downturn in 2014 can be seen as the start of a new cycle of low oil prices.[10] Lower oil prices have a direct impact on the economies of the Arab Gulf states; as these nations' budgets depend heavily on oil revenues to finance fiscal spending, low oil prices require them to find new sources of capital.

Reducing spending through austerity has been a trend across the Gulf region since 2014.[11] One way of raising capital is through bond issuances in the international marketplace, but identifying sources of foreign direct investment (FDI) is even more crucial. With East Asia as the main market for exports, the role of China's Belt and Road Initiative (BRI) presents opportunities for major FDI flows.

These demand and supply dynamics will continue, as will a progressive integration between the Arab Gulf states and southern and eastern Asia, driven by energy. The result will be greater engagement with China and growth in its strategic importance in the Gulf region. This is all the more noteworthy given the existing and growing isolationism of the United States. These contextual forces can be expected to accelerate diplomatic and commercial engagement with China.

The Context of the COVID-19 Pandemic

The arrival of the COVID-19 pandemic in 2020 had an immediate impact on the global demand for oil. The three areas where its influence was felt most strongly in the energy market were the domestic automobile, international aviation, and international shipping sectors.[12] The combined decline in consumption in those sectors resulted in a marked fall in the price of crude oil as oil inventories reached full capacity.

Beyond the public health crisis, the sharp decline in demand for oil accelerated the Gulf states' economic challenges. The fiscal challenge in particular became more intense and difficult to overcome. In the longer term, the reduced prospects for any growth in demand for oil and natural resources will have a direct effect on foreign revenue in the region. In addition, the effects of domestic economic contraction on fiscal spending will also result in more pronounced austerity measures. Achieving a more sustainable economic model regionwide will be made more difficult; yet, as indicated, greater engagement and FDI through China's BRI may help counter the economic headwinds.

Oil Market Manipulation: The Changing Role of OPEC?

It may be tempting for some to say that the pandemic could breathe new life into the Organization of Petroleum Exporting Countries (OPEC) as oil-producing states face lower revenue streams from the depressed price of crude oil. However, the indications are that OPEC may lack the ability to have a meaningful impact, and it faces politically charged challenges of its own. Many analysts were taken by surprise when Qatar announced that it would formally withdraw from OPEC on January 1, 2019. Qatar was an early member of the organization, yet it was always a marginal player as an oil exporter. OPEC remains essentially a Saudi-led cartel, with less global relevance given the shale revolution. The exploitation of shale has allowed the United States to overtake Saudi Arabia as the world's largest oil producer. While Saudi Arabia's ability to manipulate the market through OPEC has certainly weakened, OPEC will need Russian support to deliver on its promises. It is, therefore, the Saudi-Russian oil axis that matters for OPEC, which means smaller oil producers will have even less influence on decisions. In essence, it is OPEC plus Russia that matters, but it is unclear if this would be sufficient to have a discernible impact on the global price of crude oil, particularly in the context of the pandemic.[13]

The future of OPEC should be understood in the context of rising concern about Saudi Arabia following the premeditated murder of Saudi journalist Jamal Khashoggi in Istanbul. The US Congress may adopt antitrust legislation—the No Oil Producing and Exporting Cartels (NOPEC) Act—which will open the doors to litigation against Arab and non-Arab member states of OPEC. Although the COVID-19 pandemic has seen that legislation fade in importance, it remains an evergreen issue for whichever political party has power in the US Congress. Indeed, if such legislation were to pass, the price of oil could be expected to drop further.

Concluding Observations

The relationship between the United States and the Gulf region is going through a period of change and is being affected by the changing energy landscape at a geopolitical level. This has implications for regional stability, as well as for how key states in the region conduct their foreign policy. Indeed, the change is affecting the regional security architecture and underscores the need for a new definition of regional order.

It is also striking that, given the hostility directed toward Saudi Arabia by members of the US Congress, the central pillars on which energy geopolitics in the Middle East have been shaped have entered a new phase, which can be viewed as the most challenging historically since the United States' strategic interests in the region crystallized during the Richard Nixon administration (1969–1974). The extraordinary criticism and scrutiny of Saudi Arabia holds the potential to recalibrate the way the United States engages with close traditional partners in the region, in addition to its role as the major international powerbroker in the Gulf.

Although global energy prices have been low since 2014, one of the key differences in the current cycle is the advent of a new age through the exploitation of deposits of oil and gas in shale and tight formations. These efforts have allowed the United States to become increasingly energy secure and to position itself as an oil and gas exporter, even as the commercial viability of shale producers acts to depress global oil prices. The higher the price of shale goes, the more commercially viable it is for producers to exploit, and therefore the subsequent greater production of oil leads to a price depression. It is true that national oil companies have lower production costs and can compete on price, but their economies remain dependent on oil and gas revenues. Therefore, the new energy landscape serves to dampen prices for the foreseeable future, which has clear implications for the Arab Gulf region and further drives an eastward orientation. China's Belt and Road Initiative thus gains importance by becoming a key source of finance for pressing development needs, driven by a changing energy landscape and depressed economic conditions caused by a pandemic. These energy and geopolitical factors, coupled with the ever-evolving outlook and interests of the United States, are shaping a new era for the Gulf.

Notes

1. Matt Egan, "America Is Now the World's Largest Oil Producer," *CNN Business*, September 12, 2018 (https://money.cnn.com/2018/09/12/investing/us-oil-production-russia-saudi-arabia/index.html).

2. British Petroleum (BP), "Statistical Review of World Energy 2020, 69th Edition," June 2020 (www.bp.com/content/dam/bp/business-sites/en/global/corporate/pdfs/energy-economics/statistical-review/bp-stats-review-2020-full-report.pdf?utm_source=BP_Global_GroupCommunications_UK_external&utm_medium=email&utm_campaign=11599394_Statistical%20Review%202020%20-%20on%20the%20day%20reminder&dm_i=1PGC%2C6WM5E%2COV0LQ4%2CRQW75%2C1).

3. Agnia Grigas, *The New Geopolitics of Natural Gas* (Harvard University Press, 2017).

4. Bryan T. Stinchfield, Ted Auch, and Eve Bratman, "Energy Security, International Investment, and Democracy: The Case of the United States Shale Oil and Gas Industry," *Democracy and Security* 16, no. 4 (2020), pp. 309–29 (https://doi.org/10.1080/17419166.2020.1811969).

5. Grigas, *The New Geopolitics of Natural Gas*, pp. 234–69.

6. Michal Meidan, "How COVID-19 Has Changed the Long-Term Outlook for China's Oil Demand," *Oxford Energy Forum*, no. 125 (September 2020), pp. 36–39 (www.oxfordenergy.org/wpcms/wp-content/uploads/2020/09/OEF-125-1.pdf).

7. Linda Capuano, "International Energy Outlook 2020," US Energy Information Administration, October 14, 2020 (www.eia.gov/pressroom/presentations/capuano_ieo2020.pdf).

8. Michael Xiaobao Chen, "Potential and Challenges of China's Second-Tier LNG Importers," *Oxford Energy Forum*, no. 125 (September 2020), pp. 25–28 (www.oxfordenergy.org/wpcms/wp-content/uploads/2020/09/OEF-125-1.pdf).

9. Mike Fulwood and others, "Emerging Asia LNG Demand," Oxford Institute for Energy Studies, September 2020 (www.oxfordenergy.org/wpcms/wp-content/uploads/2020/09/Emerging-Asia-LNG-demand-NG-162.pdf).

10. BP, "Statistical Review of World Energy 2020."

11. Tokhir N Mirzoev and others, "The Future of Oil and Fiscal Sustainability in the GCC Region" (Washington, International Monetary Fund, February 6, 2020), pp. 17–20 (www.imf.org/en/Publications/Departmental-Papers-Policy-Papers/Issues/2020/01/31/The-Future-of-Oil-and-Fiscal-Sustainability-in-the-GCC-Region-48934).

12. Malcolm Keay and David Robinson, "COVID-19: Glimpses of the Energy Future?," *Oxford Energy Forum*, no. 123 (July 2020), pp. 29–32 (www.oxfordenergy.org/wpcms/wp-content/uploads/2020/07/OEF123.pdf).

13. Bassam Fattouh, "COVID-19, The Energy Transition and Oil Companies' Adaptation Strategies," *Oxford Energy Forum*, no. 123 (July 2020), pp. 41–44 (www.oxfordenergy.org/wpcms/wp-content/uploads/2020/07/OEF123.pdf).

FIVE

An Integrated Approach to Climate Change and Economic Diversification

SAMANTHA GROSS

CLIMATE CHANGE POSES A two-pronged challenge for the countries of the Gulf Cooperation Council (GCC). The GCC countries stand to suffer in a warming world, through extreme temperatures and rising sea levels, and the effects these will have on human health, agriculture, tourism, and other industries. Several of the region's largest and fastest-growing cities, such as Doha, Abu Dhabi, and Dubai, lie on coastal plains or islands. Temperature rise combined with extreme humidity could make coastal areas near the Arabian Gulf and the Red Sea nearly uninhabitable during the hottest times of the year.[1] Qatar points out its vulnerability to climate impacts in its Nationally Determined Contribution to the Paris Agreement: "Qatar is extremely vulnerable to sea level rise as it is liable to inland flooding of 18.2% of its land area, at less than 5m rise in sea level, along with the associated adverse impacts on the population as 96% are living on the coastal areas."[2] Food security could be a challenge; heat and shortages of water are harmful for agriculture, and fish stocks are already declining in the Arabian Gulf, which could lose up to 12 percent of its biodiversity before the end of the century.[3]

The economies of the GCC could also be adversely affected by the world's efforts to mitigate climate change. GCC economies are highly dependent on revenues from fossil fuels, the primary source of the world's greenhouse gas (GHG) emissions. Customers around the world are striving to move toward fossil fuel alternatives. Since oil production costs in the GCC are among the lowest in the world, production is likely to continue for years to come, even if the overall demand for oil declines. However, this is cold comfort since prices are also likely to decline in this low-demand scenario.

GCC countries are in a difficult position—expected to suffer severe environmental harm from inaction on climate and economic harm from the world's efforts to mitigate climate change through reduction in fossil fuel use. Nonetheless, the two-pronged nature of the challenge can drive them toward solutions that address both sides of the equation. Instead of zero-sum thinking that pits the climate challenge against economic growth, GCC countries must think of climate change as a driver of economic diversification and change that will ultimately benefit their economies, making them more sustainable for the twenty-first century. The response to climate change must be global and the GCC countries' participation in that global effort will help to spare them from their own painful climate impacts.

Reform of Fossil Fuel Prices and Production

GCC countries have long had a rentier structure, wherein the government distributes the proceeds of oil and gas sales through a number of mechanisms, including extremely low prices for energy and energy-intensive goods like water. These low energy prices represent forgone revenue rather than actual subsidies. Nonetheless, they are often so low that consumers and businesses have little incentive to conserve energy or make investments in energy efficiency. In addition, even though prices for wind and solar energy have been dropping rapidly, it is more difficult for them to compete against underpriced fossil fuels. Other parts of the world are rapidly increasing the share of renewable power generation. Wind and solar will make up 76 percent of the new generation installed in the United States in 2020, and today wind and solar account for 21 percent of California's electricity generation.[4]

Low energy prices and a hot climate contribute to very high GHG emissions in the GCC. The six GCC countries are among the world's highest per capita emitters of GHG. Five of the countries are in the top ten, with Oman coming in at number eleven (see table 5-1). Annual emissions per capita range from a high of 45.4 tons in Qatar to 15.4 tons in Oman; in comparison, the Organization for Economic Cooperation and Development

Table 5-1. *Top Ten Country Emitters of Greenhouse Gases, 2014, Metric Tons of Carbon Dioxide (CO_2) Per Person Per Year*

Country	Tons of carbon dioxide
1. Qatar	45.42
2. Trinidad and Tobago	34.16
3. Kuwait	25.22
4. Bahrain	23.45
5. United Arab Emirates	23.30
6. Brunei	22.12
7. Saudi Arabia	19.53
8. Luxembourg	17.36
9. United States	16.49
10. New Caledonia	16.01

Source: Index Mundi, "CO2 Emissions (metric tons per capita) - Country Ranking," 2014 (www.indexmundi.com/facts/indicators/EN .ATM.CO2E.PC/rankings).

(OECD) average is 9.0 tons.[5] However, since most of the GCC countries have small populations, only Saudi Arabia claims a place in the world's largest emitters by volume, at number eight, and the region emits just over 3 percent of the global total.[6]

Clearly there is room for emissions reductions while still maintaining a high standard of living. The United Arab Emirates (UAE) is the least energy-intensive economy in the GCC, but still requires 10 percent more energy to create a dollar of output than the world average. Energy demand in the region has also been growing rapidly, at more than twice the world average rate since 2000.[7] Inefficient energy consumption also reduces the amount of oil and gas available for export.

All six GCC countries have increased their energy prices, both to improve their fiscal positions and to encourage more efficient energy use among their populations. Energy price reform is one of the most powerful ways to decrease GHG emissions. For example, a 2019 study found that full deregulation of fuel prices in Saudi Arabia would deliver larger reductions in GHG emissions than policies that focused on clean energy deployment. Energy price deregulation could also provide more than $900 billion in net economic benefits, the study found, mostly through fuel savings.[8] Raising prices to international levels is politically difficult, and price increases for energy and water have been unpopular around the GCC, and in some cases reversed.[9] However, the overall economic benefits of such policies are large enough to allow governments to help industries and citizens that face hardship as GCC energy prices rise.

GCC countries can also contribute to climate goals in their oil and gas production. The region's generally low oil production costs represent the small amount of energy needed to recover the oil, and in turn the relatively small carbon footprint per barrel. However, more can be done to reduce emissions in some fields.

Methane, the primary component of natural gas, is more than fifty times more powerful than carbon dioxide as a GHG over a twenty-year timeframe.[10] Eliminating methane emissions from oil and gas production has large climate benefits and avoids wasting salable product. The International Energy Agency (IEA) estimates that 40 percent of methane emissions could be eliminated at no net cost, once the recovered methane was sold.[11] GCC countries have made significant efforts to eliminate flaring of natural gas and to reduce methane leaks, and further efforts in this area could deliver important GHG benefits.[12]

As oil fields age, energy-intensive secondary and tertiary recovery methods are often applied to extend the field's productive life. In Oman, one project is in operation using solar energy instead of natural gas to produce steam for enhanced oil recovery.[13] This technology reduces GHG emissions while preserving natural gas for other uses or for export. A total of 360 MW of solar thermal capacity is in operation at the Miraah project, but the following phase was cancelled amid the turmoil of the Covid-19 pandemic.[14]

Economic Diversification Brings Climate Benefits

GCC countries are pushing to diversify their economies in order to reduce dependence on fossil fuel revenue, given the world's push to mitigate climate change and the need to provide jobs and opportunity to their growing populations. These efforts can contribute to climate change mitigation as well.

Development of low-carbon energy provides a prime example. The GCC region is rich in renewable energy resources as well as hydrocarbons, potentially providing a new area of competitive advantage. GCC countries have some of the highest solar irradiances in the world. Nearly 60 percent of the area of the GCC has excellent suitability for deployment of solar photovoltaic (PV) systems.[15] The UAE has nearly 80 percent of the GCC's installed solar PV capacity and has attracted very low-cost projects without offering subsidies.[16] Kuwait, Oman, and Saudi Arabia also have good wind resources, although wind developments lag far beyond solar.

Despite the rich resources, renewables made up less than 1 percent of total electricity capacity in the GCC at the end of 2018.[17] Greater renewable electricity is particularly important since air-conditioning is a very large energy consumer in the region. Energy consumption for space cooling has tripled since 2000, and the changing climate will only exacerbate this trend.[18]

Looking forward, the GCC is set to see a major acceleration in renewable energy deployment. Led by the UAE, Oman, and Kuwait, a total of nearly 7 GW in renewable power generation capacity is planned to come online by the early 2020s.[19]

Renewable energy projects create jobs and attract private investment, key goals of economic diversification. Analysis from the International Renewable Energy Agency (IRENA) found that achieving national renewable energy targets in the GCC would create more than 220,500 direct jobs through 2030. GCC countries are also leveraging their endowment of renewable resources to invest in the renewable energy value chain. Kuwait, Oman, and Saudi Arabia have local content requirements for renewable energy projects, and Qatar and Saudi Arabia have announced plans for polysilicon production facilities, for use in solar panels and electronics.[20]

Because fresh water is a scarce commodity in the GCC, desalinated sea water is an important water source. Desalination is very energy-intensive, accounting for about 5 percent of total energy consumption in the Middle East.[21] Older desalination plants often use thermal technology, relying on inexpensive fossil fuels. However, newer plants use reverse osmosis technology powered by electricity. The region can become a leader in designing and executing projects that pair renewable electricity generation with production of fresh water. Desalination facilities can serve as a form of demand response and electricity storage, running during times of excess renewable electricity production and storing water for times when renewable electricity is not available. Such technology will become more important as climate change makes fresh water scarcer and grid operators look for ways to integrate intermittent renewable generation into their systems.[22]

Notes

1. Jeremy S. Pal and Elfatih A. B. Eltahir, "Future Temperature in Southwest Asia Projected to Exceed a Threshold for Human Adaptability," *Nature Climate Change* 6 (2016), pp. 197–200 (https://doi.org/10.1038/nclimate2833).

2. State of Qatar Ministry of Environment, "Intended Nationally Determined Contributions (INDCs) Report," November 19, 2015 (www4.unfccc.int/sites/sub missions/INDC/Published%20Documents/Qatar/1/Qatar%20INDCs%20Report %20-English.pdf).

3. University of British Columbia, "Climate Change to Cause Dramatic Drop in Persian Gulf Biodiversity and Fisheries Potential," *Phys.org*, May 2, 2018 (https://phys .org/news/2018-05-climate-persian-gulf-biodiversity-fisheries.html).

4. United States Energy Information Administration, "New Electric Generating Capacity in 2020 Will Come Primarily from Wind and Solar," January 14, 2020 (www .eia.gov/todayinenergy/detail.php?id=42495); California Energy Commission, "2019 Total System Electric Generation" (www.energy.ca.gov/data-reports/energy-almanac /california-electricity-data/2019-total-system-electric-generation).

5. Henry Bewicke, "Chart of the Day: These Countries Have the Largest Carbon Footprints," World Economic Forum, January 2, 2019 (www.weforum.org/agenda /2019/01/chart-of-the-day-these-countries-have-the-largest-carbon-footprints/).

6. Iman Ghosh, "All the World's Carbon Emissions in One Chart," *Visual Capitalist*, May 31, 2019 (www.visualcapitalist.com/all-the-worlds-carbon-emissions-in-one -chart/); Hannah Ritchie and Max Roser, "CO2 and Greenhouse Gas Emissions," *Our World in Data*, revised August 2020 (https://ourworldindata.org/co2-and-other-green house-gas-emissions).

7. See International Energy Agency (IEA), "Outlook for Producer Economies," Country Report, October 2018, pp. 30, 32.

8. David Wogan, Elizabeth Carey, and Douglas Cooke, "Policy Pathways to Meet Saudi Arabia's Contributions to the Paris Agreement," King Abdullah Petroleum Studies and Research Center, February 2019 (www.kapsarc.org/file-download.php?i =27843).

9. Samantha Gross and Adel Abdel Ghafar, "The Shifting Energy Landscape and the Gulf Economies' Diversification Challenge," Brookings, December 2019 (www .brookings.edu/wp-content/uploads/2019/12/FP_20191210_gcc_energy_ghafar _gross.pdf); Tom Moerenhout, "Fuel and Electricity Reform for Economic Sustainability in the Gulf," in *When Can Oil Economies Be Deemed Sustainable?*, edited by Giacomo Luciani and Tom Moerenhout (Singapore: Palgrave Macmillan, 2020) (https://doi.org/10.1007/978-981-15-5728-6_8).

10. See Intergovernmental Panel on Climate Change, "Climate Change 1995: The Science of Climate Change—Summary for Policymakers and Technical Summary of the Working Group I Report," 1995, p. 22 (https://wedocs.unep.org/handle /20.500.11822/29956).

11. IEA, "Methane Tracker 2020," *Fuel Report*, March 2020 (www.iea.org/reports /methane-tracker-2020/methane-abatement-options).

12. IEA, "Policies Database: Middle East and Methane" (www.iea.org/policies ?topic=Methane&region=Middle%20East).

13. Glasspoint, "Oman has Pioneering Enhanced Oil Recovery in the Middle East" (www.glasspoint.com/markets/oman/); SolarPACES, "Glasspoint Signs up 2nd Oman Solar EOR Project at Twice the Size: 2 GWth," November 13, 2018 (www .solarpaces.org/glasspoint-signs-up-2nd-oman-solar-eor-at-twice-the-size-2-gwth/).

14. Solarthermalworld, "Shareholders Force Glasspoint into Liquidation," May 27, 2020 (https://solarthermalworld.org/news/shareholders-force-glasspoint-liquidation/).

15. IRENA, "Renewable Energy Market Analysis: The GCC Region," 2016 (www.irena.org/-/media/Files/IRENA/Agency/Publication/2016/IRENA_Market_GCC_2016.pdf).

16. IRENA, "Renewable Energy Market Analysis: GCC 2019" (https://www.irena.org/publications/2019/jan/renewable-energy-market-analysis-gcc-2019).

17. Ibid.

18. See IEA, "Outlook for Producer Economies," p. 68.

19. IRENA, "Renewable Energy Market Analysis: GCC 2019."

20. Ibid.

21. See IEA, "Outlook for Producer Economies," p. 71.

22. Mohammad Al-Saidi and Sally Saliba, "Water, Energy and Food Supply Security in the Gulf Cooperation Council (GCC) Countries—A Risk Perspective," *Water* 11, no. 3 (2019), p. 455 (https://doi.org/10.3390/w11030455).

SIX

Sino-GCC Relations

Past, Present, and Future Trajectories

ADEL ABDEL GHAFAR

OVER THE PAST TWO decades, the countries of the Gulf Cooperation Council (GCC) and China have worked to build up their economic, political, and security relations. In 2020, China replaced the EU as the GCC's largest trading partner with bilateral trade valued at USD 161.4 billion.[1] Massive infrastructure projects in the region, such as Qatar's Lusail Stadium and high-speed rail lines in Saudi Arabia, provide lucrative opportunities for Chinese companies.[2] The United Arab Emirates (UAE) is China's largest export market and the largest non-oil trading partner in the Middle East and North Africa (MENA) region,[3] and the country has also been a hub for Chinese COVID-19 vaccine production.[4] China is also the largest customer of Omani crude oil, importing approximately 78.4 percent, a substantial increase from 17.8 percent in 2002.[5] Oman is slated to play a significant role in China's Belt and Road Initiative.[6]

Increasing levels of engagement, while disturbing policymakers in the United States,[7] demonstrate that both sides are seeking to deepen their ties

This chapter is published as Adel Abdel Ghafar, "Sino-GCC Relations: Past, Present, and Future Trajectories," Issue Brief, Middle East Council on Global Affairs, 2022.

over the coming decades. The visit in January 2022 by the head of the GCC and several GCC ministers to China has been described as "unprecedented."[8] The joint statement released following the meeting was ambitious, calling for the establishment of a strategic partnership, promotion of the free trade agreement negotiations, and implementation of a free trade area.[9] As GCC states and China deepen their engagement, they will have to navigate a complex set of regional and international factors that may constrain closer ties.

Historical Context: China's Balancing in the Gulf

The GCC's earlier relationship with China can be viewed in the context of Sino-Iranian relations, established in 1971 during the Shah's era. At the time, GCC states viewed these ties with suspicion, which only increased after the removal of the Shah and the flourishing of the relationship under the Islamic Republic. After GCC states established their own diplomatic relations with China during the 1980s, they continued to be suspicious of its intentions in Iran, especially since the two states were growing closer in several fields, including arms technology and energy.[10] While publicly holding a neutral position, China had in fact provided covert support to the Islamic Republic during its conflict with Iraq (1980–1988).[11]

Despite these concerns, the GCC stance toward China has shifted considerably over the years. As one ex-GCC official commented, "The Chinese relationship with the Islamic Republic 30 years ago was seen as a major shift and threat to us. But the GCC saw a requirement to engage, which is our historical norm."[12] In 1993, a visit to the Gulf countries by Li Lanqing, China's deputy premier, marked the beginning of China's efforts toward energy cooperation with GCC countries,[13] and thus energy security became a critical factor in GCC-China relations. In addition, China wanted to expand and diversify to new markets for its labor-intensive products, and so ever since the 1990s the UAE has become a more critical location for China's manufactured products to be re-exported to countries in the MENA region.[14]

By the 2000s, the GCC's economic engagement with China had arguably brought some balance to Beijing's Iran policy,[15] and since 2001 both Saudi Arabia and Iran have become the twin pillars of China's approach to the Gulf,[16] with both set to play a role in the BRI. China is the world's largest importer of crude oil, and imports from the key exporters and Iran (figure 6-2) are critical for its economy.

While China has avoided entanglements in regional disputes and conflicts, the growing Saudi-Iranian rivalry over the past two decades has made

Figure 6-1. China's Exports to the GCC, 2000–2019

Value of exports (in billions of dollars)

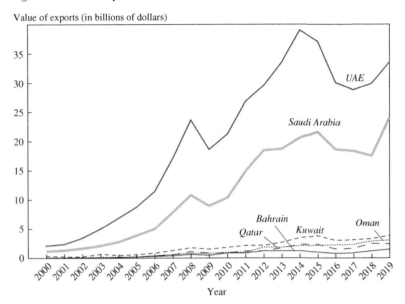

World Integrated Trade Solution, World Bank.

Figure 6-2. China's Fuel Imports from Saudi Arabia, the UAE, Oman, and Iran, 2000–2019

Value of imports (in billions of dollars)

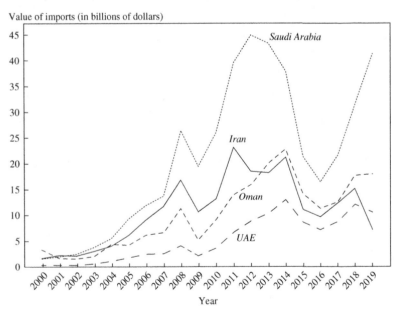

World Integrated Trade Solution, World Bank.

it increasingly difficult for Chinese policymakers to balance China's relationship with both regional powers. In addition to establishing a Comprehensive Strategic Partnership with Saudi Arabia,[17] China has also pursued a strategic partnership with Iran, which expands its economic footprint in several sectors across the country, including finance, agriculture, telecommunications, ports, and railways. In exchange, China is reportedly set to receive heavily discounted Iranian oil over the next twenty-five years.[18] The agreement was first proposed by President Xi Xinping during a state visit to Iran in 2016 after the Joint Comprehensive Plan of Action (JCPOA) was signed but was on hold during the Trump presidency after he withdrew from the nuclear agreement and adopted the "maximum pressure" policy on Iran. Xi's proposal was finally signed in 2021 after Joe Biden's election and in the final months of the Rouhani presidency.

The agreement, which has entered its implementation stages under President Raisi, has raised concerns in Saudi Arabia that its security interests are not being considered given that Iranian-backed proxies such as the Houthis continue to attack the kingdom. China has sought to alleviate this concern with Foreign Minister Wang Yi, stating that China "understands and supports the legitimate concerns of Saudi Arabia in safeguarding its national security."[19] China has also backed the new JCPOA negotiations and wants the nuclear accords reinstated. However, any deal that does not address Iran's destabilizing regional activities may engulf China in a conflict between two of its key strategic allies in the Gulf.

Pandemic Diplomacy and Beyond

COVID-19 presented China with an opportunity to increase its influence and its outreach to MENA governments and their citizens. As public health systems came under pressure in US and European countries in 2020, China had reacted to the pandemic quickly and was able to begin sending medical supplies to countries across the world. GCC countries initially sent supplies to China, but as the crisis dragged on, they became recipients. According to one analyst, China's pandemic diplomacy won over Gulf states who were grappling with the economic and medical fallout from the pandemic.[20]

Overall, China's pandemic diplomacy should be viewed within the broader context as another soft-power tool to further entrench its presence in countries where it seeks diplomatic and economic influence and to supplant its Western rivals. It also underscores its efforts to cast itself as a global leader in health care. To reboot the impression that it was the source of the virus, through its vaccine and health care diplomacy efforts China wants to be seen as a responsible global leader that is capable of fighting the virus domestically and globally.

Building on its success at increasing its soft power during the pandemic, China sought to deepen its relations as the world slowly recovers. In early 2021, Wang Yi traveled to six Middle Eastern countries, including Saudi Arabia, the UAE, Bahrain, and Oman.[21] The visit can be viewed in the context of China's objectives in the region as it adjusted to the Biden administration. Following the tense exchange between the US and Chinese delegations in Alaska in early 2021,[22] and the Biden administration's efforts to strengthen alliances with democracies around the world and forge a China strategy that combines engagement with containment, it is unsurprising that China is seeking to cement its relationships and alliances around the world, including in the Gulf. Yi's visit to Saudi Arabia was not only important for both countries' energy and trade partnerships; it also highlights the Saudi political cover and support of China's approach to Xinjiang. Chinese media reported that during this meeting Crown Prince Mohammad bin Salman said: "Saudi Arabia firmly supports China's legitimate position on affairs related to Xinjiang and Hong Kong, opposes interference in China's internal affairs under any pretext, and rejects the attempt by certain parties to sow dissent between China and the Islamic world."[23]

Yi's stop in the UAE underscores the importance of deeper ties between Abu Dhabi and Beijing. As a regional trade hub and major oil exporter to the Asian market, the UAE has prioritized its relationship and deepened its engagement with China earlier than other GCC states. The UAE's strategy of controlling access to key maritime chokepoints in the Indian Ocean, the Horn of Africa, and the Red Sea made Abu Dhabi an indispensable partner for Beijing.[24] The ties are focused not only on trade and energy, but now also on global health and vaccine diplomacy, with the UAE becoming a hub of production for the Sinopharm vaccine.[25]

The GCC's Balancing between China and the US

Historically, balancing between the US and China was not a critical issue for GCC states. However, the growing US-China rivalry and China's expanding global footprint has increasingly compelled them to do so. Navigating this change is particularly delicate for GCC states given their reliance on US security commitments. The perception of US withdrawal from the region has prompted GCC states, working on their own and less within the framework of the GCC, to diversify their security partnerships and sources of armaments. But can China replace the US as a security partner in the region?

The short answer is no. Indeed, while China has been touted as a potential security partner, its primary interests in the MENA region continue to be expanding its commercial reach and locking in energy supplies, all while avoiding any security entanglements. Some prominent Chinese commentators, such as Wang Jisi, have periodically advocated a foreign policy more focused on security concerns in the Middle East and Western Asia,[26] but this view is in the minority in a Chinese state that may be interested in somewhat more security coordination in the Middle East yet has little desire to play the kind of intense militarized goal that the US does.

China does maintain a small base in Djibouti, with 400–1,000 troops providing logistical support for antipiracy operations in the Gulf of Aden and humanitarian programs in Africa.[27] However, the base is largely focused on China's relations with sub-Saharan Africa rather than the MENA region. China has also periodically contributed forces to peacekeeping efforts in the region.[28]

China has sought to play a security role through the export of defense technology. A 2019 report about Saudi Arabia cooperating with China to develop missiles, for example, provoked considerable debate in the United States, even though Saudi Arabia sources only a tiny portion of its overall arms purchases from China. In the past, Saudi Arabia has turned to China for access to ballistic missile technology only when the United States was unwilling to provide it.[29]

The US Congress has warned Saudi Arabia against weapons purchases from Russia or China, while the US administration under President Donald Trump used this point to argue for extensive US arms sales to the kingdom.[30] In 2022 these reports were confirmed by US satellite imagery showing that Saudi Arabia has built a facility and is already manufacturing ballistic missiles with the help of China. This development has raised concerns in Washington that the Saudi ballistic missile program could alter the regional power dynamics and complicate efforts to renegotiate the JCPOA.[31]

The UAE's relationship with China has also alarmed Washington, which had wanted the UAE to exclude the information technology firm Huawei from its 5G network and limit its defense cooperation with the country, fearing that China will use its relationship with the UAE to obtain sensitive technologies, including that in the F35 fighter, which the UAE was slated to acquire. The US Congress even introduced the "Monitoring China-UAE

Cooperation Act."[32] The UAE in response decided to freeze the F35 deal and instead purchased a French-made Rafale fighter jet to signal to the US that it will not be pressured on its ties with China, and that it has other options when it comes to defense procurement.

These challenges in Saudi-US and UAE-US relations highlight a dynamic that works to China's advantage in the Gulf. While both UAE's Crown Prince Mohammed bin Zayed and Saudi Arabia's Crown Prince Mohammad bin Salman enjoyed a close relationship with the Trump administration, this clearly did not continue under Biden. In contrast, China, with its authoritarian model, enjoys continuity of leadership and policies, even when presidents change. China has been able to present itself as a long-time dependable partner unperturbed by the instability of a revolving door of governments in the US and Europe.

Having said that, the US continues to be the key security underwriter in the region. Despite its withdrawal from Afghanistan, the US still maintains a sizable military presence in the region. In Qatar, the US maintains the Udeid Air Base, which was expanded in 2021[33] and played a critical role in the withdrawal from Afghanistan. Manama continues to be the base of the US Fifth Fleet and US Naval Forces Central Command (CENTCOM).[34] In the UAE, the US has a presence at the Al Dharfa Air Base, where its personnel fired Patriot missiles to defend the UAE from Houthi attacks in 2022.[35] There is no realistic scenario in which China can step in and fill these gaps should the US withdraw completely from the GCC.

Future Trajectories and Policy Challenges

The successful implementation of BRI projects in the MENA region, specifically in the Gulf, will entail closer political engagement—which China has long avoided—because these investments highlight some of the contradictions in China's approach to the region.[36] As argued, it will prove increasingly difficult for China to both develop closer relations with Saudi Arabia and maintain its strategic and economic relations with Iran.[37]

Regardless, there is considerable demand for Chinese capital in the region, as various GCC monarchies seek to implement "vision" plans of big-push economic development and diversification.[38] China's authoritarian model of economic development no doubt also holds appeal to MENA rulers, who are averse to making any democratic concessions. This model of authoritarian development finds resonance in the Gulf, which showcased itself as a bastion of stability during the Arab uprisings in 2010 and 2011.

As GCC policymakers seek to deepen their relationships with China, incremental and well-defined engagement will be key. The US-China rivalry will likely shape the twenty-first century, and although the rivalry will play out primarily in Asia, it is likely to have effects across the MENA region.[39] Just as Chinese policymakers will have to carefully balance their relationship between Saudi Arabia and Iran, GCC policymakers will have to do balancing of their own between China and the United States.

The United States has long been the primary external actor in MENA security and is likely to continue to be in the immediate future. Saudi Arabia, like other GCC states, relies on security guarantees from the United States. Their inability to develop comprehensive self-defense capabilities has made US security assurances vital. In addition to its military presence in GCC countries, the United States conducts exercises in partnership with all six GCC states, provides combined training for their militaries, and assists in making purchased US hardware more interoperable.[40] To that end, US security guarantees will always be more important to the GCC than stronger economic relations with China, unless Chinese policymakers decide to become a part of the security architecture of the region. Overall, GCC policymakers will be well served to deepen their engagement with China in a coordinated fashion. The ability to speak with one unified GCC voice will likely produce more positive outcomes for political, economic, and security engagement with China.

Notes

1. Frank Tang, "China Meets Gulf Oil Bloc with Sights Set on Trade Deal, Energy Security," *South China Morning Post*, January 12, 2022 (https://www.scmp.com /economy/china-economy/article/3163121/china-meets-gulf-oil-bloc-sights-set-free -trade-agreement-and).

2. Camille Lons and others, "China's Great Game in the Middle East," Policy Brief (London: European Council on Foreign Relations, 2019) (www.ecfr.eu/publi cations/summary/china_great_game_middle_east).

3. Ali Obaid Al Dhaheri, "The UAE-China Relationship in 2021: A Golden Year, a Golden Future," *China Daily*, December 2, 2021 (https://www.chinadaily.com.cn /a/202112/02/WS61a817dfa310cdd39bc78c9a.html).

4. Reuters and Lisa Barrington, "UAE Launches COVID-19 Vaccine Production with China's Sinopharm," Reuters, March 29, 2021 (https://www.reuters.com/world /middle-east/new-abu-dhabi-plant-manufacture-covid-19-vaccine-chinas-sinopharm -2021-03-29/).

5. Sophie Smith, "China's Increasing Economic Presence in Oman: Implications for Oman's Economy," Euro-Gulf Information Center (https://www.egic.info/china -economic-presence-oman).

6. Mordechai Chaziza, "The Significant Role of Oman in China's Maritime Silk Road Initiative," *Contemporary Review of the Middle East* 6, no. 1 (March 2019), pp. 44–57.

7. Jonathan Fulton, "China Is Trying to Create a Wedge between the US and Gulf Allies. Washington Should Take Note," Atlantic Council, January 27, 2022 (https://www.atlanticcouncil.org/blogs/menasource/china-is-trying-to-create-a-wedge-between-the-us-and-gulf-allies-washington-should-take-note/).

8. Francesco Salesio Schiavi and Mattia Serra, eds., "The Gulf and China: A Broadening Partnership?," ISPI, January 14, 2022 (https://www.ispionline.it/en/pubblicazione/gulf-and-china-broadening-partnership-32872).

9. Cao Siqi and Wan Hengyi, "China, Gulf Countries Pledge Advancing Partnership, FTA Talks," *Global Times*, January 12, 2022 (https://www.globaltimes.cn/page/202201/1245800.shtml).

10. Theodore Karasik, *The GCC's New Affair with China*, Middle East Institute, February 24, 2016 (https://www.mei.edu/publications/gccs-new-affair-china).

11. Kristin Huang, "China and Iran: A Relationship Built on Trade, Weapons and Oil," *South China Morning Post*, January 9, 2020 (https://www.scmp.com/news/china/military/article/3045253/china-and-iran-relationship-built-trade-weapons-and-oil).

12. Ibid.

13. Gafar K. Ahmed, "In Search of a Strategic Partnership: China-Qatar Energy Cooperation, from 1988 to 2015," in *The Arab States of the Gulf and BRICS: New Strategic Partnerships in Politics and Economics*, edited by Tim Niblock, Degang Sun, and Alejandra Galindo (Berlin: Gerlach Press, 2016), p. 193.

14. Joseph Y. S. Cheng, "China's Relations with the Gulf Cooperation Council States: Multilevel Diplomacy in a Divided Arab World," *China Review* 16, no. 1 (Spring 2016), p. 38 (www.jstor.org/stable/43709960).

15. Karasik, *The GCC's New Affair with China*.

16. Cheng, "China's Relations with the Gulf Cooperation Council States," p. 39.

17. Jonathan Fulton, "Strangers to Strategic Partners: Thirty Years of Sino- Saudi Relations," Atlantic Council, August 2020 (https://www.atlanticcouncil.org/wp-content/uploads/2020/08/Sino-Saudi-Relations_WEB.pdf).

18. Farnaz Fassihi and Steven Lee Myers, "Defying U.S., China and Iran Near Trade and Military Partnership," *New York Times*, September 24, 2021.

19. Riyaz ul Khaliq, "China Says Ties with Saudi Arabia a Priority in Its Middle East Diplomacy," *Anadolu Ajansı*, October 18, 2021 (https://www.aa.com.tr/en/asia-pacific/china-says-ties-with-saudi-arabia-a-priority-in-its-middle-east-diplomacy/2395341).

20. See, for example, Y. H. Zoubir, and E. Tran, "China's Health Silk Road in the Middle East and North Africa amidst COVID-19 and a Contested World Order," *Journal of Contemporary China* (2021), pp. 1–16; Jonathan Fulton, "China's Soft Power during the Coronavirus Is Winning over the Gulf States," Atlantic Council, April 16, 2020 (https://www.atlanticcouncil.org/blogs/menasource/chinas-soft-power-during-the-coronavirus-is-winning-over-the-gulf-states/).

21. Illari Papa, "China's Foreign Minister Tours the Middle East: Outcomes and Implications," PolicyWatch 3468 (Washington: Washington Institute for Near East Policy, 2021) (https://www.washingtoninstitute.org/policy-analysis/chinas-foreign -minister-tours-middle-east-outcomes-and-implications).

22. Barbara Plett-Usher, "US and China Trade Angry Words at High Level Alaska Talks," BBC, March 19, 2021 (https://www.bbc.com/news/world-us-canada-56452471).

23. Xu Keyue, "Mideast States Back China's Xinjiang Stance," Global Times, March 25, 2021 (https://www.globaltimes.cn/page/202103/1219498.shtml).

24. Andreas Krieg, "The UAE's Tilt to China," Middle East Eye, October 1, 2020 (https://www.middleeasteye.net/opinion/why-security-partnership-between-abu-dhabi -and-beijing-growing).

25. Bloomberg, "China Picks UAE as Regional Production Hub for Sinopharm Covid-19 vaccine," Straits Times, March 28, 2021 (https://www.straitstimes.com/world /middle-east/china-picks-uae-as-regional-production-hub-for-sinopharm-covid-19 -vaccine).

26. See Eyck Freymann, "Influence without Entanglement in the Middle East," Foreign Policy, February 25, 2021 (https://foreignpolicy.com/2021/02/25/influence -without-entanglement-in-the-middle-east/).

27. See Degang Sun and Yahia H. Zoubir, "Securing China's 'Latent Power': The Dragon's Anchorage in Djibouti," Journal of Contemporary China, 30, no.130 (2021), pp. 677–92.

28. Sun Degang, "China's Soft Military Presence in the Middle East, King Faisal Center for Research and Islamic Studies," January 2018 (http://www.kfcris.com/pdf/ 07b46fba22562acf20bb92fb68f5ea5c5aaa11036d535.pdf).

29. Phil Mattingly, Zachary Cohen, and Jeremy Herb, "Exclusive: US intel Shows Saudi Arabia Escalated Its Missile Program with Help from China," CNN, June 5, 2019 (https://edition.cnn.com/2019/06/05/politics/us-intelligence-saudi-arabia-ballistic -missile-china/index.html); Jeffrey Lewis, "Why Did Saudi Arabia Buy Chinese Mis- siles?," Foreign Policy, January 30, 2014 (https://foreignpolicy.com/2014/01/30/why-did -saudi-arabia-buy-chinese-missiles/).

30. Dan De Luce, "Senators Warn Trump Admin Not to Bypass Congress Again on Arms Sales," NBC News, July 10, 2019 (www.nbcnews.com/politics/congress /senators-warn-trump-admin-not-bypass-congress-again-arms-sales-n1028566).

31. Zachary Cohen, "CNN Exclusive: US Intel and Satellite Images Show Saudi Arabia Is Now Building Its Own Ballistic Missiles with Help of China, CNN, De- cember 23, 2021 (https://edition.cnn.com/2021/12/23/politics/saudi-ballistic-missiles -china/index.html).

32. Congress.gov. "Text - H.R.6269 - 117th Congress (2021–2022): Monitoring China-UAE Cooperation Act," December 14, 2021 (https://www.congress.gov/bill /117th-congress/house-bill/6269/text).

33. Farah AlSharif, "Qatar's Defence Ministry 'Modernises' Al-Udeid Air Base in Latest Expansion Project," Doha News, August 4, 2021 (https://www.dohanews.co /qatars-defence-ministry-modernises-al-udeid-air-base-in-latest-expansion-project/).

34. Commander, Navy Installations Command Notification (https://www.cnic.navy.mil/BAHRAIN/).

35. Jon Gambrell and Howard Altman, "US Troops Sheltered, Fired Patriot Missiles during Yemen Houthi Attack on UAE," *Military Times*, February 1, 2022 (https://www.militarytimes.com/flashpoints/2022/02/01/us-military-fired-patriot-missiles-during-yemen-houthi-attack-on-uae/).

36. Yoram Evron, "The Challenge of Implementing the Belt and Road Initiative in the Middle East: Connectivity Projects under Conditions of Limited Political Engagement," *China Quarterly* 237 (March 2019), pp. 196–216 (https://doi.org/10.1017/S0305741018001273).

37. Liu Zhen, "China, Iran to Forge Closer Ties due to Common Threat from United States, Analysts Say," *South China Morning Post*, May 23, 2019 (www.scmp.com/news/china/diplomacy/article/3011573/china-iran-forge-closer-ties-due-common-threat-united-states).

38. Fulton, *China's Changing Role*, pp. 10–11.

39. See, for example, Thomas J. Wright, *All Measures Short of War: The Contest for the Twenty-First Century and the Future of American Power* (Yale University Press, 2017); Thomas J. Christensen, *The China Challenge: Shaping the Choices of a Rising Power* (New York: W. W. Norton, 2016); Lars Erslev Andersen, "China, the Middle East and the Reshaping of World Order: The Case of Iran," Working Paper 14 (Copenhagen: Danish Institute for International Studies, 2019) (https://pure.diis.dk/ws/files/3166089/DIIS_WP_2019_14_China_the_Middle_East_and_the_reshaping_of_world_order.pdf).

40. Daniel Benaim and Michael Wahid Hanna, "The Enduring American Presence in the Middle East," *Foreign Affairs*, August 7, 2019 (www.foreignaffairs.com/articles/middle-east/2019-08-07/enduring-american-presence-middle-east); Jerome H Kahan, "Security Assurances for the Gulf States: A Bearable Burden?" *Middle East Policy* 23, no. 3 (2016), pp. 30–38.

SEVEN

The COVID-19 Pandemic in the Gulf

Impact, Response, and Implications

TARIK M. YOUSEF

OVER THE PAST DECADE, the Gulf Cooperation Council (GCC) countries have faced growing challenges to their security and prosperity. Since the Arab Spring protests, leaders have placed a strong emphasis on internal stability and the need to manage reform. They have sought to lessen their dependence on hydrocarbon revenues while diversifying economies. They have responded to perceived external threats and a changing geopolitical environment. And they faced these challenges most recently during a period of relatively low oil prices, which has strained financial resources and pushed them to adopt fiscal reforms. The COVID-19 pandemic has compounded many of these challenges and is likely to have a long-term impact on the region's economies.

The Spread of COVID-19

On January 29, 2020, health authorities in the United Arab Emirates (UAE) confirmed the country's first case of COVID-19 in a visitor who had arrived

This chapter is published as Tarik M. Yousef, "The COVID-19 Pandemic in the Gulf: Impact, Response, and Implications," Policy Note, Middle East Council on Global Affairs, 2022.

Figure 7-1. New Daily Confirmed COVID-19 Cases in GCC States, February 2020–October 2021

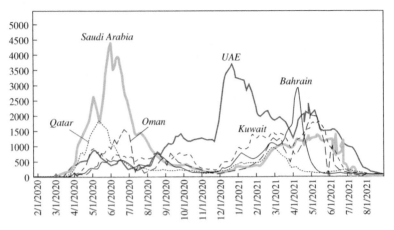

Source: Hannah Ritchie and others, "Coronavirus Pandemic (COVID-19)," OurWorldInData.org (https://ourworldindata.org /coronavirus).

from China fourteen days earlier. Bahrain saw its first case on February 21. Oman and Kuwait confirmed cases on February 24, Qatar on February 27, and Saudi Arabia on March 2; all of them seem to have originated in Iran. Incidence of the virus initially grew slowly in each of these countries, but confirmed cases of COVID-19 accelerated in mid-March as the virus gained a foothold among the resident population and the number of daily cases rose precipitously (see figure 7-1). From a combined 114 confirmed cases on March 1, the number of cases in the GCC grew to 844 by March 15 and to 4,056 by April 1, 2020.[1]

Confirmed cases in the GCC continued to grow rapidly through the spring of 2020, then began to level off over the course of the summer. Still, the total number of cases in the GCC reached over 1 million in early January 2021 and 2 million by the beginning of June as the Gulf experienced repeated waves of the virus. By mid-September 2021, total cases across the GCC leveled off at 2.5 million as vaccination rates increased. On a per capita basis, by the end of October, this amounted to 42,334 cases per million people (figure 7-2). This infection rate is lower than in the Organization for Economic Cooperation and Development (OECD) countries (85,669 cases per million), but higher than the number of cases per capita in the broader Middle East and North Africa (MENA)

Figure 7-2. COVID-19 Cases per Million Population in GCC States and Comparators, February 2020–October 2021

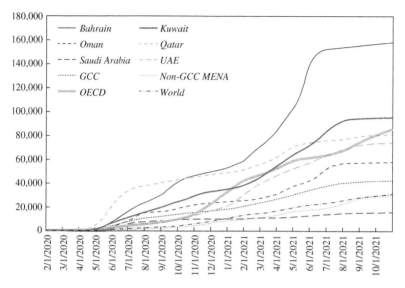

Source: Calculated by the author using data from Hannah Ritchie and others, "Coronavirus Pandemic (COVID-19)," OurWorldInData.org (https://ourworldindata.org/coronavirus).

region, where non-GCC MENA countries reported 31,133 cases per million.[2] Notably, Saudi Arabia—with 15,523 cases per million population— saw lower rates of infection than its GCC neighbors, while Bahrain experienced one of the highest rates of infection in the world (158,342 per million).[3]

Across the GCC, mortality rates associated with the virus remained low. By the end of October 2021, the Gulf region had documented 19,505 deaths associated with COVID-19 or, on a per capita basis, 327 deaths per million population. By comparison, COVID-19 deaths across the OECD averaged 1,602 deaths per million, while in the non-GCC MENA region, they averaged 615. In part, the low fatality rate associated with COVID-19 in the GCC countries reflects widescale testing and the ability of health authorities to identify cases of the virus, including asymptomatic cases and those with less critical symptoms within a largely youthful population. It also reflects the relative strength of Gulf healthcare systems and the efficacy of the public health response.

Pandemic Response

Initially, authorities across the GCC attempted to control the domestic spread of the virus by tightening border controls, conducting regular health checks, and suspending flights to high-risk countries. Building on their experience with the Middle East Respiratory Syndrome (MERS) virus in 2012, governments readied isolation units in hospitals and expanded testing and contact-tracing efforts. Through mid-March 2020, these initial measures seemed effective in controlling the virus's spread. However, as the number of cases ramped up, governments began implementing more rigorous restrictions. These varied from country to country, but they typically included travel bans, school closures, restrictions on public gatherings, closures of mosques and nonessential businesses, suspension of public holiday celebrations, and implementation of nightly curfews and mobility restrictions. Even after easing restrictions, Gulf states enforced a mask mandate and physical distancing requirements where possible.

While Gulf governments enforced closures and implemented other policy responses around the same period, they diverged in the easing of restrictions and the reopening of economies, reflecting both trends in the incidence of the virus and economic pressures.[4] Bahrain, for example, initially maintained the least rigorous restrictions in the GCC but has been careful in returning to full openness. The UAE took early steps to reopen the economy to ease pressures on private sector businesses. Oman, having imposed significant lockdown measures, kept these restrictions in place longer than other countries but then opened up more than other countries toward the beginning of 2021. Kuwait, Qatar, and Saudi Arabia began emerging from strict lockdowns with the most cautious approaches at around the same period. Each of these countries had to periodically reimpose restrictions as new waves of the virus emerged.

Over the summer and early autumn of 2021, the Gulf states made strides in expanding vaccination coverage, ensuring ready access to vaccines while implementing strict vaccine mandates requiring individuals to be fully vaccinated in order to return to normal economic life. While some vaccine hesitancy remains, vaccination rates across the Gulf grew quickly, and several GCC states lead the world in shares of their populations that are inoculated. In turn, daily new cases of COVID-19 dropped precipitously.

To manage the economic fallout from the pandemic, GCC countries have spent significant sums on stimulus packages to support workers and private sector firms. These packages have included reductions in official fees, rents, and social insurance contributions, wage subsidies for nationals in the private sector, and concessional loans to small and medium-sized enterprises (SMEs).[5] Authorities have worked with banks to increase liquidity and facilitate access to loans as well as allow loan payment deferrals. As a share of total gross domestic product (GDP), these outlays have been relatively small in comparison with those in OECD countries, ranging between 1.5 percent in Kuwait to 6 percent in Bahrain. Qatar's fiscal response—worth a reported 14 percent of GDP—is an international exception. Overall, these efforts appear to have focused mostly on providing direct support to national workers and companies but only indirect support to guest workers. More important, the overall efficacy of these efforts remains unknown given the limited transparency on policy implementation and outcomes.

Understanding Outcomes

Several factors ensured that COVID-19 was able to take root so strongly in the GCC. First, GCC states are more closely tied to the global economy than their MENA neighbors, particularly through air travel. Dubai's airport itself has the world's fourth largest number of international arrivals, and airports across the region are important transit points for international and regional flights. This global and regional connectivity made it possible for the virus to spread in the GCC earlier than in most other countries. Moreover, initial bans on flights from the early hotspot countries proved ineffective at stopping the virus because screening mechanisms were unable to identify infected but asymptomatic individuals.

Second, an initial lack of decisiveness on the part of policymakers may have given the disease room to spread. From international experience, two response methods seem to have been most effective. The first, followed by South Korea and others, focused on early and extensive testing and tracing rather than economic closures.[6] The second, exemplified by New Zealand, included rapid and comprehensive lockdowns to restrict community spread.[7] GCC states deployed a mix of these approaches, which were generally effective over time. However, having depended on procuring COVID-19 test capabilities from abroad, governments were only able to ramp up testing regimes gradually. At the same time, governments took incremental steps in implementing closures. The hesitation to shutter the local economy and the delayed implementation of robust testing and tracing allowed the virus to proliferate.

The GCC's Unique Vulnerabilities

The GCC's large guest worker population further created an environment that was conducive to the rapid spread of the virus. Private sector firms typically house low-skilled guest workers in crowded dormitories, often co-located in densely populated "industrial zones" with workers from several firms. Across the GCC, health authorities inspecting these labor camps found them to be hotspots for the virus. Moreover, they found it impossible to quickly reorganize these housing arrangements to allow for the physical distancing needed to contain the spread of the virus. Instead, they resorted to camp lockdowns and district isolation that raised concerns about the rights of workers and led to workers going without pay or access to services for extended periods.[8]

The broader dependence of these GCC economies on guest workers—both low skilled and high skilled—left their private sectors vulnerable to the economic costs of the pandemic response. Notably, governments have provided wage subsidies that cover only nationals, a minority of the private sector workforce in the GCC. Firms and guest workers responded in multiple ways. Some transitioned—where possible—to telework arrangements. Others waited out lockdowns, with firms often covering housing costs but not wages. With the prolonged duration of the pandemic, many workers were laid off or resigned and returned to their countries of origin. The loss of human capital for government and the private sector is a cause for concern about the future costs of bringing talent back after the pandemic.

The COVID-19 pandemic has also raised concerns about food security in the GCC. Every country in the region relies heavily on imports to meet their food requirements. During past international crises, like the 2008 Great Recession, GCC countries experienced shortages when major producers of rice and other staples imposed quotas on exports. Similar export quotas were put in place during the early stages of the pandemic. These export quotas, along with other disruptions to food supply chains, elevated worries in the GCC about the steady availability of food supplies. While they have been able to keep stores well stocked, owing largely to government stockpiling, the pandemic has renewed policymakers' attention to ensuring food security during times of crisis.

Finally, the pandemic has underlined the continued dependence of the GCC economies on hydrocarbons and the vulnerability of the region to price shocks. After a five-year period of relatively low but steady oil prices, the pandemic triggered a sharp decline in global demand and a dramatic collapse in oil prices, which have only partially recovered. Thus, at a time of dire need for additional fiscal space to stimulate the local economy and support an eventual recovery, GCC governments have had to draw on their sovereign wealth funds and raise sovereign debt abroad while slashing costs wherever possible. Budgetary pressures have triggered massive cuts in capital spending, delayed implementation of planned projects, and forced reductions to expatriate staff wages and numbers.

Rebuilding for the Future

With the development of several efficacious vaccines for COVID-19, the global community is shifting its priorities from combatting the virus to economic recovery. Across the globe, policymakers, having focused in 2020 on stabilizing household incomes and employment, are planning a post-pandemic future. Those countries that are being strategic about government investments in rebuilding will be the most competitive and will rebound the fastest in the wake of the pandemic. GCC countries have an opportunity to emerge from the COVID-19 pandemic better positioned to sustain their high standards of living and meet a host of potential future challenges, including public heath crises, the impact of climate change, and the retreat of globalization.

First, it is essential that GCC governments carry out a comprehensive assessment of their COVID-19 response. While the vaccines in process will likely resolve the current crisis, the world remains vulnerable to unknown future pandemics. A comprehensive review of the response will help GCC governments refine their epidemic scenario planning and crisis management. This review would pave the way for future investments in the capabilities and preparedness of public health systems. Given the proximity and relative integration of GCC countries, notwithstanding the effects of the 2017 rift, such investments could become a focus for cooperation. More ambitiously, a regional center for disease control would improve coordination in tackling future pandemics and other health crises.

Securing the future also requires pushing forward with policy and institutional reforms more generally. Governments have implemented some reforms in the context of COVID-19 responses that bode well in both regards.[9] The nature of the COVID-19 crisis has forced ministries to collaborate and take an all-of-government approach in a region known for vertical integration and weak coordination. Governments also have set up task forces to address various aspects of the crisis, working across ministries and business sectors to address specific challenges, such as supporting private sector companies and protecting trade flows. Moreover, the closure of government offices has pushed authorities to make more rapid strides in advancing e-government and m-government. Along with investments underway in financial, information, and communication technologies, these efforts should have a long-term positive impact on service delivery and economic diversification.

Finally, post-pandemic rebuilding should steer investments and reforms toward addressing structural economic priorities.[10] These include expanding the fiscal revenue base and preparing for disruptive acceleration in the energy transition. They also involve strengthening corporate governance, improving government transparency, and promoting competition in the domestic economy, as well as the promotion of SME development, technology upskilling for the national workforce, and labor mobility for guest workers. Also, in alignment with food security concerns, investments in agrobusiness and agricultural technology, both locally and internationally, meet a variety of development objectives.

Given the ongoing fiscal pressures associated with low and volatile oil prices, governments should also consider moving away from public sector employment guarantees as a means of redistributing oil revenues to the possible implementation of a minimum basic income for citizens.[11] The surge in international oil prices over the course of 2022 may undermine incentives for such reform in the short-term as countries prioritize recovery from the pandemic recession. However, long-term prospects for the oil sector, amid a growing global consensus on the need to reduce dependence on fossil fuels and combat climate change, suggest a need for Gulf states to prioritize diversification and public sector reform while they can.[12]

Notes

1. Data on COVID-19 referred to in this chapter are calculated using country-level information reported by Hannah Ritchie and others in "Coronavirus Pandemic (COVID-19)," OurWorldInData.org (https://ourworldindata.org/coronavirus).

2. One should bear in mind, however, concerns regarding low testing rates and potential underreporting in many states.

3. Later, it brought its rates of spread under control through vaccinations.

4. This figure tracks results from the Oxford COVID-19 Government Response Tracker's stringency index. The index quantifies the strictness of regulations associated with closures of schools, businesses, and public venues, as well as travel restrictions (although it does not account for enforcement or compliance).

5. International Monetary Fund, "Policy Responses to COVID-19" (www.imf.org/en/Topics/imf-and-covid19/Policy-Responses-to-COVID-19).

6. Paul Dyer, *Policy and Institutional Responses to COVID-19: South Korea*, Middle East and North Africa COVID-19 Response Project Report (Doha, Qatar: Brookings Doha Center, June 15, 2021) (https://www.brookings.edu/research/policy-and-institutional-responses-to-covid-19-south-korea/).

7. Paul Dyer, *Policy and Institutional Responses to COVID-19: New Zealand*, Middle East and North Africa COVID-19 Response Project Report (Doha, Qatar: Brookings Doha Center, January 24, 2021) (www.brookings.edu/research/policy-and-institutional-responses-to-covid-19-new-zealand/).

8. Omer Karasapan, "Pandemic Highlights the Vulnerability of Migrant Workers in the Middle East," *Future Development* (blog), Brookings, September 17, 2020 (www.brookings.edu/blog/future-development/2020/09/17/pandemic-highlights-the-vulnerability-of-migrant-workers-in-the-middle-east/).

9. Robert P. Beschel Jr. and Tarik Yousef, "Public Sector Reform in MENA: The Achievable Governance Revolution," Economic Research Forum, May 4, 2021 (https://theforum.erf.org.eg/2021/04/26/public-sector-reform-mena-achievable-governance-revolution/).

10. International Monetary Fund, *Trade-Offs Today for Transformation Tomorrow: Middle East and Central Asia*, Regional Economic Outlook (Washington, October 14, 2021) (https://www.imf.org/en/Publications/REO/MECA/Issues/2021/10/14/regional-economic-outlook-october).

11. Steffen Hertog, "The Case for an Arabian Universal Basic Income," *Project Syndicate*, December 9, 2020 (https://www.project-syndicate.org/commentary/gulf-states-case-for-universal-basic-income-by-steffen-hertog-2020-12).

12. Justin Alexander, "The Implications of COVID-19 for the Gulf States' Development Models," in *The Strategic and Geo-economic Implications of the COVID-19 Pandemic* (Manama, Bahrain: International Institute for Strategic Studies, 2020) (https://www.iiss.org/blogs/research-paper/2020/12/strategic-geo-economic-implications-covid-19-pandemic).

PART 2

ECONOMIC TRANSITION

EIGHT

GCC Economic Integration in the Aftermath of the Qatar Crisis

NADER HABIBI

THERE HAS BEEN A visible deterioration in intra-GCC relations since 2017. While tensions among the Gulf Cooperation Council (GCC) members (Bahrain, Kuwait, Oman, Qatar, Saudi Arabia, and the United Arab Emirates) have existed since the organization's inception in 1981, GCC leaders did not allow these tensions to get out of hand and overshadow the postures of cooperation and unity. For example, the episodes of bilateral tension, such as the 2004–2005 disagreement between Saudi Arabia and Bahrain over the latter's decision to sign a free trade agreement with the United States, were gradually overcome after a few years and the GCC was able to present a unified face to the international community.[1]

After the Arab Spring, the sharp disagreements between Qatar and the two largest GCC members, Saudi Arabia and the United Arab Emirates (UAE), over regional policies and treatment of the Muslim Brotherhood increased intra-GCC discord to new and unprecedented levels.[2] Their differences led to the blockade of Qatar in June 2017, which further weakened the economic and political links between GCC countries.

As a formal organization, the GCC is still alive and no member has officially withdrawn. The six member countries have continued their annual summits, although some rulers decided to send a minister or representative to the thirty-ninth and fortieth summits in 2018 and 2019 instead of attending in person.[3] This collective interest in preserving the GCC was evident in Saudi foreign minister Adel Al-Jubeir's comments during the thirty-ninth GCC summit in Riyadh in December 2018: "Members of the council are determined that the crisis with Qatar does not have a negative effect on the council in general and its structure. . . . The goal is to preserve all of these important structures, until the crisis ends, hopefully soon."[4]

The purpose of this essay is to assess the level of economic cooperation among GCC countries as measured by intra-GCC trade and investment with a focus on how these economic relations have evolved since the Qatar crisis. Since its inception in 1981, the GCC has approved several important economic coordination and cooperation agreements (see table 8-1). Most of the formal steps were taken before 2010, but some of them, such as the GCC customs union, were implemented with considerable delay. These formal achievements, however, have been inconsistent, and some member countries have been selective in the implementation of these agreements.[5]

Despite these impressive formal agreements, the political and economic institutions of GCC countries have proven unsuitable for a high level of economic integration in practice. Observers have identified four major factors that led to slow progress in GCC economic integration. First, the composition of the export products and import needs of GCC countries are very similar.[6] All are oil exporting countries, and many of the industrial and agricultural products that they need are not available in other member nations.

Second, the strong imbalance of demographic, economic, and military power in favor of Saudi Arabia has been a concern for smaller GCC countries, which are very sensitive about their sovereignty. Saudi Arabia expects other GCC members to accept its role as the natural leader of the bloc, but the smaller members have repeatedly rejected this demand.

Third, by developing bilateral military and security relations with the United States, smaller GCC countries are less dependent on larger members (and particularly on Saudi Arabia) for protection against regional threats. Furthermore, reliance on the US security umbrella has enabled the smaller GCC nations to insist on equal weight in GCC affairs, and their behavior has reduced the incentives of Saudi Arabia and the UAE to pursue deeper GCC economic integration.

Fourth, the "equalizing" influence of the United States has allowed the ruling monarchy in each GCC country to develop and sustain its own ideological and foreign policy vision even when these visions contradict each other. These disagreements have become obstacles to economic cooperation.

Table 8-1. *Timeline of GCC Economic Agreements, 1981–2015*

1981	Inauguration of the Gulf Cooperation Council; economic integration set as a top priority
1982	Establishment of the Gulf Investment Corporation (based in Kuwait) with $2.1 billion in initial capital
1983	Easing of travel and customs regulations for GCC nationals; lifting of customs duties on a list of domestic products
1985	Harmonization of policies and regulations on agriculture, industrial development, environmental protection, and education
1986	Citizens granted access to banking services and bank loans in other GCC countries
1987	Launch of negotiations for the creation of a common market and harmonized customs tariffs
1988	GCC citizens and entities allowed to trade in all GCC stock markets (implemented in 1990)
1995	GCC leaders approve a proposal to link GCC power grid; coordination established on several banking reforms
1998	GCC approves freedom of movement for citizens in all member states, approves several measures to reduce restrictions on trade and flow of commodities
1999	GCC approves the creation of a customs union by March 2005
2000	GCC citizens allowed to engage in economic activity and work in other member countries
2001	GCC approves a common 5 percent tariff for external trade and abolishes all tariffs among member states; agreement on creation of a single currency monetary union by 2010 (never implemented)
2002	GCC approves a regional emergency plan for petroleum products
2003	GCC approves a customs union agreement
2005	GCC approves a common external trade policy in order to engage in free trade agreements with major economic partners as a unified bloc
2006	GCC approves coordination and cooperation among member states toward development of peaceful nuclear technology
2008	GCC common market goes into effect, granting GCC citizens equal economic rights and legal protection in all member states (full labor, commodity, and capital mobility for citizens)
2009	Four GCC members agree on a monetary union (Oman and the UAE refuse to join)
2015	GCC customs union, which was approved in 2003, is declared fully operational

The opposing views of the Qatari and Saudi ruling families about the legitimacy of the Muslim Brotherhood is a good example of how these conflicting visions have persisted.

Intra-GCC Trade

For the reasons noted earlier, intra-GCC trade is relatively small as a share of total trade of GCC members. Focusing on trade data since 2000, figure 8-1 shows that the other members' share in total exports of each GCC country has remained below 15 percent for all except Bahrain. For Kuwait and Qatar, this ratio does not even exceed 5 percent. Figure 8-1, however, shows an increase in the GCC's share in the total exports of Bahrain, Oman, and the UAE between the first and second decades of the twenty-first century. Figure 8-1 also shows that GCC partners' share in total imports of each member country is equally small, with the exception of Oman and Bahrain. This is partly because in recent decades the UAE and Saudi Arabia have achieved more economic diversity and have become more important as sources of products and services to the other four members.[7] There has also been an increase in the GCC's share in the total imports of Bahrain, Oman, Kuwait, and Saudi Arabia over time.

Not only was the volume of trade among GCC countries on the rise before the Qatar crisis; in addition, the progress of economic diversification programs had enabled each member country to generate more goods and services for intra-GCC trade. The Qatar blockade, for example, revealed the large volume of bilateral trade between Qatar and Saudi Arabia in food and non-oil commodities. It also revealed Qatar's heavy dependence on the UAE as its main reexport hub. Overall, Saudi Arabia is the largest GCC partner of other members.

For GCC countries as a group, non-oil exports to other GCC countries accounted for 13 percent of total non-oil exports from 2007 to 2016, but most of these were destined for the Saudi market. (Saudi Arabia's share of the total non-oil exports of Bahrain, Oman, and Kuwait averaged 25, 11, and 9 percent, respectively, in this time interval).[8]

The blockade caused a severe reduction in Qatar's imports from the GCC (83 percent of which originated in Saudi Arabia and the UAE in 2016). A similar but smaller disruption occurred in Qatar's exports to the GCC. Qatar's exports to the UAE fell from $3.8 billion in 2016 to $1.5 billion in 2018 and $1.1 billion in 2019.[9] The blockade did not reduce the volume of Qatar's bilateral trade with Kuwait and Oman (neither participated in the

Figure 8-1. Other GCC Countries' Share in Total Imports and Total Exports of Each GCC Member, 2000–2019
Percent

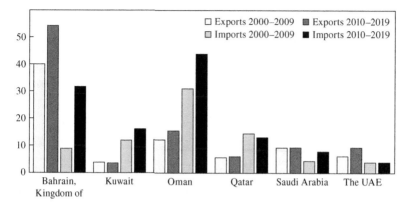

Source: IMF, Direction of Trade Statistics Dataset (https://data.imf.org/?sk=9d6028d4-f14a-464c-a2f2-59b2cd424b85). Percentages calculated by the author.

Saudi-led blockade). Furthermore, a comparison of the GCC's share of each country's total value of trade (exports plus imports) with the world during the two years before (2015–2016) and after (2018–2019) the Qatar crisis makes it clear that for Kuwait, Saudi Arabia, and the UAE the GCC's share of total trade increased. For Qatar and Bahrain, this share decreased by 65 percent and 36 percent respectively.[10]

Intra-GCC Investment and Business Relations

The GCC countries opened their stock markets to other members in 1990, while freedom of travel and business ownership were implemented in 2000. Ever since, there has been growth in intra-GCC investment and business relations. Intra-GCC foreign direct investment (FDI) accounted for 23 percent of total FDI from 2009 to 2011, which was a significant increase from only 3 percent in the period 1990–2003.[11] Among the GCC countries, Saudi Arabia was both the largest recipient and the largest source of FDI for other GCC countries. As of 2015, the FDI investments of other GCC countries in Saudi Arabia stood at $35 billion (equivalent to 10 percent of Saudi non-oil GDP); the comparable figures for Bahrain and Kuwait were $15 billion and $7 billion respectively.[12]

Intra-GCC equity investments in stock markets and financial institutions also grew significantly after 2000. In 2015, Emirati and Qatari investments in the Saudi stock market stood at $9 billion and $6 billion respectively, which was equivalent to 3.2 percent and 6 percent of their respective GDPs.[13] As a result of these cross-investments, empirical studies have detected positive correlations among the GCC stock market indexes. A 2019 study found that the Qatar blockade, however, has reduced the interdependency of Qatar's stock market with other GCC markets.[14] There has also been a significant amount of intra-GCC banking investment in terms of both ownership and deposits. Emirati and Qatari banks had strong cross-exposures before the blockade, which caused sizable asset and deposit losses for some banks and businesses in both countries.[15]

Looking Forward

The level of economic integration that the GCC had achieved before the Qatar crisis was moderate, but it offered many tangible benefits to the member states. It gave each of them a regional market to help diversify their non-oil economic sectors, as well as strong collective bargaining power in trade negotiations with the European Union and Asia.[16] As the GCC economies move forward with their diversification programs they will be able to produce a larger volume of tradable goods and services. As a result, the potential benefits of GCC economic integration will increase.

Yet most scholars are pessimistic about the prospects for a resolution to the Qatar crisis, without which there is little hope for further progress on economic integration.[17] If the crisis continues, what might emerge is deeper integration of Saudi Arabia, the UAE, and Bahrain as a GCC subgroup. Oman and Kuwait are likely to continue their neutrality in the Qatar crisis and try to contain it. This position will allow them to preserve their economic ties with both sides.

Like the rest of the world, GCC countries have been affected by the coronavirus pandemic since March 2020. The pandemic has had a mixed impact on intra-GCC relations. Since all GCC rulers have been preoccupied with the pandemic's healthcare and economic consequences, they have been distracted from the Qatar crisis temporarily. Although there has been no further escalation of tensions, the mediation attempts of Kuwait and Oman were also placed on hold. On a positive note, the GCC secretary general was able to organize several pandemic response coordination meetings at the ministerial level in 2020, and all six members participated in these meetings.

The pandemic has also affected the region through its adverse effect on the price of crude oil. Weak oil and gas revenues will also have a mixed effect on the pace of economic diversification in GCC countries (which will increase their capacity for economic integration in the long run). On the one hand, lower oil revenues will further give GCC ruling monarchies an incentive to pursue economic diversification. On the other hand, lower revenues have reduced the amount of resources that are available to finance economic diversification projects.

Notes

1. David Price, "Built upon Shifting Sands—Warning Signs for the United States' Middle East Free Trade Area Strategy," *International Review of Business Research Papers* 4, no. 2 (2008), pp. 231–42.

2. Rory Miller, "Managing Regional Conflict: The Gulf Cooperation Council and the Embargo of Qatar," *Global Policy* 10, S2 (June 2019), pp. 36–45 (https://doi.org /10.1111/1758-5899.12674).

3. "Qatari Emir to Skip Saudi-Hosted GCC Summit," *Arab Weekly*, December 9, 2018 (https://thearabweekly.com/qatari-emir-skip-saudi-hosted-gcc-summit).

4. "GCC Summit Ends without Roadmap to Resolve Ongoing Crisis," *Al Jazeera*, December 10, 2018 (www.aljazeera.com/news/2018/12/gcc-summit-ends-roadmap -resolve-ongoing-crisis-181210074639694.html).

5. For example, although the internal tariffs were removed with the creation of the GCC customs union, some GCC countries use nontariff barriers to limit imports from other members.

6. Subhadra Ganguli, "Economic Diversification and Intra-GCC Merchandise Trade: An Empirical Analysis during 1995–2015," *World Journal of Entrepreneurship, Management and Sustainable Development* 14, no. 1 (2018), pp. 25–40 (https://doi.org /10.1108/WJEMSD-06-2017-0028).

7. The economy of Bahrain is also more diverse because of its very small oil resources and because its primary exports are financial and tourism services.

8. Olumuyiwa S. Adedeji, Sohaib Shahid, and Ling Zhu, "Saudi Arabia's Growth and Financial Spillovers to Other GCC Countries: An Empirical Analysis," Working Paper 18/278 (Washington: International Monetary Fund, December 2018) (www .imf.org/en/Publications/WP/Issues/2018/12/11/Saudis-Growth-and-Financial-Spill overs-to-Other-GCC-Countries-An-Empirical-Analysis-46440).

9. International Monetary Fund (IMF), Direction of Trade Statistics Dataset (https://data.imf.org/?sk=9d6028d4-f14a-464c-a2f2-59b2cd424b85).

10. Ibid.

11. Jeffrey Martini and others, "The Outlook for Arab Gulf Cooperation," (Santa Monica, CA: Rand Corporation, 2016) (www.rand.org/content/dam/rand/pubs/research _reports/RR1400/RR1429/RAND_RR1429.pdf).

12. Adedeji, Shahid, and Zhu, "Saudi Arabia's Growth and Financial Spillovers to Other GCC Countries."

13. Ibid.

14. Lanouar Charfeddine and Hisham Al Refai, "Political Tensions, Stock Market Dependence and Volatility Spillover: Evidence from the Recent intra-GCC Crises,"

North American Journal of Economics and Finance 50 (November 2019) (https://doi .org/10.1016/j.najef.2019.101032).

15. "Qatar Blockade Plays Out in Battle over UAE Banks," *Al Jazeera*, November 25, 2018 (www.aljazeera.com/news/2018/11/qatar-blockade-plays-battle-uae-banks -181125080522958.html).

16. Ashraf Mishrif and Salma Said Humaid Al-Naamani, "Regional Integration, the Private Sector and Diversification in the GCC Countries," in *Economic Diversification in the Gulf Region, Volume I,* edited by Mishrif and Yousuf Al Balushi (Singapore: Palgrave Macmillan, 2018), pp. 209–33.

17. See Abdullah Baabood, "The Future of the GCC Amid the Gulf Divide," in *Divided Gulf: The Anatomy of a Crisis,* edited by Andreas Krieg (Singapore: Palgrave Macmillan, 2019), pp. 161–78.

NINE

The GCC's Evolving Financial Markets

JEAN-FRANÇOIS SEZNEC

THE FINANCIAL MARKETS OF the Gulf are becoming as sophisticated as those of the Western world, but their growth is limited by fragmentation. They are also hampered by major changes in technology that render local institutions less necessary to the Gulf public, which can easily work directly with the markets of New York, London, or Hong Kong. The changes have resulted in a number of mergers in the commercial banking area. The markets' fragmentation is also responsible for the very modest growth of the stock markets and local investment banking institutions, in spite of the initial December 2019 public offering (IPO) of Saudi Aramco on the Riyadh stock market.

However, two main characteristics of the Gulf markets are still very much in place. First, the markets are dominated by the US dollar because the local Gulf currencies are pegged to the dollar. Second, all of the Gulf's financial markets are dominated by the states in which they operate. The regulators have a strong say in how the banks are managed. In many cases, the states de facto control their ownership. Furthermore, the companies floated on the stock markets are often directly or indirectly controlled by the states.

Link to the Dollar

The parity of Gulf Cooperation Council (GCC) currencies with the US dollar has remained stable for decades. From time to time, financial reporters argue that currency devaluations, especially of the Saudi riyal, will be necessary should the price of oil decline substantially. However, the local financial authorities have always discarded this argument. Indeed, most GCC state income comes from dollar-denominated oil and gas sales. Furthermore, most GCC state imports, even from China and Japan, are denominated in dollars. Devaluing the local currencies would not improve the terms of trade for the local economies.

One could argue that GCC countries are exporting more non-crude oil products than they used to. Indeed, Saudi Arabia, the United Arab Emirates (UAE), and Qatar are increasingly producing and exporting basic and advanced chemicals, fertilizers, aluminum, and, in the case of Saudi Arabia, manufactured goods such as steel structures, air conditioners, electric and phone cables, and agricultural products. However, most of these products are made using materials that are themselves bought with US dollars. Only the cost of labor could benefit from the devaluation of local currency, and labor is a minimal percentage of the final cost of the modern industrial products produced in the Gulf.

Thus it is most unlikely that the region's financial markets would substantially move away from their strong link to the US dollar in the near future. The rise of China in GCC trade is remarkable and could slowly bring about changes, but not much will change until the Chinese renminbi becomes fully convertible. This would certainly help China develop its renminbi-denominated Shanghai oil exchange and decrease China's dependence on the US dollar. Making the renminbi convertible would have momentous implications for China's ability to control its currency and its economy, but would be necessary for this currency to become a major tool of trading. Chinese financial institutions are taking baby steps in this direction, such as opening some branches in the Gulf to facilitate Chinese companies' activities in the region and decrease their need for US dollars. However, convertibility implies a loss of control by the central government and the Communist Party over the economy, which is unlikely to become policy anytime soon. The US dollar will therefore remain the de facto currency of the Gulf.

The Future of the Gulf Stock Markets

The Gulf stock markets are still very small relative to enormous US and European exchanges. Even though Gulf companies and richer individuals have large amounts of liquidity, they use the local exchanges sparingly and mainly use the London and New York markets.

The largest of the region's stock markets is the Tadawul in Riyadh with a capitalization of about $500 billion, a mere fraction of the New York and London stock exchanges. Even though the Saudi Aramco IPO of 1.5 percent of its shares on the Tadawul found buyers very easily and the offering was vastly oversold, the Riyadh market remains small by world standards.

The Saudi riyal, like the other currencies of the Gulf, is freely convertible, which is a necessity for foreign investors to consider any investments in the region. Furthermore, the companies traded on the Tadawul must be transparent in their disclosures and provide balance sheets using internationally recognized standards. Thus the Tadawul has now been recognized by the providers of emerging market indexes, which means that large foreign investors can buy and sell shares on the market in Riyadh, which analysts said would bring up to $50 billion to the market. This is indeed a very important development, but the amounts are still modest.

A major limitation of Gulf stock markets is that there are more markets than there are countries when there should only be one for the whole region. Each country developed its own market according to its needs and capacities; but without a major effort by Gulf financial authorities to centralize share trading in one platform, the markets will remain internationally irrelevant. Without a common GCC currency, central bank, or monetary union, it is unlikely that a unified stock market could be established. However, it does not appear that the disagreements between GCC states on these currency and monetary policy issues will be resolved any time soon.

The lack of a unified stock market leads to the fragmentation of local capital and limits the markets' attractiveness for foreigners. In a region where the local currencies are proxies for the US dollar and where flows of capital have no restrictions, it does not appear necessary to have markets in Bahrain, Qatar, Oman, Kuwait, and the UAE, all with a fraction of the Tadawul's capitalization.

Still, despite all of the efforts to develop and integrate the GCC economies, each country is seeking to grow its own stock market. Even in the small UAE there are two competing platforms, one in Dubai and one in Abu Dhabi, which both seek to attract foreign investors with free trade zone advantages and legal systems based on English common law.

If all these markets were to merge, they could offer foreign and local investors alike an attractive platform. Merged markets would have a capitalization of over $1.5 trillion, not including the value of Saudi Aramco. Unless they are aggregated, the Gulf markets will remain minor players unable to compete with New York, London, or even Singapore or Hong Kong.

Another factor that may limit the development of Gulf stock markets is the fact that the region's economies are still mostly dependent on state-controlled entities. The companies traded are often partially owned by the states (Saudi Basic Industries Corporation, Saudi Aramco, Ma'aden, Aldar, Etisalat, Qatar National Bank, and others). Even the private companies are mostly dependent on state contracts. In other words, the markets are still very closely tied to the states' ability to sell their oil or natural gas internationally. Only Dubai has a diversified base not dependent on energy prices worldwide, but its stock market has remained very small and unable to compete with the larger markets of Saudi Arabia and Kuwait.

Commercial and Islamic Banks

Both traditional and Shariah-compliant banks have greatly benefited from the huge inflow of capital in the Gulf for the past seventy years. Banks have gone from being mere branches of colonial establishment in the 1960s to highly sophisticated, locally owned establishments today.

A corollary of their growth is that the banks have become increasingly regulated to ensure that shareholders and depositors are protected. Thus regulators like the Saudi central bank have ensured that the banks used proper accounting and developed proper lending standards and quality governance. In the process, the regulators have had to intervene on a number of occasions to protect the banks' integrity. This has led Gulf states to become increasingly influential in the banking industry.

In particular, Saudi Arabia has provided large amounts of capital to banks that at one point or another ran into difficulty. The Saudi Ministry of Finance used the Public Investment Fund (PIF) and General Organization for Social Insurance (GOSI), the state-controlled pension fund, to take a substantial, often controlling, interest in seven of the eight commercial banks and two of the four Islamic banks in the kingdom, thereby giving the state a strong say in how the banks are managed. In other Gulf countries, the states also have direct or indirect control of the banks. In Qatar, all banks are linked to the Al Thani ruling family, either through board chairmen or, in the case of Qatar National Bank, through control by the Qatar Investment Authority (QIA). In Kuwait, most banks have strong links to the government as a major depositor and client, while in the UAE many banks have strong links to royal families or the country's sovereign wealth funds (SWFs).

A major trend in the Gulf today is competition with domestic and foreign banks. Competition is made more intense by the vast extension of technology needed by the banks to remain relevant in the age of the internet. More and more transactions take place online, regardless of the location and history of the banks. To match the need for technology and market strength, many banks have merged, and many more will likely do so in the near future. The UAE's three largest banks—Emirates NBD, First Abu Dhabi Bank (FAB), and Abu Dhabi Commercial Bank (ADCB)—came from mergers. In Saudi Arabia, Alawwal Bank and the Saudi British Bank (SABB) merged in January 2020, while the National Commercial Bank (NCB) and the Samba Financial Group (the kingdom's largest and fourth largest banks) announced their merger in October 2020.[1] There are even some inter-GCC mergers, such as that of Kuwait Finance House (KFH) with Bahrain's Ahli United Bank (AUB).

Most merger arrangements have been during the Covid 19 restrictions. However, the very impressive and drastic policies taken by GCC states to limit the spread of the virus allowed countries to reopen and should be reflected in financial markets reviving and merger deals being revisited.

Sovereign Wealth Funds

Each of the Gulf countries has its own sovereign wealth fund. The Abu Dhabi Investment Authority (ADIA), Saudi Arabia's Public Investment Fund, the Kuwait Investment Authority (KIA), and Qatar's Qatar Investment Authority have grown to control close to $2 trillion and manage a large percentage of the region's oil and gas earnings. The SWFs were created to maximize returns and usually to invest outside the countries themselves. Their growth is also due in part to the leadership of the countries directing the oil earnings to them. The SWF platform gave the leadership (mainly the royal families) the ability to manage the funds outside the traditional low-risk, low-return policies of the central banks and ministries of finance, whose purview is to protect the countries' assets.

In Saudi Arabia, the Saudi central bank and the PIF co-manage the country's money. The central bank invests in highly conservative, liquid, safe foreign state securities with the goal of protecting the kingdom's nest egg, while the PIF invests in high-tech, high-risk technologies to promote a new twenty-first-century economy to benefit the country's youth. In the UAE, ADIA claims to invest conservatively along the lines of all global indexes, but also invests as its leadership sees fit for longer-term gains. The UAE's Mubadala, with assets of $260 billion, is the only transparent SWF in the Gulf. It invests in technology, industry, and energy. In Kuwait, the KIA invests the funds of the Future Generations Fund, which by law receives 10 percent of the country's gross oil income. It invests both abroad and within Kuwait and, like the other SWFs, operates less than transparently. The ultimate prize for opacity belongs to the QIA, which has investments in large local and multinational banks, real estate developments, and some industrial firms, but whose total holdings and returns are unknown to the public.

The opacity of the Gulf's SWFs works against them and their countries. They unwittingly give the impression to global financial markets that they are managed according to the whims of unaccountable leadership. Because of their opacity, they cannot borrow easily to leverage their investments. They will also suffer from being shunned by other investors in large projects and ultimately make foreign direct investment (FDI) more difficult in Gulf countries, as potential investors will not understand the actual competitive framework they have to deal with.

Policy Prescription

For Gulf financial markets to play a bigger role in the region's development, it would behoove the states to remove themselves from the various financial institutions, promote intra-Gulf mergers to make each market more globally competitive, and promote private sector investments. For instance, the banks should be truly privatized and encouraged to merge across GCC borders and beyond to become the new Citibank, Barclays, or BNP Paribas of the world.

By the same token, the stock markets could become more attractive to world buyers if they merged regionally. It would make sense to have only one exchange in the Gulf, which then could take a large volume of a sizable IPO and be much more attractive to local and foreign investors than they are as the small emerging country markets they are today.

Finally, the SWFs should become fully transparent and removed from the direct control of the royal families. Doing so would allow them to attract foreign capital, deal with banks and companies at arm's length, and provide the local citizenry with a vested interest in the welfare of each nation.

Note

1. Reuters, "NCB-Samba to Merge into Saudi Banking Heavyweight," October 11, 2020 (https://uk.reuters.com/article/us-saudi-ncb-samba-m-a/ncb-samba-to-merge-into-saudi-banking-heavyweight-idUKKBN26W0KX).

TEN

Economic Diversification in GCC Countries

MARTIN HVIDT

THE GRAND VISION BEHIND the development plans and visions published by the Gulf states—including Bahrain Vision 2030, Kuwait Vision 2035, Oman Vision 2040, Qatar National Vision 2030, Saudi Vision 2030, and United Arab Emirates (UAE) Vision 2021—is to transform their oil-dependent economies into advanced, technological post-oil economies with solid and economically sustainable foundations. Although economic diversification has been a stated goal for successive generations of policymakers in the Gulf Cooperation Council (GCC) states, the results have generally been meager, at least outside of the oil and gas sector itself.[1]

Gulf states stand to gain many benefits from diversifying their economies, as clearly spelled out in the Qatar National Development Strategy 2011–2016: "A more diversified economy is inherently more stable, more capable of creating jobs and opportunities for the next generation and less vulnerable to the boom and bust cycles of oil and natural gas prices."[2] In the Gulf context, diversification is a generic term for the efforts and reforms undertaken to broaden the productive basis in GCC economies, and thus to reduce their dependence on income from the oil and gas sector. Diversification implies the creation of multiple sources of income within economies, an effort that increasingly is seen to imply an expanded role for the private sector.[3]

Over the past five decades, GCC states have taken a number of important steps on the route to diversifying their economies. They have built infrastructure, created education and health systems, and established a broad range of manufacturing industries primarily serving the domestic market— for example, with food items, building materials, and advanced technological products. The region has been relatively successful in diversifying within the oil and gas sector—that is, in producing downstream products such as liquified natural gas (LNG), petrochemicals, fertilizers, and chemicals, as well as in using oil and gas as cheap fuel for energy-intensive industries, such as aluminum and steel production.

Furthermore, Dubai has spearheaded efforts to diversify into new sectors, including industries and activities with high growth potential, such as aviation, tourism and hospitality, real estate, logistics, business services, manufacturing, and "high-technology-content products" like smart or green technologies. These types of activities have been undertaken, but they contribute relatively little to state budgets and job creation for young nationals in the region as a whole.

Data show that revenues from the sale of oil and gas continue to make up the bulk of export earnings (80 to 95 percent) for GCC countries and remain the only notable source of income in Gulf states' national budgets.[4] In Qatar, a full 94 percent of current state revenues come from hydrocarbon sales. In other words, incomes from the hydrocarbon sector continue to dominate the GCC economies.[5]

The Current Oil Price Shocks

The two recent oil price shocks—the so-called 2014 oil price collapse and the 2020 COVID-19-induced price reductions—both act as stark reminders of exactly how dependent the Gulf states are on oil incomes. The 2014 oil price collapse saw the price of oil drop from around $100 per barrel in 2014 to the $40–60 range in the following years. To counter this, governments introduced a variety of ad hoc measures aimed at trimming budgets and achieving fiscal consolidation, including reduced subsidies on fuel, water, and electricity, coupled with large direct budget cuts to both recurring costs and development projects. However, the reforms implemented did not touch upon deeper economic structures.[6]

On top of the unfinished business of adjusting to the 2014 oil price collapse, 2020 posed new challenges. In addition to the health aspects of the coronavirus pandemic and the havoc caused by economic lockdowns, Gulf states witnessed yet another steep drop in oil prices, from around $60 per barrel to $40 per barrel in 2020 and 2021, and then an upswing of close to $70 to $80 per barrel due to the deferred demand caused by the coronavirus crisis. Gulf states faced a reduction in their oil income by one-third from 2019 to 2020, a loss of $160 billion, according to World Bank estimates.[7]

Needless to say, these two events represent a significant blow to Gulf economies. Since 2014, the price of oil has been substantially lower than the price Gulf countries need to balance their budgets, and as such, all countries in the region (except Qatar) have suffered sizable budget deficits every year. In addition to cutting spending, countries have also had to draw down reserves and incur debt. In June 2018, they held reserves of around $3 trillion in sovereign wealth funds, an amount that is likely to be closer to $2 trillion in 2021.[8] These reserves have enabled serious reforms to be postponed by partly making up for sizable state budget deficits. In addition to drawing down assets, states have incurred debt.[9] According to the Institute of International Finance, Gulf states' debt increased from $30 billion in 2014 to $220 billion by the end of 2019 and another $180 billion during 2020 and early 2021.[10]

Standard & Poor's estimates that GCC governments will face an aggregate central government deficit of about $180 billion in 2020/2021, which will be financed with $100 billion in extra debt and $80 billion in drawdown of own assets. It further estimates that the countries will post deficits until 2023 and that those deficits will accumulate to around $490 billion before then, with 60 percent of the deficits to be covered by debt and the rest by asset drawdowns. Saudi Arabia alone will be accountable for more than half of this debt.[11]

So, while fluctuations in oil prices are a common phenomenon, the situation in the early 2020s differs because the most likely scenario does not foresee a rebound of oil prices in the medium or longer term. Despite an estimated rise in world population to 9.8 billion by 2050, oil prices will be dampened by increasingly efficient oil production techniques, the availability of new supplies like shale oil, and not least by the worldwide emphasis on replacing hydrocarbons with other energy sources in order to reduce carbon emissions and prevent global warming.[12] In other words, while the debt is manageable because of the large reserves held by GCC states, the size of the yearly budget deficits is of concern and needs urgent adjustments. It may therefore no longer be possible to avoid tough choices in order to achieve economic balance.

The Future Diversification Agenda

Although the development and wider uptake of coronavirus vaccines will gradually reduce the impact of the pandemic, it is expected that the global travel (airlines) and hospitality sector will face severe economic difficulties in the years to come. For places like Dubai, this will affect the economy negatively and dampen possibilities for further diversification.

The economic downturn is, however, only partially caused by the drop in oil prices and the pandemic. There are more fundamental structural problems related to oil-driven economies. First, rapid demographic growth places pressure on Gulf societies to create large numbers of new jobs that are attractive to the local population in order to accommodate the many new working-age entrants to the labor market. Second, an economy that lacks diversification leaves state budgets very dependent on oil incomes. Third, the dominant role of the public sector in these economies in effect crowds out private businesses. Fourth, a deep segmentation of the labor market implies that nationals generally work in the public sector in well-paid and secure jobs, while migrants hold low-paying jobs in the private sector. This implies that nationals refrain from seeking private sector employment. In combination, these structural issues effectively counteract both further diversification and private sector growth.

The oil-driven economies worked well as long as oil incomes were plentiful and populations were small. However, this is not the case anymore. The economic model built on those factors has run out of steam, and GCC states must focus now on accelerating the structural reform agenda and taking steps toward a new growth model that actively promotes diversification and private sector development.

A key element in this effort is to integrate the large number of successively better-educated nationals into the economy. First, tackling the youth bulge necessitates making approximately 500,000 jobs available each year by 2035.[13] Second, it requires making economic use of the national labor force—for example, by replacing expatriate workers (mostly in higher-ranking positions) with nationals.

In order to make the private sector more attractive to the national population, the wage levels in the public and private sector have to be evened out. On the one hand, public sector wages could be lowered. On the other, productivity in the private sector could be increased so that jobs are transformed from low-skilled and low-paid to those requiring higher knowledge content and providing higher salaries. This, however, presupposes that the younger generation of Gulf Arabs possesses the qualifications and motivation to undertake such jobs.

While recognizing individual differences and similarities between the six GCC countries, forward-looking policies related to diversification should be based on the following concepts:

- Governments must leave more economic space for the private sector to become larger and stronger and accelerate job creation—for example, through privatization of public entities.

- Labor market reforms must be undertaken to provide incentives to larger parts of the national population to participate in the labor force and to make it attractive for nationals to pursue jobs in the private sector.

- Reforms must increase productivity in the private sector in order to move production up the value chain beyond simple production processes and products. The aim is to provide jobs with higher knowledge content and higher pay for the national population.

- Reforms in the educational system must be undertaken not only to better prepare young people to become competitive and productive members of the workforce, but also more broadly to change incentives for educational attainment and the acquisition of professional qualifications.

- Fiscal reforms must be undertaken to make the state budgets of GCC countries less dependent on incomes from oil and gas—for example, by implementing taxation systems.

- Institutional reforms must be devised to strengthen the capacity of the public sector to undertake planning and implement the resultant plans and development strategies.

Facing the challenges of fluctuating oil revenues, fiscal unsustainability, and strong demographic growth, GCC states are left with no other choice than to act now in order to prevent deeper and more severe crises in the future.

However, on the positive side, the austerity policies—and not least past reforms that led to removing subsidies on fuel, electricity, and water—have shown that Gulf citizens are in fact tolerant of some level of increased hardship. In addition, there are signs that the region's governments are taking advantage of the current crisis to initiate long overdue reforms, such as those related to redressing the size of the migrant population.

Notes

1. Kristian Coates Ulrichsen, *Qatar and the Gulf Crisis* (London: Hurst, 2020), p. 146.

2. Qatar National Vision and General Secretariat for Development Planning, "Qatar National Development Strategy 2011–2016," March 2011, p. 10 (www.psa.gov .qa/en/nds1/Documents/Downloads/NDS_EN_0.pdf).

3. For an elaborated definition and discussion of the concept of diversification, see Martin Hvidt, "Economic Diversification in GCC Countries: Past Record and Future Trends," Research Paper 27 (London School of Economics and Political Science, January 2013), pp. 4–5 (http://eprints.lse.ac.uk/55252/1/Hvidt%20final%20paper %2020.11.17_v0.2.pdf).

4. Ibid., p. 13. The most recent figures are from Qatar, where 89 percent of exports and 94 percent of total state revenues come from the oil and gas sector. See also Qatar National Vision and Ministry of Development Planning and Statistics (MDPS), "Qatar Second National Development Strategy 2018–2020," September 2018, p. 19 (www.psa.gov.qa/en/knowledge/Documents/NDS2Final.pdf).

5. Qatar National Vision and MDPS, "Qatar Second National Development Strategy 2018–2020," p. 19.

6. Karen E. Young, "The Difficult Promise of Economic Reform in the Gulf" (Houston, TX: James A. Baker III Institute for Public Policy of Rice University, 2018) (www.bakerinstitute.org/files/13571/).

7. Jihad Azour, "Middle East and North Africa Regional Economic Outlook" (PowerPoint presentation, International Monetary Fund, April 27, 2020), slide 15 (www.imf.org/-/media/Files/Publications/REO/MCD-CCA/2020/April/English /menap-ppt-042020.ashx).

8. Sovereign Wealth Fund Institute, "Top 94 Largest Sovereign Wealth Fund Rankings by Total Assets" (www.swfinstitute.org/sovereign-wealth-fund-rankings/).

9. IMF, "Regional Economic Outlook: Middle East and Central Asia, October 2017," World Economic and Financial Surveys, October 2017, p. 23 (www.imf .org/en/Publications/REO/MECA/Issues/2017/10/17/mreo1017).

10. "Report: Gulf States' Debts Hit $220bn," *Middle East Monitor,* March 11, 2020 (www.middleeastmonitor.com/20200311-report-gulf-states-debts-hit-220bn/); Sebastian Castelier, "How Are Gulf States Allocating COVID-Related Spending?" *Al-Monitor,* March 23, 2021.

11. Reuters, "S&P Ratings Sees GCC Debt Rising by a Record $100bn This Year," *Al Jazeera,* July 20, 2020 (www.aljazeera.com/economy/2020/7/20/sp-ratings-sees-gcc -debt-rising-by-a-record-100bn-this-year).

12. United Nations Department of Economic and Social Affairs, "World Population Projected to Reach 9.8 Billion in 2050, and 11.2 Billion in 2100," June 21, 2017

(www.un.org/development/desa/en/news/population/world-population-prospects -2017.html).

13. Martin Hvidt, "Socio-Econonomic Outlook for the Arab Gulf Countries: Figures & Forecasts" (Abu Dhabi: Emirates Policy Center and Arab Strategy Forum, 2018), p. 30 (www.arabstrategyforum.org/en/stream-report/socio-economic-outlook -for-the-arab-gulf-countries-figures-forecasts).

ELEVEN

The Governance of Fiscal and Economic Policy within the GCC

ROBERT P. BESCHEL JR.

MOST GULF COOPERATION COUNCIL (GCC) countries find themselves in a curious situation with regard to economic policymaking. As monarchies, their governance structures are inherently authoritarian, and the emir or prime minister often chairs the apex decisionmaking body. Only Kuwait has a parliament that is empowered to play a substantive role. Their central banks do not fare well on most established indexes of independence. In principle, this means that it should be relatively easy to pursue a consistent and coherent policy over time. And in some areas, such as monetary and exchange rate policy, this has indeed been the case.

Yet in other areas, such as the integration between planning and the recurrent budget, coordination has been anything but smooth. GCC countries often lack the dense network of interagency coordination mechanisms at the working level found in Organization for Economic Cooperation and Development (OECD) countries. The lack of political parties means that ministers often enter office without a strong sense of collective responsibility (unlike in parliamentary systems) or fidelity to a particular party program. Various vision documents provide an anchor of sorts for policy, yet many are not explicitly tethered to specific implementation plans. The net result is that ministries can work at cross purposes or end up in turf battles to the

Figure 11-1. Fiscal Deficit Is Set to Widen on Back of Lower Oil Receipts
(Percent of GDP)

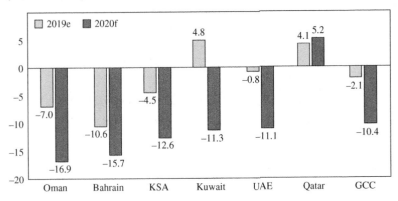

Source: Marmore MENA Intelligence, "GCC Fiscal Deficits and Financing Post COVID-19," May 7, 2020 (www.marmoremena
.com/gcc-fiscal-deficits-and-financing-post-covid-19/).

detriment of coordinated action. The result, as noted by the International Monetary Fund (IMF), is that "Weak fiscal institutions have contributed to spending inefficiencies, rising debt and deficits, and procyclical fiscal policy."[1]

On paper, many GCC countries have quite similar institutions for formulating and managing economic policy. They typically include a high-level body or economic cabinet charged with policy decisionmaking, such as the Council of Economic and Development Affairs (CEDA) in Saudi Arabia or the Economic Development Board (EDB) in Bahrain. They include a central bank charged with monetary policy, managing the currency, and banking supervision and regulation. They also include a finance ministry that oversees the annual recurrent budget (including preparation, execution, and reporting), as well as international economic relations and cash management. In five of the six GCC countries, these institutions include a ministry of economy and/or planning that is responsible for formulating a national development vision and managing the capital budget. And they include other agencies and institutions that are responsible for a range of related functions, such as gathering statistics or monitoring performance.

GCC countries also confront many similar economic and developmental challenges. Most are heavily dependent upon hydrocarbon exports and are working with varying degrees of vigor to diversify their economies away from oil and natural gas. As figure 11-1 indicates, the recent decline in oil prices has created large fiscal challenges and chronic deficits, as efforts to expand non-oil revenues have not kept pace with expenditures. The recent conflict in Ukraine and higher oil and gas prices associated with it will give GCC countries a reprieve of sorts, although it is impossible to predict the duration of this surge and whether it marks a temporary aberration or a more significant shift in the global supply curve.[2]

Spending in GCC countries has historically been procyclical, which has tended to reinforce the "boom or bust" commodity cycles in the energy market. Their large public sectors are the principal employer for many nationals, creating bifurcated labor markets that place upward pressure on wages and reduce the attractiveness of employment in the private sector. Many countries have ambitious national development programs and capital expenditure plans that have required pruning back.

Although there are many commonalities, the alignment of institutional roles and functions between countries is not perfect. Bahrain has integrated its finance and planning functions in a single ministry, whereas many other GCC countries have opted to keep them separate. The federal structure of the United Arab Emirates (UAE) gives emirates considerable autonomy over their own budgets. It is important to note that the institutions governing fiscal and economic policy have been subject to considerable historical evolution, which continues to this day. The Ministry of Finance in Kuwait, for example, has at various times been the Ministry of Finance and Economy, the Ministry of Finance and Industry (along with the Ministry of Customs and Ports), the Ministry of Finance and Oil, and the Ministry of Finance and Economy again (with responsibility for the Public Investment Authority) before assuming its current focus on finance in 1986.[3]

Central Bank Independence

For decades, the need for an independent central bank insulated from political pressure has been taken as a given by economists and senior policymakers. A number of indexes have been developed for measuring central bank independence, covering topics such as freedom from political interference, accountability, and transparency. Global trends have revealed a marked improvement in the evolution of central bank autonomy in recent decades in both the OECD and the developing world.[4]

Central banks within the GCC are relatively new institutions, with the most recent established only in 2006. They evolved from currency boards and have expanded their roles over time to include broader monetary policy and banking supervision and regulation, as well as electronic payments and anti–money laundering. A 2019 analysis revealed that, in comparison with other high-income commodity exporters, most GCC countries rank rather low on central bank independence.[5] Their boards generally lack the statutory protections found in other high-income countries, and transparency is modest. With exceptions, many dimensions of economic policy, ranging from monetary policy to banking supervision, may be shared with other government entities. Only two GCC central banks (those of Qatar and the UAE) have final authority over their economic policy objectives.

However, there are also questions about how important central bank independence really is for these countries. All maintain a long-standing currency peg to the dollar, supported by massive reserve accumulations and, until recently, significant fiscal surpluses from oil exports. They have delivered external exchange rate stability and low inflation. In this case, the dollar peg may have ultimately mattered more than the standard political and economic metrics of institutional independence.

Vision Plans and Programs

To provide broader coherence and direction to economic planning, many GCC countries have developed national vision or strategy documents. Such approaches began in the 1990s, starting with Bahrain and Oman (the two countries with the lowest oil reserves) and then expanding into Qatar, Kuwait, Saudi Arabia, and the UAE.[6] Some of these documents remain largely aspirational, articulating objectives such as "robust economic growth that benefits the people," or a "just and thriving society." Several have been overtaken by events, such as the decline in oil prices after 2014.

Saudi Arabia's "Vision 2030" is perhaps the best example of a serious transformational effort on the part of national leadership. Beyond the traditional ministries of finance and planning, the kingdom has put in place an elaborate set of institutions to support the realization of Vision 2030, including the Strategic Management Office, which is charged with translating vision objectives into action plans and managing tradeoffs between various initiatives; the National Center for Performance Measurement (or Adaa), which is tasked with monitoring and measuring performance; and the National Project Management, Operation, and Maintenance Organization (Mashroat), which is responsible for supporting project management for major infrastructure projects. Below these institutions, the government has set up Vision Realization Offices in various line departments to facilitate the implementation of Vision 2030 priorities in individual sectors. This complex administrative environment has frequently led to conflicts over turf and a Darwinian institutional evolution of sorts. In 2016, for example, the kingdom set up the Delivery and Rapid Intervention Center (DARIC) to support implementation, but it was dissolved in 2018, and its functions were transferred to other entities. Efforts are ongoing to determine whether further consolidation is necessary.

Economic Decisionmaking and the Integration of Planning and Budgeting

The challenge of coordinating economic and fiscal policy—and particularly of ensuring that the planning and finance components are well integrated—extends well beyond the GCC. Over the past twenty years, the IMF and World Bank have pushed for combining these functions (often within an empowered ministry of finance) for a variety of reasons. There was a need to reduce the chronic lack of integration between capital and recurrent budgets; to push for a more holistic treatment of both revenues and expenditures; and to remove institutional fragmentation. There were concerns that traditional planning approaches were fiscally expansionary and did not properly account for related downstream expenditures. A consensus prevailed within the broader development community that a better approach would incorporate a strong focus on sectoral plans (including integrated capital and recurrent expenditures) in the context of a robust medium-term budget, fiscal, or expenditure framework.

Yet in many countries the planning function never really went away. In fact, it accelerated globally between 2006 and 2018, from around sixty-two countries to 134.[7] Developments within the Middle East and North Africa (MENA) region have reflected these broader trends, and many GCC countries have retained a traditional planning function that is institutionally distinct from their ministries of finance. The reasons for this approach can range from the substantive (it arguably allows GCC governments to better pursue diversification and other priority economic goals) to the bureaucratic (it is the product of institutional inertia and resistance to change, as well as lack of capacity to assume this role within many ministries of finance).

This bifurcation has placed a heavy burden on external mechanisms to coordinate between these two functions, which have not always been up to the task. The example of Oman provides an interesting illustration. From a legal and institutional vantage point, Oman has in principle a powerful coordination committee in the Supreme Council for Planning (SCP). It is chaired by the sultan and vested with a wide array of powers, ranging from setting long-term strategy to approving the annual development budget. Yet in practice, most observers have noted chronic dysfunction in the interactions between the major economic players for several reasons. The underlying legislation is relatively general and would benefit from a more detailed clarification of roles and responsibilities. Oman's five-year plans should be clearer in setting forth their objectives, targets, and sector linkages. The absence of a medium-term workplan and Oman's basic monitoring and evaluation (M&E) systems have also had an impact. Data flows are heavily centralized and largely vertical in nature, and the SCP General Secretariat lacks the capacity to assume many of the roles and duties stipulated in its mandate.

Achieving Greater Efficiency in Expenditures

In the wake of the recent collapse in oil prices, many GCC countries are now facing the challenge of how to institutionalize efforts to rein in recurrent and capital expenditures. This task would typically fall within the domain of the budget department in the ministry of finance, yet such units often lack the analytic capacity and technical expertise to play this role effectively.

Saudi Arabia has arguably gone the furthest in addressing this challenge through the creation of its new Center of Spending Efficiency (CSE), which plays a critical role in analyzing the scope for savings in recurrent and capital expenditures. CSE has a unique governance structure, reporting both to CEDA and to the Ministry of Finance. It has a broad focus on both capital and recurrent expenditures as well as workforce compensation. CSE is exempted from traditional civil service rules, which has allowed it to attract top talent from the Saudi public and private sectors. Its methodologies are consistent with international best practices and avoid mechanistic and ad hoc approaches to cost reduction. Through a comprehensive analysis of operational efficiency that incorporates agency outcomes and outputs, CSE has managed the tricky balance of improving agency performance while simultaneously delivering substantial cost savings.

Short of major institutional upgrades such as the CSE, other GCC countries have been able to make significant inroads mainly by focusing on the capital budget. Between 2000 and 2017, Qatar's capital budget increased thirtyfold, leading to lax standards in investment and project management and the expectation of nearly unlimited funding among line departments.

In 2012, the Ministry of Finance established a small public investment management unit of around seven staff to enhance its oversight and set up a national portfolio of prioritized projects. The unit scaled back a large number of projects to a smaller number of "necessary" investments. Capital spending continued to increase for a couple of years, reflecting both legacy projects and spending associated with Qatar's World Cup bid. But it has since leveled off and declined, falling by over 17 percent between 2016 and 2020.[8]

The Way Forward

How should GCC countries best improve the quality of their economic governance and strengthen policy integration and cohesiveness? As the discussion here indicates, these governments have frequently resorted to institutional reorganization and realignment as their strategy of choice. Such measures may on occasion be necessary, but they are hardly the only factors. Arab policymakers have highlighted a large number of challenges to effective policy management and coordination in MENA, including the complexity, ambiguity, and contradictory nature of legislative acts; systemic gaps in human resource management; the lack of reliable data and information for policymakers; and the lack of standardized systems of communication.[9]

Yet there are also some genuine success stories that can serve as a model for others. Between 2018 and 2019, Saudi Arabia made impressive progress in improving its ranking in the World Bank's Doing Business index, jumping from ninety-second to sixty-second, and becoming the world's most improved reformer.[10] The kingdom made gains in a broad number of areas, from establishing a one-stop shop and streamlining investment procedures to introducing a new insolvency law to strengthening protections for minority investors. Credit for this success belongs to the Ministry of Commerce, which spearheaded the effort, and to the Executive Committee for Enhancing the Business Environment (Tayseer Committee). The Tayseer Committee is an innovative interagency coordination mechanism that brings together over thirty-five government agencies and over 213 reform initiatives through the use of a broader committee and sub-committee structure.

The word *tayseer* means "seamless activity" in Arabic, and the committee's operations have demonstrated that fully joined-up government operations can be achieved in ways that will yield impressive results. The next great challenge for GCC governments in the area of economic governance will be learning from this and similar experiences and effectively scaling them to implement other needed reforms. Such activities will empower

GCC countries to address the pressing developmental challenges more holistically, systematically, and ultimately more successfully.

Notes

1. International Monetary Fund (IMF), "Regional Economic Outlook: Middle East and Central Asia," World Economic and Financial Survey (Washington, October 2019), p. 47 (www.imf.org/en/Publications/REO/MECA/Issues/2019/10/19/reo-menap-cca-1019).

2. Marmore MENA Intelligence, "GCC Fiscal Deficits and Financing Post COVID-19," May 7, 2020 (www.marmoremena.com/gcc-fiscal-deficits-and-financing-post-covid-19/).

3. See the Kuwait Ministry of Finance website (https://web.archive.org/web/2013 1224105859/ http://en.mof.gov.kw/MOFInfo/MOFBrief/MOFBrief.aspx).

4. Marco Arnone, Bernard J. Laurens, and Jean-François Segalotto, "Measures of Central Bank Autonomy: Empirical Evidence for OECD, Developing, and Emerging Market Economies," Working Paper 06/228 (Washington: IMF, October 2006) (www.imf.org/en/Publications/WP/Issues/2016/12/31/Measures-of-Central-Bank-Autonomy-Empirical-Evidence-for-OECD-Developing-and-Emerging-Market-19833).

5. Hoda Selim, "Does Central Bank Independence in Arab Oil Exporters Matter?" in Institutions and Macroeconomic Policies in Resource-Rich Arab Economies, edited by Kamiar Mohaddes, Jeffrey B. Nugent, and Hoda Selim (Oxford University Press, 2019), pp. 119–48.

6. Kristian Coates Ulrichsen, Insecure Gulf: The End of Certainty and the Transition to the Post-Oil Era (Oxford University Press, 2015).

7. Admos O. Chimhowu, David Hulme, and Lauchlan T. Munro, "The 'New' National Development Planning and Global Development Goals: Processes and Partnerships," World Development 120 (August 2019), pp. 76–89 (www.researchgate.net/publication/332448322_The_'New'_national_development_planning_and_global_development_goals_Processes_and_partnerships).

8. IMF, "Qatar: 2019 Article IV Consultation—Press Release; Staff Report," Country Report 19/146 (Washington, June 2019) (www.imf.org/en/Publications/CR/Issues/2019/06/02/Qatar-2019-Article-IV-Consultation-Press-Release-Staff-Report-46956). See also Qatar Ministry of Finance, Public Budget Statement 2021 (https://www.mof.gov.qa/en/Shared%20Documents/Public%20Budget%20Statement%20Report%20Full%20Report%202021.pdf), as well as data on capital spending from Haver Analytics.

9. Rania Al-Mashat, "Economic Policy Management: A New Framework for MENA Countries," Economic Research Forum Policy Portal, November 7, 2017 (https://theforum.erf.org.eg/2017/11/07/economic-policy-management-new-framework-mena-countries/).

10. World Bank Group, "Doing Business 2020: Comparing Business Regulation in 190 Economies," October 24, 2019 (www.doingbusiness.org/en/reports/global-reports/doing-business-2020).

TWELVE

The Response of Gulf Sovereign Wealth Funds to Fluctuating Oil Prices

SARA BAZOOBANDI

THEODOSIA ROSSI

OVER THE PAST THREE decades, sovereign wealth funds (SWFs) have become a key element of the global financial system, with Gulf SWFs playing an especially sizable role. SWFs are broadly defined as government-owned investment funds or arrangements that "hold, manage, or administer assets to achieve financial objectives, and employ a set of investment strategies that include investing in foreign financial assets."[1] Governments have operated SWFs since as far back as the 1950s, but the size of these institutions began to rise sharply beginning in the 1990s.[2] In 1990, SWFs likely held a maximum of $500 billion globally; this figure had ballooned to $8.34 trillion in total assets under management (AUM) by 2019.[3]

Of the fifteen SWFs in the world with the largest total assets, six are located in Gulf Cooperation Council (GCC) states: the Abu Dhabi Investment Authority; the Kuwait Investment Authority; Saudi Arabia's Public Investment Fund; the Investment Corporation of Dubai; the Qatar Investment Authority; and the United Arab Emirates' (UAE) Mubadala Investment Company.[4] SWFs play a crucial role in the Gulf, serving as the main mechanism through which these countries manage their wealth.[5] Gulf states have deployed SWFs to achieve a range of political, social, and economic aims, including state building, promoting the longevity of ruling families, creating national identity, increasing international recognition, and enhancing resilience.[6]

Gulf SWFs are distinct from others globally in that they are funded entirely by oil and gas revenues.[7] As such, GCC governments must nimbly shape their investment strategies in response to oil and gas prices. The overarching question of this chapter is, How have Gulf SWFs shifted their investment strategies in response to oil price fluctuations from the early 2000s through the present day? First, we survey the rise of Gulf SWFs in the early 2000s; second, we assess the shift in SWF strategies that occurred around the 2010s; third, we consider the decisions made by Gulf SWFs in response to the 2020 oil price crash; and last, we recommend policies that will allow Gulf states to sustain and grow their SWFs in the coming years. We argue that Gulf SWFs have been adept, innovative, and sometimes aggressive in shifting their investment strategies in the face of fluctuating oil prices; their actions have ultimately enabled them to grow and enhance their global profiles, even in the most challenging of circumstances.

The Ascent of SWFs in the Early 2000s

Between 2003 and 2008, oil prices rose suddenly in what the World Bank refers to as a "commodity supercycle," shooting up from $28 to $134 per barrel.[8] This increase is generally attributed to increased demand for crude, promoted by an expanding global economy and by shifting consumption trends in Asia.[9] During the 2008 financial crisis, oil prices crashed, from $134 per barrel in June to $39 in February 2009; however, oil demand recovered later that year and prices returned to around $100 per barrel.[10] By the end of 2011, the total current account balance of oil exporting economies had risen to $630 billion.[11] In response to the sky-high oil prices of the early 2000s and the increased power of emerging market economies, oil exporting countries expanded existing SWFs and created new ones so that they could better leverage their growing assets.[12]

Several of the Gulf SWFs were established long before the oil supercycle of the early 2000s. The Kuwait Investment Authority was established in 1953, making it the oldest SWF in the world; Saudi Arabia's Public Investment Fund was established in 1971; and the Abu Dhabi Investment Authority was established in 1978.[13] However, most of the Gulf SWFs were established in quick succession as oil prices skyrocketed: Abu Dhabi's Mubadala Investment Company was established in 2002; the Qatar Investment Authority in 2005; the Investment Corporation of Dubai in 2006; Sharjah Asset Management Holding in 2008; the Bahrain Mumtalakat Holding Company in 2006; and Abu Dhabi's Emirates Investment Authority in 2008.[14] The Oman Investment Authority is an outlier of sorts, having been established in 2020 through a merger of two older SWFs: the State General Reserve Fund and the Oman Investment Fund.[15] Gawdat Bahgat notes that the Gulf SWFs established in the early 2000s made riskier investments during this period than the older SWFs, deriving confidence from high oil prices.[16]

The GCC SWFs drew significant attention across the global financial system in the early 2000s for the growth of their wealth, but also for their investment in so-called trophy assets. The latter included a number of high-profile deals, such as the Abu Dhabi Investment Council's acquisition of the Chrysler building in 2008 and the Qatar Investment Authority's acquisition of Harrods department store in 2010.[17] Gulf SWFs also acquired stakes in a number of prominent Western financial institutions during this period. In 2007, the Qatar Investment Authority acquired a 20.9 percent stake in the London Stock Exchange.[18] That same year, the Abu Dhabi Investment Authority purchased a 4.9 percent stake in Citigroup, becoming the company's largest shareholder.[19] These high-profile purchases were widely viewed as an attempt by Gulf leaders to enhance their positions in the international financial community.

Shifts in SWF Strategies during the 2010s

Following the dramatic rise in oil prices during the early 2000s came the 2008 financial crisis, and with it the beginning of a new period of dramatic price fluctuations. The average annual OPEC crude price dropped to $61 per barrel in 2009, rising over the next three years, only to drop again each year from 2013 to 2016. In the years since, oil prices have continued to vary year-on-year, with the advent of the COVID-19 pandemic causing prices to plummet to an annual average of $41 per barrel in 2020.[20]

By 2014, ongoing regional crises, slow global growth caused by various uncertainties (Brexit, the US-China trade war, and the eurozone crisis), and the decline of oil prices prompted a shift in GCC sovereign wealth investments.[21] During this period, SWFs globally began to redirect their investments away from luxury businesses toward the hotel sector and private markets, with the aim of generating more sustainable income; investments in trophy assets reportedly declined from $13 billion in 2009 to $1.4 billion in 2015.[22] This strategy appears to have worked, given that the assets of global SWFs rose more or less steadily over the course of the 2010s, from $4.89 trillion in December 2010 to $7.82 trillion in June 2018.[23]

GCC policymakers in particular began to move away from efforts to gain a more reputable position in the global financial system, toward strategies focused on economic diversification, as well as socioeconomic and political stabilization. As oil prices fluctuated in the wake of the 2008 financial crisis, Gulf SWFs adjusted their strategies away from the risky, high-profile international investments of the early 2000s and began to invest more assets domestically and within the Middle East.[24] In the years since, unstable oil prices and increasing domestic spending needs have led Gulf SWFs to double down on this new strategy, focusing their investments domestically and, in certain cases, drawing down funds.[25] For example, 2015 marked the first time in eight years that the Emirati government did not give Abu Dhabi's Mubadala new money.[26]

Despite fluctuating oil prices in the 2010s, Gulf SWFs held some of the largest assets globally as of 2019, both in an absolute sense and in relation to their gross domestic products (GDPs). Although the size of SWF assets in each Gulf country differs and is not usually disclosed, Fitch Ratings estimated at the time that Qatar's SWF assets were worth approximately 120 percent of its GDP and Kuwait's were worth over 400 percent.[27] Before the outbreak of the COVID-19 pandemic in 2020, it was estimated that SWFs in the Middle East had over $2 trillion in combined assets.[28]

How Gulf SWFs Responded to the 2020 Economic Crisis

The COVID-19 pandemic and the accompanying drop in oil prices posed a significant, and largely unforeseen, challenge to Gulf SWFs in 2020. Early on in the pandemic, the Institute of International Finance projected that Gulf SWFs could see their assets plunge by $300 billion over the course of the year.[29] However, by December 2020, Fitch reported that the SWF assets of Abu Dhabi, Kuwait, and Qatar had likely risen compared to 2019.[30] Saudi Arabia's Public Investment Fund, meanwhile, increased its assets from around $300 billion in mid-2019 to $400 billion by the end of 2020.[31]

So, how did Gulf SWFs manage not only to survive the crises of 2020, but to thrive? While Fitch Ratings attributes the projected 2020 rise in Gulf SWF assets to "supportive market returns," it is also clear that several Gulf SWFs deployed aggressive and innovative investment strategies in response to the crash in oil prices.[32] Two Gulf SWFs in particular invested more in

2020 than in 2019: Saudi Arabia's Public Investment Fund and Abu Dhabi's Mubadala.[33] This section considers these two examples of how Gulf SWFs successfully responded to shifting oil prices and took advantage of the opportunities offered by an economic crisis.

Saudi Arabia's Public Investment Fund purchased billions of dollars in stocks while prices were at record lows during the first quarter of 2020, as part of a stated effort to leverage "any opportunity" provided by the COVID-19 pandemic.[34] In May 2020, the central bank transferred $40 billion in foreign reserves to the Public Investment Fund—a move that the finance minister said was an "exceptional one-off transaction that came after a lot of deliberation."[35] The SWF continued to buy up stocks over the course of the year, raising its US stock holdings from $7 billion in the third quarter of 2020 to almost $12.8 billion in the final quarter.[36] In January 2021, Crown Prince Mohammad bin Salman announced that the Public Investment Fund was aiming to double its assets to around $1.07 trillion by 2025, thereby becoming one of the largest SWFs in the world.[37]

Abu Dhabi's Mubadala pursued a similarly bold investment strategy in response to the economic turbulence triggered by the pandemic. Over the course of 2020, Mubadala charged forward with new private-equity partnerships and investments, wagering on an eventual global economic recovery. Mubadala's head of venture capital, Ibrahim Ajami, said that the fund would not have invested so quickly before the pandemic, noting that COVID-19 had "enabled unbelievable growth." By early December, the SWF had invested over $11 billion—46 percent more than it did over the full year of 2019. Another key element of Mubadala's pandemic response strategy was to move quickly into the lending sector, based on the belief that the economic uncertainty of 2020 would "tighten borrowing standards."[38] In December 2020, Reuters reported that Mubadala's new strategy was "to become more of an investment-led, financially-minded, commercial sovereign wealth fund, rather than the development, strategic fund it has been doing more of since its early years."[39] These strategies quickly reaped returns for Mubadala: in June 2020, the fund reported total assets of 388.7 billion UAE dirhams (AED), up from AED378.4 billion in December 2019.[40]

Policy Recommendations

Gulf SWFs have adroitly and successfully responded to fluctuating oil prices over the years, enabling them to grow their assets and raise their global profiles since the early 2000s. These funds managed to turn the pandemic-triggered oil price crash to their advantage, succeeding against the predictions that many analysts made in early 2020. A number of Gulf SWFs were able to increase their assets in 2020, even as they expended billions of dollars in foreign assets and deposits to meet government funding needs amid the COVID-19 crisis. That said, Fitch Ratings has projected that Gulf countries "stand to substantially deplete their SWF assets in the long term without some combination of recovery in oil prices, growth in production, fiscal adjustment and supportive financial market returns," emphasizing the issue of insufficient economic diversification.[41]

So, what steps should Gulf states take in the coming years to maintain and grow their SWFs? First, they should continue and intensify their economic diversification efforts in order to build their resilience to future oil price shocks. So far, Gulf SWFs have been able to respond and ride through oil price fluctuations, but this is likely to become more and more difficult (if not impossible) as oil reserves deplete. Second, GCC states should take steps to enhance regional cooperation among their SWFs, particularly with respect to knowledge sharing and joint investments. Gulf SWFs will be better able to handle future oil price drops and other economic challenges if they work together, presenting a united front while drawing on one another's strengths and resources. The recent steps taken to resolve the Gulf crisis have opened up new opportunities for intra-GCC cooperation, from which SWFs could benefit and to which they could contribute. If Gulf states are able to successfully diversify their economies and enhance regional cooperation, their SWFs have the potential to continue their remarkable growth and to move into central positions on the international stage.

Notes

1. International Working Group of Sovereign Wealth Funds (IWG), "Sovereign Wealth Funds: Generally Accepted Principles and Practices, 'Santiago Principles,'" October 2008, p. 3 (www.ifswf.org/sites/default/files/santiagoprinciples_0_0.pdf).

2. Simon Johnson, "The Rise of Sovereign Wealth Funds," International Monetary Fund, Finance & Development, September 2007, p. 56 (www.imf.org/external /pubs/ft/fandd/2007/09/pdf/straight.pdf).

3. Ibid.; IE University Center for the Governance of Change, "Sovereign Wealth Funds 2019," edited by Javier Capapé, 2019, p. 24 (https://docs.ie.edu/cgc/research /sovereign-wealth/SOVEREIGN-WEALTH-RESEARCH-IE-CGC-REPORT _2019.pdf).

4. Sovereign Wealth Fund Institute, "Top 95 Largest Sovereign Wealth Fund Rankings by Total Assets" (www.swfinstitute.org/fund-rankings/sovereign-wealth-fund).

5. Hanan Naser, "The Role of the Gulf Cooperation Council's Sovereign Wealth Funds in the New Era of Oil," International Journal of Economics and Financial

Issues 6, no. 4 (2016), p. 1658 (www.econjournals.com/index.php/ijefi/article/view/2760/pdf).

6. Sara Bazoobandi, "Managing Gulf Sovereign Wealth: Transition to the 'Modernised Economic Era,'" *Gulf Affairs* (Summer 2019), pp. 26–27 (www.oxgaps.org/files/commentary_-_bazoobandi.pdf).

7. Karen E. Young, "Sovereign Risk: Gulf Sovereign Wealth Funds as Engines of Growth and Political Resource," *British Journal of Middle Eastern Studies* 47, no. 1 (2020), p. 97 (https://doi.org/10.1080/13530194.2020.1714866).

8. These are the West Texas Intermediate (WTI) benchmark prices. John Baffes and others, "The Great Plunge in Oil Prices: Causes, Consequences, and Policy Responses," Policy Research Note 15/01 (World Bank Group, March 2015), p. 4 (https://openknowledge.worldbank.org/bitstream/handle/10986/23611/The0great0plun0and0policy0responses.pdf?sequence=1&isAllowed=y); Christiane Baumeister and Lutz Kilian, "Forty Years of Oil Price Fluctuations: Why the Price of Oil May Still Surprise Us," *Journal of Economic Perspectives* 30, no. 1 (Winter 2016), p. 147 (https://pubs.aeaweb.org/doi/pdf/10.1257/jep.30.1.139).

9. Baumeister and Kilian, "Forty Years of Oil Price Fluctuations," p. 147.

10. Ibid.

11. Naser, "The Role of the Gulf Cooperation Council's Sovereign Wealth Funds," p. 1658.

12. Ibid.; Javier Santiso, "Sovereign Development Funds: Key Financial Actors of the shifting Wealth of Nations," Emerging Markets Network Working Paper (Paris: OECD Development Centre, October 2008), p. 7 (www.oecd.org/dev/41944381.pdf).

13. Santiso, "Sovereign Development Funds," p. 7; Sovereign Wealth Fund Institute, "SWF Profiles" (www.swfinstitute.org/fund-rankings/sovereign-wealth-fund).

14. Sovereign Wealth Fund Institute, "SWF Profiles"; Sharjah Asset Management, "Who We Are," 2020 (https://sam.ae/).

15. Turki Al Balushi, "Oman Shifts Wealth Funds into New Entity with $17 Billion Assets," Bloomberg, June 4, 2020 (www.bloomberg.com/news/articles/2020-06-04/oman-shifts-wealth-funds-into-new-entity-with-17-billion-assets).

16. Gawdat Bahgat, "Sovereign Wealth Funds in the Gulf: An Assessment," Research Paper 16 (London School of Economics and Political Science, July 2011), p. 5 (http://eprints.lse.ac.uk/55015/1/__Libfile_repository_Content_Kuwait%20Programme_Bahgat_2011.pdf).

17. Sara Bazoobandi and Jeffrey B. Nugent, "Political Economy of Sovereign Wealth Funds in the Oil Exporting Countries of the Arab Region and Especially the Gulf," Working Paper 1143 (Cairo: Economic Research Forum, 2017), p. 21 (https://erf.org.eg/app/uploads/2017/10/1143.pdf); Daniel Nasaw, "Abu Dhabi Fund Buys New York City's Chrysler Building for $800m," *The Guardian*, July 9, 2008 (www.theguardian.com/business/2008/jul/09/sovereignwealthfunds.usa); Reuters, "Factbox: Qatar's Investments in Britain - Barclays, Sainsbury's, Harrods and IAG," February 19, 2020 (www.reuters.com/article/uk-iag-qatar-stake-investments-factbox/factbox-qatars-investments-in-britain-barclays-sainsburys-harrods-and-iag-idUKKBN20D1EC).

18. Freya Berry and Clare Hutchinson, "Qatar Cuts Stake in London Stock Exchange by a Third," Reuters, July 10, 2014 (www.reuters.com/article/us-qatar-holding-lse/qatar-cuts-stake-in-london-stock-exchange-by-a-third-idINKBN0FF17G20140710).

19. Eric Dash and Andrew Ross Sorkin, "Citigroup Sells Abu Dhabi Fund $7.5 Billion Stake," *New York Times*, November 27, 2007.

20. Statista, "Average Annual OPEC Crude Oil Price from 1960 to 2021," March 2021 (www.statista.com/statistics/262858/change-in-opec-crude-oil-prices-since-1960/).

21. Bazoobandi, "Managing Gulf Sovereign Wealth."

22. Javier Espinoza, "Sovereign Wealth Funds Move beyond Trophy Assets," *Financial Times*, March 19, 2017 (www.ft.com/content/ac407e16-0b30-11e7-97d1-5e720a26771b).

23. Statista, "Assets of Global Sovereign Wealth Funds from December 2010 to June 2018," August 2018 (www.statista.com/statistics/276618/volume-of-managed-assets-in-sovereign-wealth-funds-worldwide/).

24. Bahgat, "Sovereign Wealth Funds in the Gulf," p. 8.

25. Bazoobandi, "Managing Gulf Sovereign Wealth," p. 26.

26. Stanley Carvalho and David French, "UPDATE 2—Abu Dhabi to Merge Sovereign Funds Mubadala and IPIC," Reuters, June 29, 2016 (www.reuters.com/article/mubadala-ma-ipic-uae/update-2-abu-dhabi-to-merge-sovereign-funds-mubadala-and-ipic-idUSL8N19L0ZT).

27. Fitch Ratings, "Sovereign Wealth Funds Key to High GCC Ratings," Non-Rating Action Commentary, November 25, 2019 (www.fitchratings.com/research/sovereigns/sovereign-wealth-funds-key-to-high-gcc-ratings-25-11-2019).

28. Matthew Martin and Nicolas Parasie, "Gulf Sovereign Funds Seen Shedding $300 Billion in Market Mayhem," Bloomberg, March 26, 2020 (www.bloomberg.com/news/articles/2020-03-26/gulf-sovereign-funds-seen-shedding-300-billion-in-market-mayhem).

29. Ibid.

30. Fitch Ratings, "Sovereign Wealth Funds in the GCC," Special Report, December 17, 2020 (www.fitchratings.com/research/sovereigns/sovereign-wealth-funds-in-gcc-17-12-2020).

31. Public Investment Fund, "PIF Launches Five-Year Strategy Including Vision Realization Program 2021–2025," January 23, 2021 (www.pif.gov.sa/en/MediaCenter/Pages/NewsDetails.aspx?NewsID=64); Natasha Turak, "Massive Saudi Wealth Fund Zeros in on China, Plans to Open New Asia Office," CNBC, May 1, 2019 (www.cnbc.com/2019/05/01/saudi-public-investment-fund-zeros-in-on-china-despite-us-investments.html).

32. Ibid.

33. Rory Jones and Miriam Gottfried, "Abu Dhabi's $230 Billion Man Bet the World Would Overcome Covid-19," *Wall Street Journal*, December 5, 2020.

34. Pierre Paulden, "Saudi Arabia Wealth Fund Buys Boeing, Citi, Disney Stakes," Bloomberg, May 15, 2020 (www.bloomberg.com/news/articles/2020-05-15/saudi-arabia-wealth-fund-buys-stakes-in-disney-facebook-citi).

35. Natasha Turak, "The Gulf's Sovereign Wealth Funds 'Need to Be Deployed' amid Coronavirus Crisis, Expert Says," CNBC, June 2, 2020 (www.cnbc.com/2020/06/02/coronavirus-gulf-sovereign-wealth-funds-need-to-be-deployed-amid-pandemic.html).

36. Saeed Azhar, "Saudi Sovereign Wealth Fund Boosts US Equities Exposure to Nearly $12.8 Billion," Reuters, February 16, 2021 (www.reuters.com/article/saudi-pif-stocks-int-idUSKBN2AG289).

37. Marwa Rashad and Saeed Azher, "Saudi Sovereign Fund to Double Assets in Next Five Years to $1.07 Trillion: Crown Prince," Reuters, January 24, 2021 (www.reuters.com/article/us-saudi-pif-assets/saudi-sovereign-fund-to-double-assets-in-next-five-years-to-1-07-trillion-crown-prince-idUSKBN29T0MC).

38. Jones and Gottfried, "Abu Dhabi's $230 Billion Man."

39. Davide Barbuscia and Saeed Azhar, "Exclusive-Abu Dhabi's Mubadala Reviews Equities Fund in Investment Shake-up—Sources," Reuters, December 14, 2020 (www.reuters.com/article/mubadala-inv-strategy-funds-exclusive-idUKKBN28O14X).

40. Mamoura Diversified Global Holding PJSC, "Unaudited Interim Condensed Consolidated Financial Statements for the Six-Month Period Ended 30 June 2020," p. 4 (www.mubadala.com/generic/download?file=MDGH%2030%20June%202020%20FS[2].pdf&id=16272).

41. Fitch, "Sovereign Wealth Funds in the GCC."

THIRTEEN

Structural Reforms, Fiscal Sustainability, and Intergenerational Wealth as the GCC Transitions to a Post-Oil Future

IRFAN ALEEM

IN FEBRUARY 2020, BEFORE COVID-19 was recognized as a pandemic, the International Monetary Fund (IMF) published an insightful and thought-provoking paper whose main conclusion was that if Gulf Cooperation Council (GCC) countries maintained their existing fiscal stance, the region as a whole could exhaust its financial wealth in the next fifteen years (see figure 13-1).[1] A key assumption, consistent with those of other prominent agencies at the time, was that global oil demand would peak in around 2041 at 115 million barrels per day (mbd), up from its pre-COVID-19 level of around 100 mbd.[2]

Fast-forward to the end of 2020, when the onset of COVID-19 had triggered seismic shocks to the global economy and accelerated behavioral and technological changes. Federal Reserve chairman Jerome Powell put it well when he spoke in November 2020 about the long-term consequences of the pandemic: "We're not going back to the same economy . . . we're going back to a different economy."[3] Although the timeline for economic recovery is unclear, Powell conveyed his belief that the global economy would be vastly different after things finally return to "normal."

The long-term consequences of this changed world for the GCC are clearly visible. BP argued in its influential September 2020 report on

Figure 13-1. Public Wealth under the Current Fiscal Stance:
Benchmark Projection

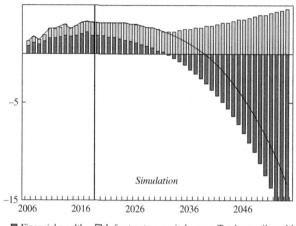

1. Real non-oil wealth (GCC total, trillions of 2018 US dollars)

Simulation

■ Financial wealth   ▢ Infrastructure capital   —— Total non-oil wealth

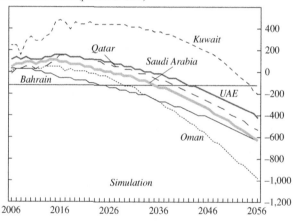

2. Financial wealth (percent of GDP)

Kuwait

Qatar

Saudi Arabia

Bahrain

UAE

Oman

Simulation

Source: Country authorities and IMF staff calculations.

the future of energy that global oil demand had already peaked. This is a
radically different position from its central 2019 scenario—the "evolving
transition"—which envisioned a peak in oil demand by 2040, similar to the
IMF's prediction. Oil will be replaced by clean electricity, BP predicts,
because demand may never recover from the COVID-19 pandemic.

The European Union (EU) made a game-changing commitment in October 2020 to lower oil and gas demand from 50 percent of primary energy currently to less than 5 percent by 2050, through enhanced use of renewable energy. Tesla successfully demonstrated in 2020 the viability of mass-produced electric vehicles (EVs); and its commitment to make substantially cheaper EVs by 2022–2023, if achieved, may hasten an end to the oil age.[4]

If global oil demand peaks much earlier than was previously expected, as assumed by the IMF, it will have profound implications for a region that has been trying to diversify away from dependence on oil and gas with limited success for many years. This chapter looks at challenges and opportunities for a transition to a post-oil future, with a focus on structural reforms to help achieve fiscal sustainability and inter-generational equity.

From a public sector fiscal balance perspective, the situation may have worsened substantially more than the IMF predicted. At the same time, more solutions may be available to meet this challenge than were considered in the IMF report or are currently being considered by government policymakers.

Impact of Game-Changing Events in the Wake of COVID-19

If oil demand peaks in 2031, a decade earlier than predicted in the IMF's benchmark scenario, owing to the game-changing events in the wake of COVID-19, a depletion of net financial wealth earlier than 2034 for the region becomes possible, especially for those GCC countries unable to significantly alter their fiscal stance through structural reforms.[5] This projection of oil demand peaking in 2031 is more conservative than alternative scenarios of faster technological innovation and regulatory response to climate change, which project oil demand peaking in 2030 or earlier, including BP's 2020 projections. The recent turmoil in oil markets is not an aberration; it is a glimpse of the future. The world has entered an era of low oil prices—and no region will be more affected than the GCC. It is of monumental consequence for the political economy of the region and its stability. Ignoring its possibility would be a tragic mistake.

In addition, as economies slowed amid the ensuing lockdown to control its spread, oil prices and tax revenues fell sharply. To contain the fall in revenues, GCC countries took steps to cut current expenditures (including public sector wages) and increase value-added taxes (VAT). They also announced stimulus packages involving increased public expenditures to provide support to their economies during the lockdowns. The net effect is that budget deficits are expected to prevail in all GCC countries in 2020.[6] This will undermine the ability of GCC countries to add to their net financial assets in 2020 and likely 2021, and adds to the urgency of addressing this issue. Another key assumption made in the IMF paper, that GCC countries maintain fiscal measures taken during 2014–2018 after the collapse in oil prices, will no long hold. Budget deficits will require countries to borrow more and/or draw down central bank and sovereign wealth fund (SWF) assets.

Broad Contours of Long-Term Fiscal Choices Facing Policymakers

Full preservation of current wealth would require a large and immediate fiscal adjustment. The IMF paper outlines a useful framework of the choices available to policymakers. For all generations to equally share the initial level of wealth, the Non-Oil Primary Balance (NOPB) must be immediately improved to a level that is consistent with keeping wealth constant over time.[7] The magnitude of the estimated adjustment for maintaining current wealth is large: the average NOPB in the GCC will need to fall from about 42 percent of non-oil gross domestic product (GDP) in 2019 to 12 percent.

A large and immediate fiscal adjustment would be a challenge in the GCC countries, which have so far opted for fiscal balances that are not sufficient to meet the saving rates implied by a strategy to maintain current wealth. The lower oil price environment has made this challenge more difficult: fiscal balances have turned negative, and countries have been unable to save any portion of their oil receipts.[8] Thus total wealth in the GCC has been declining in recent years.

Three options are shown in figure 13-2 for six GCC countries. The first option shows the adjustment required for the NOPB to maintain current levels of wealth for future generations. For example, Qatar needs to reduce its non-oil deficit from an estimated 38 percent of non-oil GDP in 2019 to 8 percent immediately. Kuwait, with a larger current asset base, needs to immediately reduce the deficit from 85 percent to 28 percent, while Bahrain, with more limited resources, must reduce its deficit from 18 percent to 2 percent. Such large adjustments are not feasible in the short run.

A slower adjustment path is possible if countries opt to pass only half the current wealth to future generations. Even on this path, significant fiscal adjustment is unavoidable. Qatar would need to reduce its NOPB by a quarter,

Figure 13-2. Non-Oil Primary Balance under Three Different Scenarios, 2019–2100
(Percent of non-oil GDP)

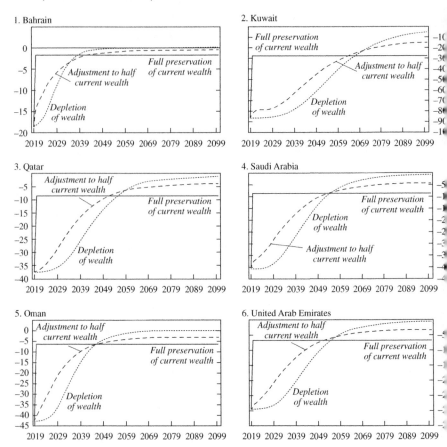

Source: IMF staff calculations.

from 38 percent of non-oil GDP in 2019 to 28 percent by 2025. Even this will not be sufficient to prevent a decline in net wealth if the peak in oil demand begins earlier (in 2031, rather than 2041). Even slower fiscal adjustment could lead to near full depletion of wealth.

Current IMF projections appear consistent with a scenario of gradual adjustment that will stabilize long-term wealth at only half its 2019 level. This will be insufficient to prevent a decline in net wealth, especially if game-changing events in the wake of the coronavirus epidemic cause the peak in oil demand to materialize a decade earlier.

Possible Policy Solutions to the Challenges
Facing GCC Policymakers

Reassessing the approach to economic diversification is, at its heart, a problem of governance. Even full replacement of the hydrocarbon industry with non-oil activity would still create a significant revenue shortfall, since the fiscal revenue that is generated from the hydrocarbon industry is much higher than what is generated from nonhydrocarbon industries.[9] Value-added and excise taxes will help enhance fiscal revenues, and consideration should be given to moving toward other broad-based taxes, such as income taxation. Changing schemes could be useful, but it represents a narrow approach because it is based on diversification in production.

Consideration should be given to a broader approach to diversification. Effective diversification would not require non-oil sectors to completely replace oil. For oil-exporting countries, what is needed is diversification in exports: an increase in non-oil exports to compensate for the decline in petroleum exports. For non-oil exports to be competitive, in turn, requires GCC countries to have access to cutting-edge technology and skills that only foreign direct investment (FDI) can bring about. However, attracting FDI to set up non-oil industries has been a challenge to date in all GCC countries for a variety of reasons.[10]

An alternative is to complement diversification in exports with diversification in income through equity investment in production facilities abroad—that is, active investments, as opposed to passive investments by SWFs. This approach, which would shift investments away from public infrastructure, might substantially increase long-term inflows of income from abroad; but increasing investment abroad would require consensus at the highest levels of government.

In the effort to diversify the sources of income, there is another reason to shift investment away from construction and other forms of domestic public investment that generated nonfinancial wealth in the past, financed from oil revenue savings. Returns to this type of investment appear to have declined and infrastructure is now largely in place.[11] Thus, fiscal consolidation to reduce domestic capital spending would have a less adverse economic impact than previously thought.

With less need to develop infrastructure, countries can turn their attention to the optimal use of financial savings generated by returns from non-oil activities. Herein lies a major challenge in governance. Much of the expenditure on infrastructure goes to firms run by the elite in the GCC.

This challenge of elite capture makes it difficult to reduce expenditures on construction in the garb of developing "world class infrastructure." Regulatory restrictions, which inhibit FDI because they require multiple and ad hoc approvals for key investments, would create another governance challenge of "coordination." For diversification to be effective, many of the Vision 2030 projects in GCC countries that were recommended by "favored" consultants should be reconsidered (such as creation of the futuristic city Neom in Saudi Arabia). They are wildly optimistic, infeasible, and their projected impact on non-oil exports is questionable.

Countries have begun cutting the public wage bill in the wake of the pandemic, but further reductions through reducing subsidies and distortions between public and private sector salaries and pension terms will be necessary; these will affect entitlements, however. If the peak in oil demand begins to materialize earlier than expected, oil prices, and with them oil export revenues, are likely to weaken significantly, undermining a key condition for the maintenance of the dollar peg. In the current environment, dollar pegs will remain intact; but if weaker oil prices increase pressure on the current account over the latter part of the 2020s, policymakers should consider more flexible exchange rates, which would aid their efforts to diversify economies by making non-oil exports more competitive, especially as fiscal policy remains tight with little scope to boost public sector employment.

The non-oil fiscal balance should also be a target in the formulation of fiscal policy. Decomposing the overall balance into an oil and a non-oil balance is critical for understanding fiscal policy developments, evaluating sustainability, and determining the macroeconomic impact of fiscal policy. Although these balances are widely available with the IMF, no GCC country regularly reports the NOPB. Many oil-producing countries can indeed afford to run potentially sizable non-oil deficits, but decisions on the appropriateness of the non-oil deficit to aim for should be based on a transparent assessment of government wealth (including oil wealth), rather than on current oil income.

The proper pricing of public land is also critical for reducing corruption and avoiding excessive and unnecessary real estate development fueled by wasteful lending of billions of dollars. Proper pricing of public land will also reduce unnecessary infrastructure—why have four-lane highways when you can do with three, given demographics? There is an opportunity cost involved in real estate development: resources that could be used for diversification, GDP growth, and increasing the SWF, instead of for physical assets that will likely be underutilized.

Notes

1. See Tokhir Mirzoev and others, "The Future of Oil and Fiscal Sustainability in the GCC Region," Departmental Paper 20/01 (Washington: International Monetary Fund, February 6, 2020) (www.imf.org/en/Publications/Departmental-Papers -Policy-Papers/Issues/2020/01/31/The-Future-of-Oil-and-Fiscal-Sustainability-in -the-GCC-Region-48934). Specific timing will vary across countries depending on initial conditions (see graph in Panel 2)

2. The IMF paper assumed that improvements in energy efficiency will have a more moderate effect on natural gas and that its global demand will likely continue to grow. However, a peak in global oil demand, even if gas demand continues to grow, will not help gas producers like Qatar if liquefied natural gas (LNG) price contracts continue to be linked to oil prices.

3. Ryan Downie, "'We're Not Going Back,' Says Fed Chair: What Investors Should Know about an Economy Forever Changed," Nasdaq, December 13, 2020 (www .nasdaq.com/articles/were-not-going-back-says-fed-chair%3A-what-investors-should -know-about-an-economy-forever).

4. Kirsten Williams, "European Council Reaches Agreement on Going Carbon Neutral by 2050," *Jurist*, October 27, 2020 (www.jurist.org/news/2020/10/european -council-reaches-agreement-on-going-carbon-neutral-by-2050/); European Commission, "Going Climate-Neutral by 2050," Brochure, July 16, 2019 (https://ec.europa .eu/clima/sites/clima/files/long_term_strategy_brochure_en.pdf).

5. Mirzoev and others, "The Future of Oil and Fiscal Sustainability in the GCC Region," p. 12, 21; William Jackson, "Recovery Faces Strong Headwinds" (London: Capital Economics, Middle East Economic Outlook, October 21, 2020), p. 16 (www .capitaleconomics.com/publications/middle-east-north-africa-economics/middle -east-economic-outlook/recovery-faces-strong-headwinds/).

6. The minimum fiscal break-even price for GCC countries in 2020 was around $40 per barrel, higher than the average crude prices expected for 2020.

7. NOPB is the primary fiscal balance net of oil-related revenues and expenditures, excluding interest payments.

8. Alternative price assumptions do not change the general outcome—that financial wealth would be depleted under the current fiscal stance once the peak in oil demand begins to materialize—but do affect its timing. A real oil price of $100 a barrel would delay the time of wealth exhaustion until 2052, while a real oil price of $20 a barrel would bring it forward from 2034 to 2027.

9. According to the IMF, fiscal revenue that is generated from the hydrocarbon industry is 80 cents from a dollar of GDP; that generated from nonhydrocarbon industries is about 10 cents from a dollar, compared to 14½ cents globally.

10. These include the relatively small size of individual GCC economies, a regulatory environment that is not conducive to private investment, lack of a skilled

workforce, and the recent split in the GCC as an economic region due to the blockade of Qatar.

11. Growth multipliers of fiscal spending in infrastructure are estimated to have declined. See Armand Fouejieu, Sergio Rodriguez, and Sohaib Shahid, "Fiscal Adjustment in the Gulf Countries: Less Costly Than Previously Thought," Working Paper 18/133 (Washington: IMF, June 13, 2018) (www.imf.org/en/Publications/WP/Issues/2018/06/13/Fiscal-Adjustment-in-the-Gulf-Countries-Less-Costly-than-Previously-Thought-45931).

PART 3

LABOR MARKETS

FOURTEEN

Labor Market Dynamics and Policy Responses in the Gulf

SAMER KHERFI

THIS CHAPTER DESCRIBES HOW the main features of the Gulf Cooperation Council (GCC) labor market interact, and how market outcomes influence and respond to policy intervention. The GCC's remarkable growth and transformation has been fueled by oil and gas revenues, as well as a huge influx of foreign workers, who constitute close to 90 percent of the labor force in some countries. The reliance on foreign labor is expected to continue, even as young nationals become more educated and skilled. The demographic reality in the GCC is that the national workforce is too small to sustain alone the needs of a growing, outwardly oriented, high-consumption economy. Despite substantial private sector job growth, the employment of nationals in the sector has remained well below potential in all GCC countries. The private sector has not been able to create enough jobs that young Gulf nationals consider suitable, or for which they are qualified, leading to rising national unemployment in different parts of the Gulf.[1]

Unemployment in the GCC is mainly a youth problem, disproportionately affecting young women, whose traditionally low labor force participation has grown rapidly. The rise in economic opportunities and female educational attainment has increased the opportunity cost of household production and led to a substantial drop in fertility. The interactions between education, economic growth, and fertility have reinforced the rise in youth labor supply across the region. A strict definition of unemployment status reveals that youth unemployment is primarily voluntary and structural; many young nationals would rather wait for better employment opportunities in the public sector than accept unattractive job offers in the private sector. Labor force participation rates, still low by global standards, suggest that choosing to remain economically inactive is a common response to the lack of jobs deemed suitable.[2]

Unemployment in the GCC is therefore not a temporary phenomenon. Quota-based job nationalization interventions have been only partially successful in the private sector. Too many nationals remain uninterested in private employment, and too few firms are interested in employing nationals. The main labor policy challenge is how to reconcile private sector conditions with the career expectations and skills of national jobseekers. Future national youth employment will depend more than ever on job creation in the private sector. Public employment is no longer capable of growing fast enough to absorb the flow of jobseekers without creating a serious underemployment problem.[3] Also, the downward pressure on oil prices has led to important public spending cuts, while government-driven investment in public infrastructure has slowed significantly, as the stock of physical capital approaches its frontier capacity.

The limited success of long-term efforts to generate national employment in the private sector can be attributed to two institutional factors: the regulatory system that governs foreign labor and the public-private sector wage gap. The GCC labor market is highly segmented by nationality and employment sector, and these lines of segmentation overlap to a large extent because nationals overwhelmingly hold public sector jobs. These two salient features not only determine how the market functions, but also set the incentive structure that governs employee and employer behavior and relations. Policies have not been effective because they tend to be incompatible with the incentives imposed by market segmentation.[4]

The sponsorship (kafala) system manages the employment of foreigners and ensures that they remain temporary residents and guest workers, with no track to permanent residency or citizenship. Under typical kafala rules, the right to reside in a country is tied to a job contract of a specific duration with a specific employer, and workers cannot change employers without the permission of the current employer. Various reforms have relaxed these restrictions, effectively granting more mobility and flexibility to skilled labor only, with the objective of attracting and retaining talent. In addition, nationals receive significantly higher salaries and benefits in the public sector, even after controlling for skills and other wage determinants. Since GCC nationality is normally a precondition for access to high-paying public jobs, this entry barrier is effective in protecting public sector benefits by insulating nationals from the competitive pressures of a global supply of work that dictates employment and pay conditions in the private sector.

Under these conditions, employers have reasons to favor foreign workers over nationals of the same caliber, and to resist the drive to nationalize private sector jobs. Foreign workers have lower reservation wages, as many of them come from low-wage, high-unemployment regions. Also, they are subject to the highly restrictive sponsorship contract. Its short duration (one to three years) and firm-specific designation (ruling out job mobility for many workers) generate asymmetric bargaining power that decidedly favors the employer. The outcome is a more manageable or docile foreign workforce that may be judged to possess better work ethics. In a nutshell, the total price of foreign labor services is significantly lower.[5] The gradual elimination of kafala rules in the region for skilled workers, essentially allowing them to change employers, generates competition that diminishes the control employers exercise over foreign workers and increases the attractiveness of national workers.

A large share of the GCC's foreign workforce fills low and semi-skilled occupations, whereas most nationals hold, or prefer to hold, managerial or government positions. Many foreign workers occupy jobs that young nationals do not want for economic reasons (low pay) or social considerations (prestige, religion, and cultural norms). The scope of substitution between domestic and foreign labor is more limited than what demographics data suggest, especially among the wealthier members of the GCC. In cases where foreign and national workers complement each other (managers need workers to manage), restricting the inflow of foreign labor may eventually depress the demand for local labor. In addition to providing production complementarity, expatriates boost the demand for all workers, including nationals, because spending by foreign residents is a major component of aggregate demand. It is interesting that short-term demand shocks have pushed governments to introduce measures to preserve national employment gains in the private sector, essentially by making it costly and complicated for firms to lay off nationals in response to business conditions. Although such steps protect jobs in the short run, they are likely to have a negative impact in the long run if firms hesitate to hire more nationals in good times in anticipation of complications associated with dismissing them in times of need.

On the supply side, public sector pay shapes the expectations of Gulf youth. Youth strongly favor public employment, with many preferring to wait for an uncertain public sector job that promises a better salary than to accept a guaranteed but low-paying job in the private sector. Some young GCC employees take a private sector job only long enough to secure a position in the public sector. In the wealthier Gulf countries (in per capita terms), only high-value-added jobs in the private sector are capable of attracting youth because their high reservation wage is conditioned on public sector compensation. The resulting higher cost of, and lower demand for, national workers, reduces private sector willingness to invest in their training and skill development.

Government-led job nationalization efforts focused for many years on the imposition of sector, occupation, or firm-specific quotas, specifying the (minimum) proportion of employment allocated to nationals. Despite some success at the sectoral level, quotas did not reach their macro targets because they were implemented without complementary measures to address the deeper problem of incentives described earlier. Furthermore, a quota itself may not be the most efficient way to increase national employment. By design, the quota does not adjust to market or firm conditions. In markets where nationals represent a small share of employees, creating enough jobs for nationals does not necessarily require reducing the percentage of foreign labor. In addition, the quota applies uniformly and therefore imposes unequal adjustment costs on firms. As a result, firms may handle national employment primarily as a minimum regulatory requirement, with no incentive to further increase job offers to nationals. Also, the quota emphasis on quantitative targets may come at the expense of job quality. The phenomenon of ghost workers, workers who appear on employers' payrolls but have limited duties or expectations, illustrates the distortions that may arise.[6] Some firms appear to have reacted to the quota on foreign workers by transferring some of their services to other companies. The outsourced services typically are support activities that are foreign-labor intensive in sectors that are subject to lower quotas. This type of restructuring raises the share of nationals in the workforce but does nothing to raise the number of national hires.

The limited success of quota regulations prompted Gulf governments to reform and expand their set of policy tools in order to address the impediments to nationalization. In addition to softening the restrictions of the kafala system, measures to tax foreign labor were enacted in all countries. In some countries, wage subsidies were introduced to bridge the gap between market realities and youth expectations, a costly intervention because the gap is large and long-standing. The tax on foreign labor was designed to particularly discourage the reliance on unskilled workers.[7] Other country-specific interventions involved offering consumer subsidies to nationals working in the private sector, as well as unemployment compensation and training programs aimed at improving the match between national workers and firms.[8]

These labor interventions are closely linked to a common drive in the region to adopt a growth model that depends much less on labor and capital accumulation. GCC countries seem determined to achieve robust long-term growth by diversifying the structure of production away from hydrocarbon and toward knowledge-based sectors, where productivity-driven growth is not constrained by diminishing returns or resource imbalances. However, the success of these plans requires that GCC firms become innovative and globally competitive, and that GCC youth acquire the skills that are attractive to such firms.

There is debate on the extent of mismatch between the skills acquired and sought. Employers frequently blame the education system for the lack of young graduates with market-oriented qualifications. Although the GCC has achieved significant improvement in educational attainment, especially among women, concerns remain about the quality and type of education in light of students' poor performance on international standardized tests and the insufficient number of nationals who pursue careers in science and technology. On the other hand, youths' preference for public employment tends to reduce the incentive to invest in market-tested skills, because public sector salaries are tied less strongly to productivity than to satisfying diploma requirements and years of service.

In the labor market, diversification efforts in resource-rich countries often collide with one aspect of the resource curse: the distribution of hydrocarbon wealth generates economic rent of various forms (government transfers, business ownership dividends, sponsorship revenue, and public wages that do not reflect productivity considerations). This rent diminishes the private return on investment in education and discourages the acquisition of market skills. Abundant natural resources create opportunities for nationals to engage in rent-generating activities that distort education and labor market signals and lead to skill shortages.

Policies to limit the flow of mostly unskilled foreign workers may not actually be popular among the national population. Gulf firms and households are more likely to worry about lower profit margins and more expensive household workers caused by restrictions on the supply of unskilled labor.

There have instead been calls to limit competition from foreign skilled workers, who command private wages comparable to the wage expectations of young nationals. The policy to attract global talent suggests that the right path is to equip GCC youth with skills that enable them to compete globally.

The ready availability of low-wage labor from abroad is a challenge to diversification, as GCC firms resist adopting costly measures to switch inputs from unskilled to skilled labor. Business owners regularly complain that imposing fees and quotas and facilitating labor mobility increases costs and reduces their ability to compete. GCC countries that rank highly on other dimensions of global competitiveness are more likely to diversify their economies easily. In countries with a well-established physical infrastructure, the next and more demanding challenge is to accumulate a human capital infrastructure capable of attracting innovation and research activities. The anticipated long-run productivity gains, and the associated short-term adjustment costs, are conditional on successful reforms to the output, labor, and education markets.

The COVID-19 pandemic led to massive layoffs and an exodus of foreign labor. Some GCC countries are estimated to have lost up to 10 percent of their populations.[9] Many workers have taken substantial salary cuts in order to remain employed. The downward flexibility of wage and employment has shifted a large share of the pandemic burden to labor-exporting countries.

The short-term domestic countermeasures taken by Gulf states to address the pandemic-driven drops in spending and oil prices have led to large fiscal imbalances, causing states to slow down or place on hold long-term growth and diversification plans. The severe drop in aggregate demand has hit the service sector hard, with the GCC economy expected to have contracted by about 6 percent in real terms in 2020.[10]

A sizable number of the jobs lost to the pandemic are not expected to return, as many firms adapt to the crisis by permanently digitizing and automating their operations, especially in labor-intensive industries.[11] These adjustments will favor the demand for intellectual and physical capital and intensify the decades-long negative effect of technological progress on unskilled labor.

The expected permanent effect of the pandemic may have a silver lining for the GCC labor market. The massive departure of mostly unskilled workers creates an opportunity to change the labor market landscape to limit the rebound in their demand. The crisis underscores the need to transition faster from a low-wage, low-productivity business model to a high-wage, high-productivity model. The accelerated, and sometimes forced, digital transformation of businesses and governments is not expected to slow down. Some GCC governments have accelerated the job nationalization drive, while others have taken steps to attract and retain global talent by offering long-term residency and possibly citizenship.[12] The challenge, however, is that GCC youth and workers might eventually bear the brunt of the crisis if efforts to minimize labor market segmentation stall and jobseekers are not offered, or ignore, the opportunity to acquire skills through proper education and training.

<h3 align="center">Notes</h3>

1. International Monetary Fund (IMF), "Labor Market Reforms to Boost Employment and Productivity in the GCC" (Washington, October 5, 2013) (www.imf.org /external/np/pp/eng/2013/100513.pdf).

2. Paul Dyer and Samer Kherfi, "Gulf Youth and the Labor Market," in *Young Generation Awakening: Economics, Society, and Policy on the Eve of the Arab Spring*, edited by Edward A. Sayre and Tarik M. Yousef (Oxford University Press, 2016), pp. 88–109.

3. Ibid.

4. Ibid.

5. Ibid.

6. Aarti Nagraj, "GCC Nationalisation Schemes Creating 'Ghost Workers,'" *Gulf Business*, January 26, 2014 (https://gulfbusiness.com/gcc-nationalisation-schemes -creating-ghost-workers/).

7. IMF, "Labor Market Reforms."

8. "UAE App Offers Special Discounts to Private Sector Employees," *Khaleej Times*, March 5, 2019 (www.khaleejtimes.com/nation/uae-app-offers-special-discounts -to-private-sector-employees); Ruba Obaid, "Campaign Promotes Employment of Saudis in the Private Sector," *Arab News*, January 14, 2020 (www.arabnews.com /node/1613181/saudi-arabia).

9. Shaji Mathew, "Oxford Economics Sees Exodus of Expat Workers from across Gulf," Bloomberg, May 22, 2020 (www.bloomberg.com/news/articles/2020-05-22 /oxford-economics-sees-exodus-of-expat-workers-from-across-gcc).

10. IMF, "Economic Prospects and Policy Challenges for the GCC Countries" (Washington, October 25, 2020) (www.imf.org/en/Publications/Policy-Papers/Issues /2020/12/08/Economic-Prospects-and-Policy-Challenges-for-the-GCC-Countries -49942).

11. Tom Standage, "New Technological Behaviours Will Outlast the Pandemic," *The Economist*, November 16, 2020 (www.economist.com/the-world-ahead/2020/11 /16/new-technological-behaviours-will-outlast-the-pandemic).

12. "Kuwait's Parliament Passes Law to Cut Expat Numbers," *Gulf Business*, October 21, 2020 (https://gulfbusiness.com/kuwaits-parliament-passes-law-to-cut-expat -numbers/); "UAE to Offer Citizenship to 'Talented' Foreigners," BBC, January 30, 2021 (www.bbc.com/news/world-middle-east-55869674).

FIFTEEN

Human Capital Development in the GCC

MARVIN ERFURTH

NATASHA RIDGE

HUMAN CAPITAL, UNDERSTOOD AS "the knowledge, skills, and health that people accumulate over their lives," is widely recognized as a key factor in increasing the economic growth and competitiveness of nations.[1] Despite high per capita gross domestic product (GDP), human capital development in the Gulf Cooperation Council (GCC) remains a key challenge.[2] Despite large investments and overall school enrollment rates of close to 100 percent, the quality of education still needs improvement. The performance of GCC students in international assessments such as the Programme for International Student Assessment (PISA), Trends in International Mathematics and Science Study (TIMMS), and the Progress in International Reading Literacy Study (PIRLS) is consistently below the mean, and well below the performance of European countries with similar per capita GDP (see table 15-4).[3] Males in particular struggle; countries in the GCC have some of the largest reverse gender gaps in the world, despite the fact that women are far more likely to be unemployed.[4] Finally, research has historically been a low priority for GCC governments, and without considerable investment in applied and basic research, attracting and developing top talent will be problematic.[5] Most GCC countries speak of a desire to transform themselves into knowledge-based economies, but doing so will be difficult unless these challenges are addressed.

The onset of COVID-19 in early 2020 has further compounded these challenges. In 2020, the World Bank projected a permanent loss of human capital among younger generations and the most vulnerable groups due to increased health risks, rising unemployment rates, and a loss of learning, in particular for low-socioeconomic-status (SES) groups (estimated at 0.6 years worldwide in 2020).[6] Although GCC countries have responded to COVID-19 by moving learning online, implementation has been inconsistent and the effectiveness is far from clear; there have been widespread allegations of cheating on national exams and parents helping students with their exams and assignments.[7] These problems, coupled with rising unemployment and the departure of many skilled and unskilled expatriate workers, will place additional pressures on human capital development.[8] This chapter explores both the challenges and the opportunities that GCC governments face at this unique moment in time.

We first discuss long-term challenges in GCC labor markets and education sectors. Given those challenges, we describe opportunities for the region, and what policymakers and leaders should do to stay ahead of them.

Challenges Facing GCC Labor Markets and Education Sectors

Despite the substantial economic development of GCC countries after the discovery of oil, the GCC faces at least four challenges that threaten sustainable human capital development. First, in higher education, tertiary graduates are narrowly clustered in business and law majors, followed by engineering. A holistic approach to national development also requires increasing the number of graduates in underrepresented fields such as education, the social sciences, and arts and humanities (see table 15-1).[9]

Second, there is a growing reverse gender gap, in which females are outperforming males at all levels of education across the region (see table 15-4).[10] Tertiary education enrollment of females exceeds that of males in most GCC countries (see tables 15-1 and 15-2). This gap is particularly relevant because males are expected to be the providers for their families but are poorly prepared for the labor market. A small number of initiatives focus on males who are at high risk of dropping out of education systems, but there are virtually no initiatives to address their lower performance and

Table 15-1. *Distribution of Tertiary Graduates by Field of Study*

Percent

Field of Study	Bahrain	Oman	Qatar	Saudi Arabia	UAE (2017)
Education	5	4	7	13	3
Arts and Humanities	9	9	15	19	6
Social Sciences, Journalism, and Information	8	1	14	7	7
Business Administration and Law	49	36	30	30	48
Natural Sciences, Mathematics, and Statistics	2	4	5	8	2
Information and Communication Technology	4	12	3	7	6
Engineering, Manufacturing, and Construction	10	28	16	7	20
Health and Welfare	9	5	8	7	7

Source: UNESCO Institute for Statistics (http://uis.unesco.org/); all data for 2019 except for the UAE; no data available for Kuwait.

Table 15-2. *Enrollment in Tertiary Education*

Thousands

Country	Public Institutions			Private Institutions		
	Men	Women	Total	Men	Women	Total
Bahrain (2020)	8,499	15,816	24,315	6,786	7,012	13,798
Kuwait (2020)	28,402	56,803	86,065	n.a.	n.a.	49,264
Oman (2020)	n.a.[a]	n.a.	63,410	n.a.	n.a.	68,350
Qatar (2018/2019)	6,461	20,276	26,737	3,976	4,531	8,507
Saudi Arabia (2020)	792,807	829,609	1,622,416	n.a.	n.a.	76,388
UAE (2018)	106,22	34,194	44,816	38,758	47,740	86,498

Sources: Bahrain: Open Data Portal (http://www.data.gov.bh/) | Qatar: Planning and Statistics Authority (https://www.psa.gov.qa/) | Kuwait: Central Statistics Bureau (https://csb.gov.kw/) | Oman: National Centre for Statistics and Information (https://data.gov.om) | Saudi Arabia: General Authority for Statistics (https://www.stats.gov.sa/) | UAE: Bayanat—The Official Data Portal (https://www.bayanat.ae/).

a. n.a. = not available.

Table 15-3. *Labor Force Participation Rates*

Percent

Country	Men	Women
Bahrain (2017)	87	44
Kuwait (2015)	53	39
Oman (2013)	59	29
Qatar (2019)	66	36
Saudi Arabia (2020)	66	31
UAE (2017)	63	32

Sources: Bahrain: Open Data Portal (http://www.data.gov.bh/); Qatar: Planning and Statistics Authority (https://www.psa.gov.qa/); Kuwait: Central Statistics Bureau (https://csb.gov.kw/); Saudi Arabia: General Authority for Statistics (https://www.stats.gov.sa/); UAE: Bayanat—The Official Data Portal (https://www.bayanat.ae/).

Note: Labor force participation rate is the percentage of employed nationals aged 15 or over. Except for Bahrain, the reported values exclude full-time students.

engagement in education more generally. This situation will create future challenges for GCC countries, as well as for individual national males.

Third, despite the increasing education levels of women, the reverse gender gap's impact creates added pressure on labor markets since women's labor market participation remains relatively low.[11] Table 15-3 provides an overview of the large disparity between male and female engagement in national labor markets.

Fourth, the quality of education, particularly public education, across the region remains low.[12] Results from international assessments such as PISA, TIMSS, and PIRLS find the GCC countries lagging behind Organization for Economic Cooperation and Development (OECD) counterparts, despite high expenditures on education (see table 15-4).[13] Each of these challenges alone, and even more so combined, reveals the need for systematic approaches to human capital development in the region.

GCC countries also share considerable mismatches between labor market supply and demand. This is problematic for human capital development in several ways. The root causes of these mismatches are seldom addressed in ways other than nationalization efforts, which can lead to an ever-expanding public sector or the implementation of private sector quotas.[14] As a result, the state-led economic model persists across the region, and the public sector remains the dominant employment preference of GCC nationals, whose participation in the private sector remains low because of the

Table 15-4. *Mean PISA Scores in OECD and GCC Countries*

	Reading			Mathematics			Science		
	Male	*Female*	*Gap*	*Male*	*Female*	*Gap*	*Male*	*Female*	*Gap*
Qatar	375	440	65	402	426	24	400	439	39
UAE	403	460	57	430	439	9	420	447	27
KSA	373	427	54	367	380	13	372	401	29
OECD	472	502	30	492	487	−5	488	490	2

Source: OECD, "PISA 2018 Results (Volume II): Where All Students Can Succeed," December 3, 2019 (https://doi.org/10.1787/b5fd1b8f-en).

Notes: PISA = Programme for International Student Assessment. No PISA data are available for Bahrain, Kuwait, and Oman.

incentives provided by the nationalization strategies.[15] Current capacity development in local communities is not strategic and makes no attempt to match crucial occupations and tasks with long-term needs; the result is continued reliance on expatriate communities.[16] The existing science, technology, engineering, and math (STEM) and entrepreneurship initiatives in GCC countries can be seen as attempts to increase the number of graduates in these fields to address particular shortages in labor market demands. For instance, the natural sciences remain particularly underrepresented in recent graduate cohorts, as table 15-1 shows. Finally, despite a multiplicity of existing strategies for diversification and modernization, the long-term benefits of research as a base for competitive and knowledge-based economies is largely undervalued. Therefore, local and regional knowledge production, such as that measured by registered patents or university-industry research projects, remains strikingly low.[17]

Opportunities for the GCC and Recommendations for Human Capital Development

Some of the challenges that GCC countries face also present opportunities. First, the populations of the GCC countries are much younger than their European and North American counterparts (see table 15-5). The GCC's relative youth could be turned into an immense opportunity to modernize if more attention were given to private sector employment.

Second, governments in the region are particularly open to new ideas and innovation, as exemplified by the United Arab Emirates (UAE) National Innovation Strategy and Saudi Arabia's information and communication technology (ICT) strategy.[18] Third, GCC economies are largely well re-

Table 15-5. *Age Structure of National GCC Populations*

Percent

Age Group	Bahrain (2015)		KSA (2015)		Kuwait (2015)		Oman (2015)		Qatar (2015)		UAE (2019)
	Nationals	Nonnationals	Nationals	Nonnationals	Nationals	Nonnationals	Nationals	Nonnationals	Nationals	Nonnationals	Total Population
0–14	32	11	30	15	36	15	36	5	38	11	15
15–29	27	25	28	18	28	15	30	33	27	27	26
30–39	14	34	16	28	13	31	16	36	12	33	31
40–49	11	19	12	25	10	24	7	17	9	20	17
50–59	9	8	7	10	7	10	5	7	8	8	8
60–69	4	2	4	3	4	3	3	1	4	2	2
70–79	2	0	2	1	2	1	2	0	1	0	1
80+	1	0	1	0	1	0	1	0	1	0	0

Sources: GCC national and foreign populations by five-year age group from "Gulf Labour Markets, Migration and Population (GLMM) Programme" (https://gulfmigration .org/); UAE total population estimates by age groups and gender from Bayanat—The Official Data Portal (https://www.bayanat.ae/).

sourced to develop and implement new ideas and potentially innovative approaches. For instance, ICT spending in Saudi Arabia totaled 111.98 billion Saudi riyals in 2014, or roughly $30 billion.[19] Likewise, the UAE invested more than 22 billion dirhams (roughly $6 billion) in its space program.[20] And fourth, governments across the region are supportive of making great leaps forward because it shines a favorable light on their national plans.[21] For instance, Saudi Arabia strives to be the "heart of the Arab and Islamic worlds, the investment powerhouse, and the hub connecting three continents."[22]

One area in the education sector that remains largely overlooked in the GCC is technical and vocational education and training (TVET), the advancement of which has immense potential to up- and re-skill workers in times of change. Although some GCC countries have developed strategies to increase TVET opportunities and attainment, some cultural constraints may hinder their development and require novel approaches. Southeast Asian countries, such as Singapore, are moving fast in this direction (see, for instance, their SkillsFuture Initiative), which is where policymakers might find answers to open questions.

Higher education opportunities are increasing, yet academic research receives too little attention. In recent years, Saudi Arabia, the UAE, and Qatar in particular have made progress building new physical higher education infrastructure, but there has been much less investment in research funding and infrastructure. Therefore, another potential opportunity could be to foster a locally relevant research culture, which would also increase the long-term benefits of research for large groups of people.[23]

Last, despite COVID-19's devastating impact on GCC economies and labor markets, the lessons learned could be used to accelerate the digital transformation of industries and introduce new ways of remote working.[24] In light of the low female labor force participation across the GCC (see table 15-3), a new remote working culture could leverage technology to better integrate women and other underrepresented groups into national and regional labor markets.

Concluding Remarks

GCC countries' human capital is underdeveloped relative to both their GDP and their spending on education. COVID-19 adds to existing challenges while also creating new ones, such as lost learning and employment opportunities for younger generations and vulnerable groups. There is also a direct loss of human capital due to the departure of many expats during the pandemic. In addition, there are significant mismatches between educational outcomes and labor market demands, compounded by ineffective social and public policy initiatives. However, the region also has a number of opportunities that policymakers could take advantage of. The regional demographics, coupled with outward-looking and well-resourced governments, could provide a great opportunity to modernize economies and increase global competitiveness. New approaches to TVET seem particularly promising, and academic research should be strengthened through the development of local research communities.

Notes

1. World Bank, "The Human Capital Index 2020 Update: Human Capital in the Time of COVID-19" (Washington, 2020), p. ix (http://doi.org/10986/34432); Gary S. Becker, *Human Capital: A Theoretical and Empirical Analysis, with Special Reference to Education* (University of Chicago Press, 1993); Amartya Sen, "Editorial: Human Capital and Human Capability," *World Development* 25, no. 12 (1997), pp. 1959–61 (www.staff.ncl.ac.uk/david.harvey/AEF806/Sen1997.pdf); Joseph E. Stiglitz, "New Theoretical Perspectives on the Distribution of Income and Wealth among Individuals," in *Inequality and Growth: Patterns and Policy,* edited by Kaushik Basu and Joseph E. Stiglitz (London: Palgrave Macmillan, 2016), pp. 1–71 (https://doi.org/10.1057/9781137554543_1).

2. World Bank, "The Human Capital Index 2020 Update," pp. 31–36.

3. Organization for Economic Cooperation and Development (OECD), "PISA 2018 Results (Volume II): Where All Students Can Succeed," December 3, 2019 (https://doi.org/10.1787/b5fd1b8f-en).

4. World Bank, "The Human Capital Index 2020 Update"; Sheikh Saud bin Saqr Al Qasimi Foundation for Policy Research (AQF), "Education in the United Arab Emirates and Ras Al Khaimah," Fact Sheet, September 2020 (https://publications.alqasimifoundation.com/en/education-in-the-united-arab-emirates-and-ras-al-khaimah); Natasha Ridge, *Education and the Reverse Gender Divide in the Gulf States: Embracing the Global, Ignoring the Local* (Teachers College Press, 2014).

5. PricewaterhouseCoopers (PwC), "Advancing Academic Research in the GCC: How to Enhance Research Operations to Drive Better Performance Outcomes in Higher Education Institutions," 2019 (www.pwc.com/m1/en/publications/advancing-academic-research-in-gcc/advancing-academic-research-in-gcc.pdf).

6. World Bank, "The Human Capital Index 2020 Update," pp. 62–83.

7. Derek Newton, "Another Problem with Shifting Education Online: A Rise in Cheating," *Washington Post,* August 7, 2020 (www.washingtonpost.com/local/education/another-problem-with-shifting-education-online-a-rise-in-cheating/2020/08/07/1284c9f6-d762-11ea-aff6-220dd3a14741_story.html).

8. Davide Barbuscia and Marwa Rashad, "'What's the Point of Staying?': Gulf Faces Expatriate Exodus," Reuters, May 7, 2020 (www.reuters.com/article/us-health

-coronavirus-gulf-jobs-idUSKBN22J1WL); Sameer Hashmi, "Coronavirus Threatening Expat Exodus from the UAE," *BBC News*, October 9, 2020 (https://www.bbc.com/news/world-middle-east-54418336).

9. GFH Financial Group (GFH), "Sector Report: GCC Education," October 2016 (www.gfh.com/wp-content/uploads/GFH-Education-Sector-Report.pdf); Alpen Capital, "GCC Education Industry," November 13, 2018 (https://argaamplus.s3.amazonaws.com/9e55ad53-477f-48f0-b202-2c2f03d6a03d.pdf).

10. Ridge, *Education and the Reverse Gender Divide in the Gulf States*; World Bank, "The Human Capital Index 2020 Update," pp. 18–21.

11. Gail Buttorff, Bozena Welborne, and Nawra al-Lawati, "Measuring Female Labor Force Participation in the GCC," Issue Brief (Rice University, Baker Institute for Public Policy, January 18, 2018) (https://scholarship.rice.edu/bitstream/handle/1911/99713/bi-brief-011818-wrme-femalelabor.pdf?sequence=1&isAllowed=y); Karen E. Young, "Women's Labor Force Participation across the GCC," Issue Paper 10 (Arab Gulf States Institute in Washington (AGSIW), December 7, 2016) (https://agsiw.org/wp-content/uploads/2016/12/Young_Womens-Labor_ONLINE-4.pdf); PwC, "Women in Work Index 2019: Turning Policies into Effective Action," March 2019 (www.pwc.co.uk/economic-services/WIWI/pwc-women-in-work-2019-final-web.pdf); Woohyang Sim, "For Love, Money and Status, or Personal Growth? A Survey of Young Emirati Women's Educational Aspirations," *Gulf Education and Social Policy Review* 1, no. 1, pp. 73–90 (https://doi.org/10.18502/gespr.v1i1.7470).

12. Ahmar Mahboob and Tariq Elyas, eds., *Challenges to Education in the GCC during the 21st Century* (Cambridge, England: Gulf Research Centre, 2017) (www.academia.edu/19123677/Challenges_to_Education_in_GCC_during_the_21st_Century).

13. National Foundation for Educational Research (NFER International), "Key Insights from International Large Scale Assessments in the Gulf," NFER Education Briefings, April 20, 2018 (www.nfer.ac.uk/media/2392/ilsa01.pdf); United Arab Emirates Ministry of Education Assessment Department, "Building Knowledge in the UAE: Findings from TIMSS 2011 & PIRLS 2011," 2012 (www.moe.gov.ae/En/ImportantLinks/InternationalAssessments/Documents/PIRLS/PIRLS%20Report%202011.pdf).

14. Antonio Carvalho, Jeff Youssef, and Nicolas Dunais, "Maximizing Employment of Nationals in the GCC: Benefits and Limits of Labour Policy Instruments" (New York: Oliver Wyman, 2018) (www.oliverwyman.com/content/dam/oliver-wyman/v2/publications/2018/october/maximizing-employment-of-nationals-in-the-gcc.pdf).

15. Hilal Halaoui and others, "Private-Sector Participation in the GCC: Building Foundations for Success" (Beirut: strategy&, 2017) (www.strategyand.pwc.com/m1/en/ideation-center/media/private-sector-participation-in-the-gcc.pdf).

16. Ibid.; Carvalho, Youssef, and Dunais, "Maximizing Employment of Nationals in the GCC."

17. PwC, "Advancing Academic Research in the GCC."

18. UAE Ministry of Cabinet Affairs, "UAE National Innovation Strategy," 2015 (www.moei.gov.ae/assets/download/1d2d6460/National%20Innovation%20Strategy

.pdf.aspx); Saudi Ministry of Communications and Information Technology, "ICT Sector Strategy 2023," 2019 (www.mcit.gov.sa/sites/default/files/strategy_summary .pdf).

19. Saudi Communications and Information Technology Commission, "ICT Report: ICT Investments in the Kingdom of Saudi Arabia," 2015, p. 7 (www.citc.gov.sa /en/reportsandstudies/Reports/Documents/ICTInvestments_EN.pdf).

20. Adelle Geronimo, "UAE Space Investments Exceed AED 22 Billion," tahawul-tech.com, January 15, 2019 (www.tahawultech.com/region/uae/uae-space-investments -exceed-aed-22-billion/).

21. Qatar General Secretariat for Development Planning, "Qatar National Vision 2030," July 2008 (www.gco.gov.qa/wp-content/uploads/2016/09/GCO-QNV-English .pdf); Kingdom of Saudi Arabia, "Vision 2030," 2016 (http://vision2030.gov.sa/down load/file/fid/417); UAE, "Vision 2021," 2014 (www.vision2021.ae/docs/default-source /default-document-library/uae_vision-arabic.pdf?sfvrsn=b09a06a6_6); Oman, "Oman Vision 2040: Vision Document," 2019 (www.2040.om/Oman2040-En.pdf).

22. Kingdom of Saudi Arabia, "Vision 2030," p. 9.

23. PwC, "Advancing Academic Research in the GCC."

24. Jad Hajj and others, "Adopting Emerging Technologies in a Post-COVID-19 World" (Beirut: strategy&, July 2020) (www.strategyand.pwc.com/m1/en/articles/2020 /adopting-emerging-technologies-in-a-post-covid-world.html); PwC, "Lessons from Lockdown: New Ways of Remote Working in Saudi Arabia," 2020 (www.pwc.com /m1/en/publications/lessons-from-lockdown-new-ways-remote-working-in-sa.html).

SIXTEEN

Women in the Workforce Across the GCC

KAREN E. YOUNG

DISCRIMINATION AND OPPRESSION ON the grounds of sex and gender are perhaps the most prevalent human rights violations in the world as they affect half of the global population, but they are by no means limited to the geography of the Middle East or Persian Gulf.[1] In a region where there has been so much economic change over the past two generations, the Gulf Cooperation Council (GCC) member states are a site of unexpected social revolution. The revolution is unexpected because it has largely been a state development project to educate, improve the health of, and increase the productivity of their citizens, with the largest shift in circumstances afforded to women citizens of the Gulf. The rights to work, to learn and acquire high-value skills, to control financial resources within the family, and to be an instrument and representative face of the state are all in line with broader national development objectives and foreign policy projections of the modern Gulf states.

Women are encouraged to enter the workforce by a range of social policies. Globally, we know that education access, public safety and antiharassment policies, legal protection for equal pay, access to childcare, and cultural norms all contribute to the ability of women to gain meaningful and productive employment. We also know that most people around the world believe it is acceptable and desirable for women to work outside the home (85 percent of women and 81 percent of men).[2]

Historically, if we consider the movement of women from home-based labor into the workforce in Western societies during the Industrial Revolution, the path has usually been through low-wage manufacturing (usually textiles) and persistent organizing and protests to pressure states to change restrictions on women's place in society, with labor and political participation demands overlapping.[3] In the GCC, it is the states themselves paving the way for citizen women outside the home and into more public-facing roles. The distinction between female citizen and female foreigner is essential here, for there remain major differences on class, race, and nationality lines in the lives of women living and working in the GCC.

There are many distortions to the oil-and-gas-rich economies of the Gulf, and the rentier paradigm has hindered labor market development with its reliance on cheap imported foreign labor and proliferation of a redundant low-wage service industry. Of the distortions of the rentier model, Michael Ross argues that oil wealth has hindered the demand for dual-income families, as well as any kind of labor organizing.[4] Although there is merit to his critique, there has also been a silver lining to the trajectory of women's economic inclusion within the Gulf.

As more recent research by Gail J. Buttorff, Nawra Al Lawati, and Bozena C. Welborne demonstrates, Gulf state diversification policies that intervene in labor markets to encourage and protect job opportunities for nationals have had an add-on effect of boosting female citizens' employment.[5] The rentier paradigm in its state-centric development has brought a new generation of women into higher education and employment, helping them avoid the toil of factory floors and street protests. Its abundance of low-wage household labor and childcare, provided on the backs of poor women from South Asia, the Philippines, and Africa has also solved the "second shift" dilemma that so many women in the developed world struggle to resolve.[6] Women citizens of the Gulf states are more likely to work in banking, education, insurance, and real estate because those sectors are nationalized as a matter of government policy. Traditional caring (often low-paid) roles in health and hospitality continue to be the domain of foreign workers.

As the GCC states seek to further reduce their reliance on foreign workers and reduce the fiscal burden of creating new public sector jobs, there remain persistent cultural and social barriers to Gulf citizens entering blue-collar and skilled work in manufacturing, construction, nursing, retail, and service sector jobs. Explaining labor force participation requires going beyond wages and the social status of service sector work. For some Gulf women, training and educational attainment is a broader goal than employment.

Survey work in the United Arab Emirates (UAE) finds that for many Emirati women, higher education is a form of self-care and empowerment as much as, if not more than, a goal for career advancement and economic independence.[7] Women in other Gulf states may find higher education tied to career opportunity more of a priority; and women surveyed at age 30 rather than age 20 may have very different perceptions of the value of a job and financial independence. In Saudi Arabia, for example, young Saudi women are actively joining the workforce even in the face of the COVID-19 pandemic and rising unemployment. October 2020 labor market reports from the Saudi investment bank Jadwa report that young women's labor force participation increased from about 10 percent in the second quarter of 2017 to nearly 25 percent by the second quarter of 2020.[8] The Saudi case is especially fast moving, as the opening of employment opportunities to women and state programs to restrict certain sectors to nationals only has increased women's labor force participation since 2016, as part of the Vision 2030 economic development plan. The global COVID-19 pandemic arrived at a particularly difficult time for Saudi women looking to work and gain financial and personal independence.

The International Labor Organization (ILO) finds that nearly 40 percent of women working globally are concentrated in sectors that are especially vulnerable to the economic effects of the COVID-19 pandemic: hotels and hospitality, food services, wholesale and retail, and professional services.[9] In Saudi Arabia, 53 percent of job losses among female workers in the first half of 2020 were in education, wholesale and retail, and professional services, according to Jadwa's second quarter 2020 report. So, while more women have been actively seeking work since 2017, these women are also adversely affected by job losses as the COVID-19 pandemic hits the sectors where they have successfully gained employment.

Women's labor force inclusion also includes participation in governance. As Hala Aldosari explains in the Saudi context, the nationalist project of the Vision 2030 reforms is a hybrid form of modernization, creating opportunity for women but under state direction:

> Vision 2030 explicitly targets an increase in women serving in senior-level positions from the current 1.27 percent to 5 percent. In addition to the need to increase women's participation by providing opportunities to gain experience, the unstated imperative also is to improve the image of Saudi Arabia internationally, as it seeks greater economic integration and foreign investment. This process is well-

Figure 16-1. Sectors with Highest Number of Female Job Losses in Q2 2020

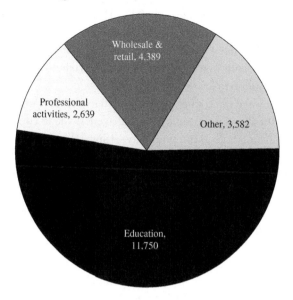

Wholesale & retail, 4,389

Professional activities, 2,639

Other, 3,582

Education, 11,750

Source: Jadwa Investment, "Saudi Labor Market Update—Q2 2020," Labor Market Report, October 8, 2020 (www.jadwa.com/en/researchsection/research/economic-research/labor-market-reports).

articulated by the theory of neopatriarchy, which posits that the patriarchal structures and gender relations of traditional Arab societies will continue to be enforced in modern states. The result is a hybrid society in which some women gain leadership positions while the state continues to enforce restrictive laws and public policies to maintain the structure of a conservative traditional society.[10]

Women's presence, in the workforce and as part of the apparatus of governance within state institutions, serves multiple purposes in state-led development models. In Saudi Arabia, women's economic inclusion pairs with a state goal to increase the availability of financial products like mortgages (which grows the financial service industry and creates jobs), and as citizens take on more credit, they will spend more on domestic goods and services. Although overall employment among Saudis did not significantly improve between 2018 and 2020, more women are entering the workforce—albeit from a low base—reaching 20.2 percent in 2018, from 19.4 percent in 2017.[11] Women are a large part of that demographic change. A one percentage point increase in the Saudi workforce every year would add about 70,000 more women a year to the labor market.[12] This would increase the demand for new products to improve financial mobility. HSBC projects that the growth in female employment has the potential to generate $33 billion in new mortgage loans, or 40 percent of the first-time buyer demand, either as independent purchases (Saudi women have long had the right to own property) or by their contribution to household income.

More difficult to uncover empirically is what motivates women to apply for and take these jobs, to assume financial agency, and to compete among male job applicants and within university settings. Women's rights activism in the GCC is also complex and dangerous.[13] The agency of Gulf women who are willing to take on new roles, learn new skills, and compete with their male counterparts deserves recognition, and they are very competitive and resilient.

Women across the GCC are better educated than their male peers and have a substantial presence in science and engineering fields in higher education, often well above female averages in the Organization for Economic Cooperation and Development (OECD) economies.[14] In the Middle East, it is estimated that 40 percent of university students specializing in computer science and information technology (IT) are women. The percentage is even higher in Saudi Arabia and the UAE, where women represent 70 to 80 percent of computer science and IT students; by comparison, the figure is 15 to 20 percent in the United States.[15]

Jennifer DeBoer and Ashley Kranov find that state education policy has dramatically improved overall enrollment, as well as the proportions of the school-going population of GCC females.[16] There is strong and growing representation of women in engineering and science, technology, engineering, and math (STEM) study and work. In fact, DeBoer and Kranov find higher proportions of the female university student cohorts enroll in science in Saudi Arabia (16.3 percent of females, 12.7 percent of males), in the UAE (8.2 percent of females, 7.9 percent of males), and in Oman (24.7 percent of females, 18.3 percent of males). For the adult population at least 25 years of age in all GCC countries, a higher proportion of women than men have attained the highest level of tertiary education.

The results, then, are impressive, but there is much further ground to take if Gulf female citizens are to increase their numbers in both private and public sector employment, and to use their achievements in in produc-

Table 16-1. Labor Force Participation
Rate, Females Age 15+

Percent

Country	2020
United Arab Emirates	52.482
Saudi Arabia	22.258
Bahrain	45.035
Qatar	56.762
Kuwait	49.339
Oman	30.983

Source: World Bank, "Labor Force Participation Rate, Female (% of female population ages
15+) (modeled ILO estimate)" (https://data
.worldbank.org/indicator/SL.TLF.CACT.FE.ZS).

tive work. Also promising is state regulation to protect women's pay equality under law. In both the United Arab Emirates and Saudi Arabia, new protections for women's wage equality became law in 2020.[17] As the regulatory environment expands to include protection of equal pay for equal work, the barriers to women's economic inclusion in the Gulf are breaking down. The overall picture, however, is a workforce in which women are less visible and less present than their male peers.

Even including noncitizens in their calculations, 2020 World Bank data finds women's participation in the labor force reaches just over half of women in only two of the six GCC states (Table 16-1). Across the GCC, most women (citizen or resident) are not employed.

If we look more closely at the data on the division between public and private sector employment among nationals and nonnationals, there is a further delineation in persistent preferences and advantages for public sector employment among nationals, and an underpresentation of national women in the workforce (Table 16-2). Women citizens in the GCC states are less visible, yet more educated and better prepared for leadership roles in both public and private sector work than many of their male peers. Governments have clear financial and political rationales to raise women's labor force participation. The challenge will be to match the skills and aspirations of young women entering the labor force with opportunities for advancement and leadership in both government and private sector organizations. As economic imperatives shift within the GCC, with mounting fiscal pressure on some states, families

Table 16-2. *Employment Demographics in Gulf Countries by Sector, Nationality, and Gender*

Percent

Country		Public Sector Employment			Private Sector Employment			Domestic Workers		Total
		Total	Nationals	Non-nationals	Total	Nationals	Non-nationals	Total	Non-nationals	
Kuwait (2018)	Female	7.43	5.90	1.50	5.80	1.10	4.80	10.70	10.70	24.00
	Male	9.02	6.10	2.90	54.40	1.20	53.20	12.50	12.50	76.00
Bahrain (2019 Q2)	Female	3.64	3.23	0.41	18.62	4.53	14.09	8.45	8.45	22.26
	Male	3.87	3.02	0.86	73.87	9.70	64.18	3.09	3.09	77.74
Oman (2019)	Female	4.46	3.88	0.58	12.61	3.28	9.33	7.37	7.37	17.07
	Male	6.25	5.24	1.02	76.67	8.92	67.76	3.77	3.77	82.93
Saudi Arabia (2020 Q2)	Female	6.13	5.73	0.40	7.94	5.51	2.43	10.85	10.85	14.07
	Male	10.01	9.32	0.69	75.92	11.39	64.53	26.47	26.47	85.93
Qatar (2019)	Female	2.64	1.52	1.11	10.88	0.34	10.54	5.25	5.25	13.52
	Male	6.76	2.62	4.14	79.72	0.62	79.10	3.14	3.14	86.48

Sources: Kuwait Central Statistical Bureau, "Population Statistics" (www.csb.gov.kw/Pages/Statistics_en?ID=1); Bahrain Labour Market Regulatory Authority, "Bahrain Labour Market Indicators" (http://blmi.lmra.bh/2019/06/mi_dashboard.xml); Oman National Centre for Statistics and Information, "Labor Market Data Portal" (https://data.gov.om/byvmwhe/labour-market); Saudi Arabia General Authority for Statistics, "Labor Force," 2020 (www.stats.gov.sa/en /814); Qatar Planning and Statistics Authority, "Labor Force Archive" (www.psa.gov.qa/en/statistics1/pages/topicslisting.aspx?parent=Social&child=LaborForce).

are more likely to need two incomes; more women will either take advantage of new opportunities or be compelled to enter the workforce.

Notes

1. United Nations Population Fund (UNFPA), "The Human Rights of Women," 2006 (www.unfpa.org/resources/human-rights-women).

2. Gallup and International Labor Organization (ILO), "Towards a Better Future for Women and Work: Voices of Women and Men," Report, March 8, 2017 (www.ilo .org/global/publications/books/WCMS_546256/lang—en/index.htm). This study provides the first-ever account of global attitudes and perceptions of women and men regarding women and work based on the 2016 Gallup World Poll. The poll, which was conducted in 142 countries and territories, is representative of 98 percent of the global population.

3. Joyce Burnett, *Gender, Work and Wages in Industrial Revolution Britain* (Cambridge University Press, 2008); Teri L. Caraway, *Assembling Women: The Feminization of Global Manufacturing* (Cornell University Press, 2007).

4. Michael L. Ross, "Oil, Islam and Women," *American Political Science Review* 102, no. 1 (February 2008), pp. 107–23 (www.sscnet.ucla.edu/polisci/faculty/ross/papers /articles/Oil%20Islam%20and%20Women%20-%20apsr%20final.pdf); Michael Ross, *The Oil Curse: How Petroleum Wealth Shapes the Development of Nations* (Princeton University Press, 2012).

5. Gail J. Buttorff, Nawra Al Lawati, and Bozena C. Welborne, "Cursed No More? The Resource Curse, Gender, and Labor Nationalization Policies in the GCC," *Journal of Arabian Studies* 8 (2018), pp. 65–86 (https://doi.org/10.1080/21534764.2018 .1546935).

6. Melissa A. Milkie, Sara B. Raley, and Suzanne M. Bianchi, "Taking on the Second Shift: Time Allocations and Time Pressures of US Parents with Preschoolers," *Social Forces* 88, no. 2 (December 2009), pp. 487–517 (https://www.jstor.org/stable /40645814).

7. Woohyang Sim, "For Love, Money and Status, or Personal Growth? A Survey of Young Emirati Women's Educational Aspirations," *Gulf Education and Social Policy Review* 1, no. 1 (July 29, 2020), pp. 73–90 (https://doi.org/10.18502/gespr.v1i1.7470).

8. Jadwa Investment, "Saudi Labor Market Update—Q2 2020," Labor Market Report, October 8, 2020 (www.jadwa.com/en/researchsection/research/economic -research/labor-market-reports).

9. ILO, "As Jobs Crisis Deepens, ILO Warns of Uncertain and Incomplete Labour Market Recovery," June 30, 2020 (www.ilo.org/global/about-the-ilo/newsroom/news /WCMS_749398/lang—en/index.htm).

10. Hala Aldosari, "All the King's Women: New Shura Council Members Stir Gender Debate," Arab Gulf States Institute in Washington (AGSIW), May 11, 2017 (https:// agsiw.org/kings-women-new-shura-council-members-stir-gender-debate/).

11. Karen E. Young, "Saudi Arabia's Housing Goals Need Empowered Women," Bloomberg, May 24, 2019 (www.bloomberg.com/opinion/articles/2019-05-24/saudi-arabia -s-ambitious-housing-goals-needs-empowered-women); data on Saudi employment

from Jadwa Investment, "Labor Market Reports" (www.jadwa.com/en/researchsection /research/economic-research/labor-market-reports).

12. Zainab Fattah, "Saudi Arabia's $90 Billion Reason to Allow Women to Drive," Bloomberg, June 24, 2018 (www.bloomberg.com/news/articles/2018-06-24/saudi -women-driving-is-seen-better-for-economy-than-aramco-ipo).

13. May Seikaly, Rahil Roodsaz, and Corine van Egten, *The Situation of Women in the Gulf States*, European Parliament, Study for the Femm Committee, 2014 (www .europarl.europa.eu/RegData/etudes/STUD/2014/509985/IPOL_STU(2014)509985 _EN.pdf).

14. Karen E. Young, "More Educated, Less Employed: The Paradox of Women's Employment in the Gulf," *Gulf Affairs* (Spring 2017), pp. 6–9 (www.oxgaps.org/files /analysis_young_spring_2017.pdf); Karen E. Young, "Women's Labor Force Partici-pation across the GCC," Issue Paper 10 (Washington: AGSIW, December 7, 2016 (https://agsiw.org/womens-labor-force-participation-across-gcc/).

15. Thuraiya Alhashmi, "Cracking the Glass Ceiling: Arab Women in Technol-ogy," AGSIW (blog), January 11, 2018 (https://agsiw.org/arab-women-technology/).

16. Jennifer DeBoer and Ashley Ater Kranov, "Key Factors in the Tertiary Edu-cational Trajectories of Women in Engineering: Trends and Opportunities in Saudi Arabia, the GCC, and Comparative National Settings," in *Science and Technology Development in the Gulf States: Economic Diversification through Regional Collabo-ration*, edited by Afreen Siddiqi and Laura Diaz Anadon (Berlin: Gerlach Press, 2017), pp. 61–62.

17. Chris Maxwell, "UAE Law Ensuring Equal Pay for Men and Women Comes into Force," *The National*, September 24, 2020 (www.thenational.ae/uae/government /uae-law-ensuring-equal-pay-for-men-and-women-comes-into-force-1.1083027); Deema al-Khudair, "Saudi Arabia Looks to Close Gender Pay Gap," *Arab News*, Sep-tember 17, 2020 (www.arabnews.com/node/1735791/saudi-arabia).

SEVENTEEN

Tackling Youth Unemployment in the GCC

NADER KABBANI

YOUNG PEOPLE IN THE Gulf Cooperation Council (GCC) face a myriad of challenges as they transition from school to work. The preceding chapters highlight a number of issues that are common across GCC countries, including deficits in education systems that contribute to poor skills development; a dual labor market that induces nationals to queue for public sector jobs; weak private sector growth as a result of overregulation and the concentration of economic activity in the hands of connected insiders; and socioeconomic barriers to the participation of young women in the labor market. These issues have profoundly affected the transition of young nationals from school to work.

This chapter presents an overview of youth unemployment in the GCC and reviews what GCC states are doing to address the challenges.[1] GCC countries face a tight window for implementing policy changes before their natural resource wealth runs out.[2] The coronavirus pandemic has created additional challenges for young nationals as they complete school and enter the labor market.

Assessing the Situation

Young GCC nationals have difficulty finding suitable work. Youth unemployment rates are higher than the global average of 13 percent in all GCC countries except Qatar.[3] In 2018, Saudi Arabia's unemployment rate among young nationals was the highest, at 37 percent.[4] Its national population is over 20 million and the public sector has not been able to employ all citizens who want a job. Indeed, 45 percent of employed nationals already work in the public sector. Given that the public sector offers wages that are 70 percent higher than in the private sector, more generous benefits, shorter working hours, and job security, it is no wonder that 80 percent of unemployed Saudis prefer a government job.[5] However, the lack of public sector jobs contributes to job queuing, which contributes to high rates of unemployment.

At the other extreme, in 2018 Qatar was the only GCC country with low youth unemployment rates among its national population, at less than 1 percent.[6] Qatar faces the same challenges as other GCC countries. However, the share of Qatari citizens in the labor force was only 5.1 percent in 2018.[7] Also, Qatar has the highest income per capita in the GCC. As a result, its public sector is able to absorb the incoming cohorts of young Qataris. Over 80 percent of Qatari nationals work in the public sector or for a public enterprise. However, they represent less than 43 percent of total public sector employment, indicating that there is room for further absorption, if needed. Practically any young Qatari who wants a decent job can find one.

The four other countries of the GCC have youth unemployment rates that fall between these two extremes. Kuwait and the United Arab Emirates (UAE) are also relatively wealthy as measured by income per capita. But because their national populations are larger than that of Qatar, the absorption capacity of their public sectors is more limited. Their youth unemployment rates are high: 28 percent in the UAE in 2009 and 22 percent in Kuwait in 2017.[8] Although the UAE is quite wealthy, its wealth and economic opportunities are concentrated in two of the seven emirates, Abu Dhabi and Dubai. Given their wealth and the absorption capacity of their respective public sectors, both Kuwait and the UAE have taken steps to reduce unemployment rates among their youth by reducing the share of foreign workers in their respective public sectors.

Bahrain and Oman are less wealthy than other GCC countries. Their capacity to absorb workers in the public sector is also limited. As in Saudi Arabia, a large share of their populations has been required to accept jobs in the private sector. Both countries have been more successful than Saudi Arabia in this regard, and their populations have accepted the need to take on even blue-collar private sector work. As such, unemployment rates among their youth are lower than the GCC average.[9] It remains to be seen how they will handle the need for further fiscal consolidation, which will push even more of their young nationals into private sector work.

Finally, there is a gender dimension to youth unemployment in the GCC. Unemployment rates are especially high among young female nationals: 52 percent for women and 31 percent for men in Saudi Arabia in 2018. In Kuwait, unemployment was 37 percent among women and 20 percent for men in 2017. Thus, even though young female GCC nationals are less likely than their male counterparts to join the workforce, those who do have more difficulty finding a suitable job aligned with their preferences and the conservative social norms of their countries. One reason for the high rates of unemployment is that most young women would rather wait for a job in the public sector than explore options in the private sector.

Policy Responses

In response to the youth unemployment challenge, GCC countries endeavored to increase the absorption capacity of their respective public sectors and offered their private sectors incentives to hire more nationals. They have worked to improve their education systems and provide training to low-skilled nationals. They have tried to diversify their economies and create more jobs by supporting private sector development and entrepreneurship and boosting the private sector participation of nationals. These policies are in line with those advocated by the World Bank, the World Economic Forum, and others.[10] The main problem has been following through on them.

ABSORBING NATIONALS INTO THE PUBLIC AND PRIVATE SECTORS

The main factor contributing to youth unemployment in the GCC is the dual market structure: a public sector with high wages, benefits, and job security, and a private sector that is mainly attractive to well-connected business owners and high-level managers who have the skills and motivation to succeed. In the UAE, the median salary of Emiratis working for the public sector is almost twice as high as the corresponding figure in the private sector.[11] GCC governments must either employ more nationals in the public sector or bring the two sectors into alignment.

As an initial step, policymakers across the GCC have redoubled their efforts to promote labor market nationalization policies. Three GCC states—Qatar, Kuwait, and the UAE—have adequate financial resources to absorb more nationals into the public sector. Indeed, their labor market national-ization policies have largely focused on replacing foreign workers in the pub-lic and semi-public sectors and in public enterprises. An employment plan announced in the UAE aimed to cut unemployment rates among UAE na-tionals in half by increasing Emiratization in both public and semi-public sectors.[12] Kuwait has gone a step further by privatizing state-owned enter-prises in order to make them more efficient and create more jobs.[13]

In Saudi Arabia, Oman, and Bahrain, the public sector is no longer able to absorb more nationals. Instead, these countries have focused on giving the private sector incentives to hire them. Saudi Arabia's quota system, Nitaqat, introduced penalties and incentives for private sector firms to hire nationals based on the estimated availability of qualified Saudi workers in each sector. However, the large wage differences between nationals and for-eign workers have limited the effectiveness of the system.[14] In the end, align-ing wages is more economically efficient than establishing quotas.[15] GCC countries have therefore taken steps to increase permit fees for foreign work-ers and provide wage subsidies for nationals in an effort to align employer costs. As part of Bahrain's National Employment Program, launched in early 2019, the country increased work permit fees by 66 percent. At the same time, its Wage Support Program contributes on average 50 percent of the salaries of Bahrainis during the first three years of employment.[16]

PRIVATE SECTOR DEVELOPMENT AND SUPPORT
FOR YOUNG ENTREPRENEURS

All GCC countries support private sector development, with an eye toward diversifying their economies and creating jobs. The private sector in the GCC is overregulated and governed by an entrenched system of clientelism and connections. In addition, much private sector activity is run through public or quasi-public enterprises, relies on government contracts, is financed through public financial institutions, and is supported by public subsidies. In this environment, it is difficult for the private sector to grow organically or for someone who is not politically connected to establish and grow a suc-cessful business.

Developing a dynamic private sector requires "changing the rules of the game."[17] GCC countries have made remarkable strides in recent years, with Dubai leading the way. In 2020, the UAE ranked sixteenth out of 190 econ-omies on "ease of doing business," followed by Bahrain, which was ranked forty-third.[18] Indeed, all GCC countries rank among the top half in the world.

However, simply creating employment opportunities in the private sector is not enough. They must also offer decent wages, benefits, and work conditions. This is not easy in the presence of foreign workers who are willing to accept lower wages and tend to be more productive. According to Oman's National Centre for Statistics and Information, over half of all Omanis who work in the private sector have monthly wages below 500 Omani rials ($1,300), which is not enough to support a comfortable lifestyle.[19]

ALIGNING EDUCATION SYSTEMS WITH THE NEEDS OF THE LABOR MARKET

In order for GCC countries to maintain living standards while diversifying their economies, they need to invest in human capital. Many GCC students complete the minimum level of schooling needed to secure a job in the public sector. These degrees provide little in the way of marketable skills. In Saudi Arabia, private firms are often unable to find nationals with the skills and motivation to fill quotas and end up hiring "ghost workers" on the books. This policy essentially taxes private firms and dampens the competitiveness of Saudi businesses, reducing job creation and growth.

GCC governments have been working to improve the skills content of their education systems. Universities have engaged with the private sector, introducing business courses and internships into their curriculums, developing career placement offices, and establishing accelerators to support entrepreneurially minded students. GCC countries are also reforming their primary and secondary education systems. These efforts have met with considerable success. Under Qatar's "Education for a New Era" initiative, Qatari students' scores on the Programme for International Student Assessment (PISA) increased by more than fifty points across reading, mathematics, and science between 2006 and 2014. Better educational outcomes are the key to improving labor market outcomes.

Conclusion

Youth unemployment is pervasive in most countries of the GCC. GCC countries with adequate financial resources, including Qatar, the UAE, and Kuwait, have focused on absorbing their young nationals into the public sector. GCC countries with fewer resources, including Saudi Arabia, Bahrain, and Oman, have focused on offering the private sector incentives to hire young nationals. Getting the private sector to do their bidding is tricky.

Quota systems have created inefficiencies in the labor market. A more effective policy has combined higher work permit fees for foreigners and wage subsidies with on-the-job training.

Notes

1. This chapter does not address the employment challenges facing young expatriates, given their extraordinarily diverse backgrounds and circumstances as well as the minimal policy interest afforded to them by their host- country governments.

2. Tokhir N. Mirzoev and others, "The Future of Oil and Fiscal Sustainability in the GCC Region," International Monetary Fund (IMF), Departmental Paper 20/01 (Washington, February 6, 2020), p. 22 (www.imf.org/en/Publications/Departmental -Papers-Policy-Papers/Issues/2020/01/31/The-Future-of-Oil-and-Fiscal-Sustainabil ity-in-the-GCC-Region-48934).

3. Nader Kabbani, "Youth Employment in the Middle East and North Africa: Revisiting and Reframing the Challenge," Policy Briefing (Doha, Qatar: Brookings Doha Center, February 26, 2019) (www.brookings.edu/research/youth-employment-in-the -middle-east-and-north-africa-revisiting-and-reframing-the-challenge/).

4. "Saudi Youth Unemployment Declines by 6% in 2018," *Saudi Gazette*, April 16, 2019 (http://saudigazette.com.sa/article/563562).

5. "Saudi Companies Pay 59% Less for Same Job in Public Sector," *Saudi Gazette*, June 23, 2019 (http://saudigazette.com.sa/article/569742); Robert Anderson, "80% of Unemployed Saudis Prefer Public Sector Jobs," *Gulf Business*, May 31, 2016 (https:// gulfbusiness.com/80-unemployed-saudis-prefer-public-sector-jobs/).

6. Qatari Planning and Statistics Authority, Labor Force Surveys for the First, Second, Third, and Fourth Quarters of 2018. https://www.psa.gov.qa/en/statistics1/pages /topicslisting.aspx?parent=Social&child=LaborForce.

7. Qatari Planning and Statistics Authority, "Labor Force Sample Survey 2018," June 2019 (www.psa.gov.qa/en/statistics/Statistical%20Releases/Social/LaborForce /2018/statistical_analysis_labor_force_2018_En.pdf).

8. United Arab Emirates (UAE) Federal Competitiveness and Statistics Centre, "Labor Force Survey 2009"; Kuwaiti Central Statistical Bureau, "Annual Statistical Abstract, 2017–2018," 2018 (www.csb.gov.kw/Pages/Statistics_en?ID=18&ParentCatID =2). The UAE government has not updated its figures since 2009, even though it conducts an annual labor force survey. As such, it is reasonable to assume that the situation has not improved much and that youth unemployment rates remain high.

9. Kabbani, "Youth Employment in the Middle East and North Africa."

10. Roberta Gatti and others, "Jobs for Shared Prosperity: Time for Action in the Middle East and North Africa" (Washington, World Bank, 2013) (https://openknow ledge.worldbank.org/handle/10986/13284); World Economic Forum, "Rethinking Arab Employment: A Systemic Approach for Resource-Endowed Economies," Regional Agenda, October 2014 (www3.weforum.org/docs/WEF_MENA14_Rethinking ArabEmployment.pdf).

11. Mouawiya Al Awad, Samer Kherfi, and George Naufal, "An Investigation into the Labor Market Behavior and Characteristics of Emirati Unemployed with Spe-

cial Emphasis on Young Unemployed," Working Paper ZU-WP 2012-001 (Zayed University, January 12, 2012) (www.zu.ac.ae/main/en/research/publications/_documents/Youth%20Unemployment.pdf).

12. Jennifer Bell, "Abu Dhabi Plan Aims to Reduce Emirati Unemployment by Half," *The National*, June 14, 2016 (www.thenational.ae/uae/government/abu-dhabi-plan-aims-to-reduce-emirati-unemployment-by-half-1.197150).

13. Noha El Chaarani, "Kuwait Aims to Create Thousands of New jobs for Its Nationals," *Gulf Business*, July 9, 2017 (https://gulfbusiness.com/kuwait-aims-create-thousands-new-jobs-nationals/).

14. Mohamed Ramady, "Gulf Unemployment and Government Policies: Prospects for the Saudi Labour Quota or Nitaqat System," *International Journal of Economics and Business Research* 5, no. 4 (2013), pp. 476–98 (www.inderscienceonline.com/doi/pdf/10.1504/IJEBR.2013.054266).

15. Al Awad, Kherfi, and Naufal, "An Investigation into the Labor Market Behavior."

16. Obeid Al-Suhaimi, "Bahrain Launches National Plan to End Unemployment," *Asharq Al-Awsat*, February 26, 2019 (https://aawsat.com/english/home/article/1608956/bahrain-launches-national-plan-end-unemployment).

17. Gatti and others, "Jobs for Shared Prosperity."

18. World Bank, "Doing Business 2020: Comparing Business Regulation in 190 Economies," 2020 (https://openknowledge.worldbank.org/handle/10986/32436).

19. "Over Half of Omanis in Private Jobs Earn Less Than OMR500," *Times of Oman*, June 24, 2019 (https://timesofoman.com/article/1504222/Oman/Government/Over—half-of-Omanis-in-private-jobs-earn-less-than-OMR500).

EIGHTEEN

Gulf Labor Migration

Between Structural Constraints
and Political Choices

IMCO BROUWER

THE SIX COUNTRIES OF the Gulf Cooperation Council (GCC) have chosen a model of development that relies heavily on foreign labor. Since the 1970s, the proportion of foreign nationals as a percentage of the total population has grown continuously; in the years 2018–2019 it ranged from around 38 percent in Saudi Arabia to 87 percent in Qatar and the United Arab Emirates (UAE). This circumstance has triggered questions about national identity and security among GCC nationals, notably in the UAE, where approximately 1.2 million Emiratis are outnumbered by approximately 3.3 million Indians.[1]

Since the early 1990s, GCC countries have announced plans to nationalize their workforces, aiming to reduce their reliance on foreign workers and increase the employment of nationals.[2] However, the policies adopted have, at most, slowed down the increase of foreign workers in absolute and relative terms.[3] Reasons for this include continuing or accelerating investments in labor-intensive sectors, such as construction and hospitality (for example, Expo 2020 in the UAE, FIFA World Cup 2022 in Qatar, and Neom in Saudi Arabia); the vast oversupply of cheap labor from Asian, Arab, and African countries; a lack of willingness to enforce better working and living conditions for foreign workers in order to keep costs low; the persistence of the sponsorship system and the financial benefits that GCC citizens derive from it; and an abundance of oil and gas revenues, which allow for unrestrained public spending.[4]

As elsewhere, the COVID-19 pandemic had an enormous immediate impact on GCC societies and economies. It has accelerated the adoption of new measures to, on the one hand, reduce the number of foreign workers and, on the other hand, attract more skilled workers by offering permanent residence and even citizenship.[5] Will COVID-19 provide an opportunity for the GCC to reduce its reliance on low-skilled foreign labor where it previously failed? This chapter briefly describes a few structural aspects of GCC societies and economies and discusses the (in)effectiveness of previously adopted policies concerning labor migration.

Growing Demographic Imbalance between Nationals and Nonnationals, 1970–2019

Since the 1970s, the GCC's reliance on foreign labor seems to have become structural. For all GCC countries, the average annual growth percentage of nonnationals has been greater than that of nationals—sometimes more than five times greater.[6]

Even though the first workforce nationalization policies were adopted in the early 1990s, the imbalance has only increased. For example, the Qatari and UAE nonnational populations doubled between 2005 and 2010. By the end of 2018, the nonnational population in Qatar had further increased by approximately 70 percent, or more than 1 million individuals. During the same period, the number of foreign nationals in Saudi Arabia increased by approximately 50 percent, or 4 million.

According to the most recent data published by the GCC countries' National Statistical Offices (NSOs), the nonnational population ranged from 37.8 percent in Saudi Arabia to 87.8 percent in Qatar. The average of the GCC countries was approximately 51.8 percent (see table 18-1).

These data do not reflect the impact of COVID-19, and official data for 2020 are limited. Between January and November 2020, 272,126 foreign workers are reported to have left Oman.[7] Uncorroborated press reports stated that 158,000 foreign nationals left Kuwait between March and July; this figure was expected to reach 1.5 million by December.[8] Other reports predict that the total population could decline by rates ranging from 4 percent in Oman and Saudi Arabia to 10 percent in Qatar and the UAE.[9]

Table 18-1. *Population of Nationals and Nonnationals in GCC Countries*

Country (date)	Total Population	Nationals	Nonnationals	Nationals (%)	Nonnationals (%)
Bahrain (mid-2019)	1,483,756	701,827	781,929	47.3	52.7
Kuwait (January 1, 2020)	4,464,521	1,365,171	3,099,350	30.6	69.4
Oman (mid-2019)	4,617,927	2,655,144	1,962,783	57.5	42.5
Qatar (November 2019)	2,774,000	338,000[a]	2,436,000[a]	12.2[b]	87.8[b]
Saudi Arabia (mid-2018)	33,413,660	20,768,627	12,645,033	62.2	37.8
United Arab Emirates (mid-2018)	9,366,829	1,214,529[a]	8,152,299[a]	13.0[b]	87.0
Total[c]	56,120,693	27,043,299	29,077,394	48.2	51.8

Source: National Institutes of Statistics and GLMM's calculations based on data published by the National Institutes of Statistics for the years indicated in the table. See Gulf Labour Markets, Migration, and Population (GLMM) Programme, "Demographic and Economic Module" (https://gulfmigration.grc.net/glmm -database/demographic-and-economic-module/).

a. Gulf Labour Markets, Migration, and Population (GLMM) Programme estimate, based on data published by National Statistical Institutes.

b. Ratio is calculated on the basis of population estimates.

c. Total is the sum and ratio of population numbers at different dates. It is not exactly the total population at any of these dates.

Fertility and Second-Generation Foreign Nationals

Given the magnitude of the demographic imbalance, high fertility rates among GCC nationals have not able to reduce it. In addition, the total fertility rates of nationals declined from above 7 percent in the 1970s to below 3 percent in 2019–2020, notwithstanding heavy subsidizing of fertility and the family.[10] In Qatar, the imbalance is growing in births: in 2018, 27.8 percent of the 28,069 births were nationals, 37.8 percent were non-Qatari Arabs, 30 percent were Asians, and 5.2 percent were Europeans.[11]

In all GCC countries, the number of second-generation foreign nationals—either born in the GCC or arriving through family reunion—has grown by 8 percent in Oman (of all aged 0–14), 23 percent in Saudi Arabia, 28 percent in Bahrain, 49 percent in Kuwait, 61 percent in the UAE, and 67 percent in Qatar (see table 18-2).[12] These individuals have to leave the country at the age of 18 unless they continue to study.

Extended Stays and Retirees

GCC countries consider the presence of foreign workers to be temporary and oblige them to leave at the end of their contracts. Relatively recently, some countries (including the UAE in 2011 and Qatar in 2020) have allowed workers to renew their contracts or change employers without leaving the country and thereby prolong their stays. Retaining workers has potential benefits for countries, employers, and workers.[13] These reforms will increase the average duration of stay of foreign workers. However, long before these reforms were introduced, many workers stayed beyond the duration of their initial contracts.[14]

The number of nonnationals aged 65 and older has increased over the years in absolute and relative terms—another indicator that one can stay in the GCC without working (see table 18-2). Of the total population over 65, the percentages of nonnationals were 17 percent in Bahrain (2019); 10 percent in Oman (2019); 19 percent in Saudi Arabia (2018); 64 percent in Kuwait (2019); and 64 percent in Qatar (2015).[15]

Irregular Migration and the Sponsorship System

Irregular migration is not unique to the GCC countries. Migrants may be in an irregular situation because they have violated a law relating to lawful entry, legal residency status, legal employment status, or any other situation

Table 18-2. National and Nonnational Populations by Age in GCC Countries, 2015–2019

Country	Date	Age Group	Nationals		Nonnationals		Total Population		Nonnationals
			Number	%	Number	%	Number	%	% in Each Age Group
Bahrain	Mid-2019	0–14	216,771	31	82,378	11	299,149	20	28
		15–64	448,356	64	692,043	89	1,140,399	77	61
		65+	36,700	5	7,508	1	44,208	3	17
Kuwait	December 2019	0–14	469,101	34	453,319	15	922,420	21	49
		15–64	834,544	61	2,537,978	82	3,372,522	76	75
		65+	61,526	5	108,053	3	169,579	4	64
Oman	Mid-2019	0–14	1,004,909	38	90,599	5	1,095,508	24	8
		15–64	1,542,141	58	1,859,672	95	3,401,813	74	55
		65+	108,094	4	12,512	1	120,606	3	10
Qatar	2015	0–14	116,225	38	240,649	11	356,874	14	67
		15–64	179,053	58	1,997,304	88	2,176,357	85	92
		65+	11,358	4	19,993	1	31,351	1	64
Saudi Arabia	Mid-2018	0–14	6,298,475	30	1,922,405	15	8,220,880	25	23
		15–64	13,598,990	65	10,517,938	83	24,116,928	72	44
		65+	871,162	4	204,690	2	1,075,852	3	19

Source: National Institutes of Statistics and GLMM's calculations based on data published by the National Institutes of Statistics for the years indicated in the table. See Gulf Labour Markets, Migration, and Population (GLMM) Programme, "Demographic and Economic Module" (https://gulfmigration.grc.net/glmm-database/demographic-and-economic-module/).

regarded by the host country or country of origin as a breach of existing laws.[16] What is unique in the GCC countries is the sponsorship system, which allows for abuses and for migrants to find themselves in irregular situations. One situation that has proven hard to eliminate is migrants entering a GCC country on a so-called free visa without a job, continuing to pay a sponsor in order to stay in the country, and trying to earn income by performing unofficial jobs.

The number of migrants in an irregular situation is by definition hard to estimate. Occasional amnesties that allow migrants to regularize their situation and either stay or leave the country are indicators that many nonnationals find themselves in an irregular situation. In Saudi Arabia, between November 2017 and November 2019, 3 million foreign workers regularized their positions. One million left the country and 2 million stayed.[17] Workers may decide not to come forward for amnesty because they prefer to continue to work and live in the country, knowing that there will be other amnesties in the future.[18] GCC nationals may have no interest in denouncing their employees for being in irregular situations. Thus, notwithstanding strict regulation (or exactly because of it), irregular migration is a common and persistent structural phenomenon in GCC countries.[19]

Persistent Employment Imbalance between Nationals and Nonnationals

In the GCC countries, the employment rate of nonnationals is higher than their proportion in the total population because the vast majority of foreign workers are unaccompanied. Despite low oil and gas prices, their percentages between 2016 and 2019 remained stable for Qatar (95.1 to 94.9 percent) and Kuwait (85.6 to 85.7 percent); decreased for Oman (80.9 to 78.4 percent); and increased for Bahrain (74.4 to 79.5 percent) and, especially, for Saudi Arabia (59.4 to 76.3 percent).[20]

The impact of COVID-19 on the employment imbalance cannot yet be assessed because of the absence of official data. It is likely, however, that the employment imbalance has shrunk since March 2020, in part because large infrastructure projects for mega-events were (almost) completed in 2020 (notably in the UAE and Qatar), though not in Saudi Arabia (Neom). Whether departing low-skilled construction workers will be replaced by low-skilled hospitality sector workers in the UAE and Qatar to provide services to millions of expected visitors depends on control over the pandemic and willingness to resume travel. And whether they will be replaced by higher-skilled foreign workers will be a test, especially for the UAE and Qatar, which seek to develop knowledge-based societies and economies.

Private versus Public Sector Employment

In the GCC countries nonnationals work almost exclusively in the private and domestic sectors. In 2019–2020, the percentage of nonnationals working in the private sector ranged from 63.4 percent in Saudi Arabia to 83.9 percent in Bahrain. The percentage in the domestic sector ranged from 8.8 percent in Qatar to 36.1 percent in Saudi Arabia. The percentage in the government sector ranged from 0.5 percent in Saudi Arabia to 6.8 percent in the UAE. The percentage of nationals working in the government and private sectors varies significantly. The percentage working in the government sector ranged from 30.5 percent in Bahrain to 84.2 percent in Kuwait, implying that the percentage working in the private sector ranged from 15.8 percent in Kuwait to 69.5 percent in Bahrain.[21]

Between 2017/2018 and 2018/2019, Bahrain, Oman, and Saudi Arabia were able to reduce employment of nationals in the government sector and increase their employment in the private sector in absolute and relative terms. In Qatar, the employment of nationals in the government sector remained the same, but employment in the private sector slightly decreased. Employment of domestic workers (exclusively nonnationals) grew in Bahrain, Oman, Qatar, and especially Saudi Arabia.[22]

The impact of the pandemic on the private-public employment breakdown for nationals and nonnationals is uncertain. It is also not clear whether there will be a reduction of employment in the domestic sector and whether the transition from live-in domestic workers to those who live outside the home will continue.[23]

Educational Background of Nonnationals and Nationals

A comparison of the educational background of nonnationals and nationals in Kuwait, Qatar, and Saudi Arabia shows that, on average, nonnationals are less educated than nationals (data for the other three GCC countries are incomplete or unavailable).[24] In both Qatar and Saudi Arabia, approximately 66 percent of nonnationals have between a primary and secondary education level. The percentage of nonnationals holding a university degree or higher is approximately 16 percent in both Qatar and Saudi Arabia.

In the UAE, according to the Organization for Economic Cooperation and Development (OECD), nonnational students perform much better than national students.[25]

At the same time, GCC countries have made enormous progress in educating their nationals. Approximately one-third of Qataris aged 15 and older in 2016 had at least a university degree, while in Saudi Arabia this figure was 18.5 percent and in Kuwait 13.4 percent.[26]

Gender Perspectives

Economic participation of nonnational women is on average double that of the national population, except in Saudi Arabia.[27] This is partially explained by the fact that most nonnational women come to the GCC to work and not as dependents. GCC women have made an enormous leap forward in education, but this has not resulted in an equal increase in workforce participation; the percentage of women in the workforce is only 39.3 percent in Kuwait, 36.9 percent in Qatar, 32.2 percent in Bahrain, 30.9 percent in the UAE, and 19.0 percent in Saudi Arabia. Lifting legislation prohibiting women to drive may have a positive impact on Saudi female employment.[28] While there may be a perceived conflict between maintaining high fertility rates and female participation in the workforce, Kuwait shows that a relatively high level of fertility can go together with a relatively high rate of female workforce participation. Increasing female employment is, of course, potentially an important factor in reducing dependence on foreign labor.

Foreign Workers' Perspectives

Over the past decade, new labor and residency laws addressing foreign workers have been adopted in all GCC countries. Generally, these aim to reduce reliance on nonnational workers, increase the employment of nationals, or improve the working and living situations of nonnational workers. Research among migrant workers has shown, however, that key problems persist.[29] These include (1) payment of hefty recruitment costs, even if officially prohibited by national GCC legislation; (2) contract substitution, with new contracts guaranteeing lower wages than initially agreed; (3) delayed payments, even if Wage Protection Systems (WPS) have been adopted in five of the GCC countries; (4) sale of free visas, through which workers enter GCC countries without jobs and need to pay a sponsor to stay in the country and accept irregular jobs; (5) poor living conditions; (6) poor enforcement (labor inspection) and no effective redress, notwithstanding the establishment of offices and procedures. The sponsorship system is widely seen as a major obstacle for effective improvement and, indeed, where the sponsorship system is reformed or partially abolished, improvements are observed.[30] The Qatari reform program concerning migrant labor is far more ambitious than any other program in the GCC.[31]

Both the employment and health of foreign workers in the GCC have been negatively affected disproportionately by COVID-19.[32]

Conclusion

Since the early 1990s, there has been an increasing discrepancy between the policies announced to reduce reliance on temporary foreign workers and the reality. At the outbreak of the COVID-19 pandemic, there were more foreign workers in the GCC countries than ever before, both in absolute and in relative terms. Foreign workers tended to stay much longer than their original contracts and the number of resident nonworking foreign nationals continued to increase. The few policies that have been introduced seem to recognize the reality (and in some cases, such as Qatar, responded to external pressures), allowing foreign workers to stay longer and giving them better working and living conditions. These changes have contributed to the impression that the GCC countries are starting to become countries of (temporary) immigration.[33] The pandemic had the immediate effect of reducing the number of foreign nationals in the GCC and provided an opportunity to call for further dramatic reductions. If the reliance on foreign workers is to be effectively reduced, GCC countries will need to critically review and revise their model of development.

Notes

I thank Françoise De Bel-Air, senior researcher at the Gulf Labor Markets, Migration and Population (GLMM) Programme (www.gulfmigration.grc.net), which is responsible for maintaining the demographic-economic database, for the data and her insights. I remain entirely responsible for the content of the chapter.

This chapter was finalized in February 2021.

1. Unless otherwise indicated, the data used in this chapter are from GLMM, "Demographic and Economic Module" (https://gulfmigration.org/glmm-database /demographic-and-economic-module/).

2. These efforts are also known as Emiratization, Omanization, Saudization, etc.

3. One example is allowing only a certain percentage of foreign workers in private sector companies and imposing fines and hiring stops of foreign nationals if noncompliant. The Saudi Nitaqat programme is a primary example; see GLMM, "The Socio-Political Background and Stakes of 'Saudizing' the Workforce in Saudi Arabia: the Nitaqat Policy," Explanatory Note no. 3, 2015 (https://cadmus.eui.eu/bitstream /handle/1814/34857/GLMM_ExpNote_03_2015.pdf?sequence=1&isAllowed=y). See also "Omanisation Targets for 2020 Announced," *Times of Oman*, December 10, 2019 (https://timesofoman.com/article/2364364/Oman/Omanisation/Omanisation-targets -for-2020-announced).

4. Every country in the Gulf manages migrant residency and employment through the sponsorship (kafala) system. Under this system, a local citizen or local company (the kafeel) must sponsor foreign workers in order for their work visas and residency to be valid. Tying a worker closely to a sponsor has been widely criticized as allowing for abuses. Reform and abolition of certain elements of the kafala system have been announced or adopted, notably in Bahrain (2009), Qatar (2020), and Saudi Arabia (2020). So far, only Qatar has effectively abolished some of its key aspects, including the requirement to have a no objection certificate (NOC) to move from one employer to another.

5. Kuwait and the United Arab Emirates (UAE) have implemented such policies. See Tom Allinson, "Kuwait's Looming Expat Bill Could Force Huge Numbers to Leave," *Deutsche Welle*, July 20, 2020 (www.dw.com/en/kuwait-expat-bill-could-mean -thousands-leave/a-54268903); "UAE Citizenship for Expats: Who Can Apply and How," *Khaleej Times*, January 30, 2021 (www.khaleejtimes.com/news/20210130/uae -citizenship-for-expats-who-can-apply-and-how).

6. In the UAE, the figures are 2.8 percent for nationals and 16 percent for non-nationals. In all Gulf Cooperation Council (GCC) countries the growth of the non-national population has been faster than that of the national population, except for Kuwait in the early 1990s after the Iraqi invasion, and Oman and Saudi Arabia in the early 2000s.

7. See "Expat Worker Numbers in Oman Down by a Quarter of a Million in 2020," *Times of Oman*, December 27, 2020 (https://timesofoman.com/article/expat-worker -numbers-in-oman-down-by-a-quarter-of-a-million-in-2020). However, the website of the Omani National Center for Statistics and Information (NCSI) reports a decline of 224,378 foreign nationals between January 1, 2020, and February 1, 2021.

8. "Kuwait Expects Nearly 1.5 million Expats to Leave by End of Year," *Arab News*, July 11, 2020 (www.arabnews.com/node/1703066/middle-east).

9. Shaji Mathew, "Oxford Economics Sees Exodus of Expat Workers from Across Gulf," *Bloomberg Quint*, May 22, 2020 (www.bloombergquint.com/onweb/oxford -economics-sees-exodus-of-expat-workers-from-across-gcc).

10. Causes for decline include rapid increases in women's education, participation in the labor market, and divorce rates. The total fertility rate does not include children from female GCC citizens and non-GCC fathers because they do not receive GCC nationality, even if they are born in the country. For detailed sources and

other metadata, see Françoise De Bel-Air, "Fertility in Qatar and in Other GCC States: Some Elements of Comparison," GLMM, 2018 (http://gulfmigration.org /media/pubs/rp/NPRP%20Project%20-%20Francoise%20De%20Bel-Air%20-%20 2019-11-26.pdf); Onn Winckler, *Arab Political Demography: Population Growth, Labor Migration and Natalist Policies* (Sussex Academic Press, 2009), pp. 62–63.

11. De Bel-Air, "Fertility in Qatar."

12. Typically, a foreign mid- to high-skilled worker with a salary above a certain threshold (generally $1,250–1,500 per month) can bring his wife and children into a GCC country. Officially, at the age of 18, foreigner nationals would have to leave the country unless they are enrolled in university. No data are available about how many actually leave. No policies exist to retain any of these foreign nationals, even if they have completed their studies and are well integrated in the local community.

13. Suresh Naidu, Yaw Nyarko, and Shing-Yi Wang, "Worker Mobility in a Global Labor Market: Evidence from the United Arab Emirates," Working Paper 20388 (Cambridge, Mass.: National Bureau of Economic Research, August 2014) (www.nber.org /papers/w20388.pdf).

14. Duration-of-stay data are not published by GCC National Statistical Offices (NSOs), but some data on Qatar show that, in 2010, more than 16 percent of non-nationals had stayed in the country for a period of five to nine years and more than 14 percent for ten years or more. Table available on the GLMM website.

15. Previous percentages were lower, indicating a growth of nonnationals aged 65 and older; these figures were 10 percent in Bahrain (2010); 42 percent in Kuwait (2013); 6 percent in Oman (2013); 47 percent in Qatar (2010); and 10 percent in Saudi Arabia (2017). For the UAE, only data for 2005 are available and are not included here. After retiring, foreign nationals are allowed to stay in a country if, for example, they have investments in the country and own property.

16. Nasra M. Shah, "Introduction: Skilful Survivals—Irregular Migration to the Gulf," in *Skilful Survivals: Irregular Migration to the Gulf*, edited by Philippe Fargues and Nasra M. Shah (Gulf Research Center Cambridge, 2017), pp. 1–11 (https:// gulfmigration.org/media/pubs/book/BookChapters/GLMM%20-%20IM%20%20-% 20Chapter%20I%20-%20Extract%20-%202017-05-16.pdf).

17. "4.17m Illegal Aliens Arrested; More Than a Million Deported," *Saudi Gazette*, November 16, 2019 (http://saudigazette.com.sa/article/582733/SAUDI-ARABIA /417m-illegal-aliens-arrested-more-than-a-million-deported).

18. Being in an irregular situation for some foreign workers is a choice because it allows them to earn more than in a regular job and, ironically, does not necessarily make the worker more vulnerable. Once they want to leave the country, they come forward during an amnesty period.

19. See Françoise De Bel-Air, "Irregular Migration in the Gulf States: What Data Reveal and What They Conceal," in *Skilful Survival* edited by Fargues and Shah, pp. 33–56. Between November 2017 and November 2019, the average number of deported irregular migrants remained approximately 43,000 per month. See "4.17m Illegal Aliens Arrested."

20. Data for the UAE are unavailable.

21. GLMM, "Demographic and Economic Module."

22. Ibid.

23. See Marie-José and Hadi Assaf, "The Future of Domestic Work in the Countries of the Gulf Cooperation Council," Secretariat of the Abu Dhabi Dialogue, May 2018 (http://abudhabidialogue.org.ae/sites/default/files/document-library/2018 _Future%20of%20Domestic%20Work%20Study.pdf).

24. GLMM, "Demographic and Economic Module."

25. See Organization for Economic Cooperation and Development (OECD), "United Arab Emirates: Student Performance (PISA 2018)," (http://gpseducation.oecd .org/CountryProfile?primaryCountry=ARE&treshold=10&topic=PI): "After accounting for socio-economic status, the difference in reading performance between immigrant and non-immigrant students is one of the largest among PISA-participating countries and economies, in favour of immigrants."

26. GLMM, "Demographic and economic module."

27. Ibid.

28. See Françoise De Bel-Air and others, "Possible Impact of Saudi Women Driving on Female Employment and Reliance on Foreign Workers," GLMM, Explanatory Note no. 4, 2017 (https://gulfmigration.org/media/pubs/exno/GLMM_EN_2017 _04.pdf).

29. See Philippe Fargues, Nasra M. Shah, and Imco Brouwer, "Working and Living Conditions of Low-Income Migrant Workers in the Hospitality and Construction Sectors in Qatar," GLMM, Research Report no. 1, 2019 (http://gulfmigration .org/media/pubs/rp/GLMM_EN_2019_RR01.pdf) and Philippe Fargues, Nasra M. Shah, and Imco Brouwer, "Working and Living Conditions of Low-Income Migrant Workers in the Hospitality and Construction Sectors in the United Arab Emirates," GLMM, Research Report no. 2, 2019 (http://gulfmigration.org/media/pubs/rp/GLMM _EN_2019_RR02.pdf).See also Ray Jureidini, "Wage Protection Systems and Programmes in the GCC," GLMM, Research Report no. 1, 2017 (https://gulfmigration .org/media/pubs/rp/GLMM_EN_2017_RR01.pdf). More recently, on Qatar see International Labour Organization (ILO), "Assessment of the Wage Protection System in Qatar," Assessment Report, June 2019 (www.ilo.org/wcmsp5/groups/public/—arab-states/—ro-beirut/documents/publication/wcms_726174.pdf).

30. See Maysa Zahra, "The Legal Framework of the Sponsorship Systems of the Gulf Cooperation Council Countries: A Comparative Examination," GLMM, Explanatory Note no. 4, 2019 (http://gulfmigration.org/media/pubs/exno/GLMM_EN _2019_04.pdf).

31. See ILO, "Annual Progress Report on the Technical Cooperation Programme Agreed between the Government of Qatar and the ILO," October 7, 2019 (www.ilo .org/wcmsp5/groups/public/—ed_norm/—relconf/documents/meetingdocument /wcms_723203.pdf).

32. Zahra R. Babar, "Migrant Workers Bear the Pandemic's Brunt in the Gulf," *Current History* 119, no. 821 (December 2020), pp. 343–48 (https://georgetown.app .box.com/s/fodsccwxqydfdvt3mlk1nxg8780xixpz); Hanan M. Al Kuwari and others, "Epidemiological Investigation of the First 5685 cases of SARS-CoV-2 infection in

Qatar, 28 February–18 April 2020," *BMJ Open* (October 2020) (https://bmjopen.bmj.com/content/10/10/e040428).

33. According to the United Nations definition, all foreign nationals in the GCC are already migrants. See GLMM, "Terminology" (https://gulfmigration.org/about/terminology/).

NINETEEN

Migrant Laborers in the Gulf

NOHA ABOUELDAHAB

DEVELOPMENTS IN THE AREA of labor reforms across the Gulf countries are encouraging signs of a much needed overhaul of protective systems for migrant laborers. Qatar's winning bid to host the 2022 FIFA World Cup drew significantly more attention to the plight of migrant laborers in the country. The COVID-19 pandemic drew renewed attention to the need for better social protection of migrant workers in Qatar and the wider Gulf region. Although legislation intended to improve the living and working conditions of migrant laborers has been adopted across the Gulf, its actual impact has been mixed.[1]

As the Gulf states attempt to transition to knowledge-based economies, it is imperative that they ramp up efforts to ensure that labor reforms, including social protection schemes, meaningfully benefit the majority of the population that contributes to their economic growth: migrant laborers. Social protection can be construed in several ways, but it is primarily a set of public policies that aim to protect against economic and social distress. In the Gulf context, the focus of such policies should be on protection against unemployment and low or unpaid wages, as well as access to remedies for

This chapter was previously published as Noha Aboueldahab, "Social Protection, Not Just Legal Protection: Migrant Laborers in the Gulf," Brookings Institution, August 23, 2021 (https://www.brookings.edu/research/social-protection-not-just-legal-protection-migrant-laborers-in-the-gulf/).

contract violations. Low-skilled migrant laborers constitute a substantial segment of working migrants who require social protection the most.[2] The heavy interdependence of foreign laborers and Gulf nationals requires that social protection measures be implemented with a view to ensuring long-term impact and sustainability. However, legal protection does not automatically ensure enforcement.

This chapter presents three key requirements for transforming legislative labor reforms from a predominantly "on paper" existence to one that is enforced and practiced. Crucially, these requirements are effective only when pursued together rather than in isolation from each other. First, there must be enforceable social protection provisions in bilateral labor agreements and in employment contracts, along with more effective state-run enforcement mechanisms. These are important in order to mitigate the ability of employers to escape accountability for violations of labor laws. Second, a socialization of reforms that targets the tripartite nexus of the notorious Gulf kafala, or sponsorship, system—the migrant worker, the employer, and the state—is needed. Finally, the establishment of localized monitoring and evaluation tools would ensure higher quality and context-specific research on labor policy reform. A better understanding of what works and what does not work in different contexts across the Gulf would better inform policy recommendations that benefit migrant workers and the state. Significant reforms have been undertaken in Qatar, spurred by the country's role as host to the 2022 FIFA World Cup. This chapter begins by outlining some of the notable developments in labor reforms there. It goes on to explain why the three interconnected requirements outlined here are necessary not only in the Qatari context, but across the Gulf region as well.

Recent Developments in Labor Reforms: Qatar

The majority of reforms to Qatar's labor laws since 2014 have aimed to ease the mobility of migrant laborers as well as to bring national legislation in line with international labor standards. Law No. 13 (2018) removed the exit permit requirement, which required foreign laborers to secure permission from their employer to leave the country.[3] The new law was extended to domestic workers by way of Ministerial Decision No. 95 in 2019, which allows them to leave the country after notifying their employers at least seventy-two hours prior to their departure.[4] Law No. 21 (2015) made it illegal for employers or sponsors to take possession of passports of foreign nationals.

Though the problem of employers confiscating passports persists, this practice has declined.[5]

A significant development in Qatar's labor law came with the adoption of Law No. 19 (2020), which allows migrant workers to change jobs before the end of their contract without first having to obtain a No Objection Certificate (NOC) from their employer. The NOC system left foreign employees at the mercy of their employers when seeking employment elsewhere. It was a central feature of the kafala system, which essentially shackled migrant workers to their sponsor or employer, leading to exploitative practices that violate international human rights laws and international labor standards. Domestic workers, who long operated within a legal vacuum because labor laws were not applicable to them, finally obtained legal protection in the form of Law No. 15 (2017), which regulates the relationship between domestic workers and their employers and grants them rights that were not previously specified.[6] That same year, Qatar passed Law No. 13 (2017), allowing for the establishment of labor dispute committees, which offer a mechanism through which workers and employers could settle their disputes.[7] Finally, a number of reforms aimed at protecting wage payment, introducing a nondiscriminatory minimum wage, and establishing the Workers Support and Insurance Fund, were introduced.[8]

Leveraging Enforcement to Tackle a Culture of Employer Impunity

While these reforms are encouraging and have even been hailed as historic in "dismantling" the kafala system, the lack of enforcement is pervasive, and impunity remains endemic.[9] Employers who fail to fulfill their obligations to their employees are the primary sources of noncompliance. Lack of enforcement of legal and social protection measures is a major challenge across the Gulf region.[10] Legal protection does not automatically ensure enforcement. Mechanisms that aim to ensure compliance with international best practices, while also ensuring that legislative and policy reforms make sense in the unique contexts of each Gulf state, are critical. The opening of the International Labour Organization (ILO) Project Office in Qatar in April 2018, which is the first in the Gulf region, is facilitating such efforts.

Nevertheless, because few bilateral labor agreements between sending and receiving states include social protection provisions, recruitment agencies and employers continue to abuse the rights of migrant workers. For example, neither the 2013 Saudi Arabia-Philippines agreement on domestic worker recruitment nor the 2008 Qatar-Sri Lanka agreement concerning Sri Lankan manpower employment in Qatar includes adequate and accessible social protection provisions for migrant workers.[11] Moreover, the COVID-19 pandemic brought to the fore the disproportionate suffering of migrant laborers at the hands of the deadly virus; their cramped living and working conditions in particular allowed the virus to flourish.[12]

The underlying vulnerabilities of migrant workers extend beyond the pandemic, however. Although strict health policies require all migrant workers to undergo health screening before they are granted a visa or employment in the Gulf, there is a social stigma surrounding the health of low-skilled migrant workers in particular and their ability to maintain employment. This stigma reflects migrants' perceived reluctance "around admitting ill-health, to their employers and supervisors," for fear of losing their jobs.[13] Given the social and economic fallout since the onset of COVID-19, Gulf states can no longer afford to exclude migrant workers from adequate access to national health frameworks. As Zahra Babar notes:

> There has not been a great deal of effort on the part of the GCC host states to mainstream labor migrants' health needs into national health policy frameworks [which is essential] when such a large population of migrants as in the GCC are present . . . there is no global commitment among state and international bodies that bind them to certain health outcomes for migrants.[14]

Enforcement mechanisms thus must take into account both living and working conditions of migrant workers in the Gulf, especially as low-skilled migrant laborers' accommodation is often provided by their employers.

The involvement of international organizations such as the ILO and the role it has played in Qatar are instrumental in ensuring that domestic legislation and practice is in line with international standards. However, bilateral labor agreements that address social protection measures are also an important channel through which migrant workers could more effectively claim their social, economic, and health rights. Through more robust bilateral labor agreements, longer-term benefits for migrant laborers could be introduced, such as sudden economic hardship relief (unemployment benefits) and pensions. While there may be little incentive for migrants' home (sending) states to develop such policies, advocacy groups such as unions in the sending states must prioritize the issue of social protection for migrant laborers and apply pressure on sending states to ensure that their citizens benefit from these basic international standards of social and economic security. Low-skilled migrant laborers in particular experience greater vulnerabilities stemming from marginalization in receiving states as noncitizens, and from economic and social hardship.

Socialization of Labor Reforms: An Opportunity in the Post-COVID-19 Era

Enforcement mechanisms and bilateral labor agreements on their own are not enough, however. A socialization of labor reforms that targets the tripartite nexus of the notorious Gulf kafala system—the migrant worker, the employer, and the state—is needed. In the absence of context-specific social movements that work toward the social protection of migrant workers, such socialization would need to take place through alternative means. This includes, but is not limited to, ensuring worker representation in policy reform processes and in monitoring and evaluation mechanisms. In April 2019, Qatar issued a decree that allows for the establishment of joint committees to resolve workplace issues: workers in companies with thirty or more employees elect their own representatives to discuss policies and grievances with management.[15] It remains to be seen whether such Joint Committees will influence policy reform, or increase discussion of the impact of legislative reforms on migrant workers in the workplace. These efforts are important, however, for fostering an environment conducive to social dialogue about issues that directly affect migrant laborers. They could also contribute to "reducing tensions between nationals and nonnationals and promoting social cohesion."[16]

The socialization of labor reforms, however, presents a challenge related to the implicit social contract between Gulf nationals and their states. As Mustafa Qadri explains, this challenge puts the state in a position where it must balance "the need to maintain a social contract based on an imbalance in labor relations in favor of employers and business owners, who are overwhelmingly citizens, with its international obligations to respect core aspects of human rights and labor rights and the need to respond to a global market increasingly sensitive to rights protections."[17] Although Qadri's discussion focuses on the United Arab Emirates, his observations are also relevant to the rest of the GCC, where a similar social contract between the state and citizen exists: one that "effectively promises the latter a ready source of revenue and significant control over migrant labor in return for reduced social and political freedoms."[18] The COVID-19 pandemic presents an un-paralleled opportunity to tackle negative stereotypes of migrant workers as well as the structural inequalities they face due to the discriminatory application of social protection schemes. Without changes targeting society, such as cultivating a respect for the rule of law as well as empathy for others at the family level, the prospects for meaningful and long-lasting improvements to the social protection of migrant workers will remain limited.[19]

Less Sensationalist, Better Informed: The Need for Representative Monitoring and Evaluation

Few mechanisms systematically assess the impact of policy reform on migrant workers in the Gulf. Instead, sensationalist headlines and reports that tend to draw conclusions based on anecdotal interviews overlook both deeper, structural problems and positive trends that are not—but should be—newsworthy. The establishment of localized monitoring and evaluation tools, such as the Qatar Guest Workers' Welfare Index (GWWI) developed by the Social and Economic Survey Research Institute (SESRI), would ensure higher quality and context-specific research on labor policy reform. The resulting understanding of what works and what does not work in context-specific cases across the Gulf would inform policy recommendations that benefit migrant workers and the state.

Abdoulaye Diop and co-authors emphasize that without valid indicators it is difficult to gauge the effect of legislative reforms on "the actual lives of workers."[20] They discuss the example of employers' confiscation of employees' passports in Qatar, a practice that is prohibited by Law No. 21 (2015).[21] In a SESRI survey conducted in 2014, more than one-third of the migrant worker respondents said they had voluntarily handed their passport to their employer for safekeeping because they feared for the security of their passports in the labor camps where they reside. Clearly, as Diop and co-authors observe, the "solution to passport withholding is not only informing workers about their rights or forcing employers not to retain passports against the will of the worker, but also *improving the security of their accommodations*."[22] This example demonstrates the importance of not only ensuring that adequate monitoring and evaluation mechanisms, such as the GWWI, are in place, but that migrant laborers are consistently afforded the opportunity to explain the nuances of their situation. Without the vital input from migrant laborers, policy reforms will remain misguided.

Conclusion

The COVID-19 pandemic has made painfully clear that not all 7.8 billion inhabitants of the planet are in the same boat. Although COVID-19 does not discriminate and has affected both rich and poor and everyone in between, the underlying difficult living and working conditions of migrant laborers in the Gulf have made it increasingly clear that they suffer disproportionately. Work and accommodation conditions are inextricably tied to labor laws and policies in the Gulf. The migrant laborer-employer-state nexus maintains the kafala system that has overwhelmingly favored the interests of employers at the expense of employees' social, economic, and human rights. As countries continue to grapple with geopolitical, economic, and public health policy challenges, the post-COVID-19 era presents an especially opportune time to address ways to ensure long-term social protection that will aid Gulf states in transitioning to sustainable knowledge-based economies. The focus on legislative and policy reforms thus far has been encouraging in the Gulf. However, policies must include effective enforcement mechanisms domestically and in bilateral labor agreements, the socialization of reforms into society, and context-specific monitoring and evaluation tools that are representative of workers' complex experiences.

Notes

I would like to thank Jihane Benamar for her research assistance on this chapter, the peer reviewers for their valuable comments, and the editors of this volume.

1. Vani Saraswathi, "The Kafala Is Alive and Kicking . . . Migrants Where It Hurts Most," Migrant-Rights.Org, October 29, 2020 (www.migrant-rights.org/2020/10/the-kafala-is-alive-and-kicking-migrants-where-it-hurts-most/).

2. Migrant Forum in Asia, "Social Protection for Low-Skilled Migrant Workers and Their Families," Policy Brief 7, September 2013 (www.ilo.org/dyn/migpractice/docs/137/PB7.pdf).

3. International Labour Organization (ILO), "Law No. 13 of 2018 amending certain provisions of Law No. 21 of 2015 in relation to organizing the entry and exit of expatriates and their residence," October 23, 2018 (http://ilo.org/dyn/natlex/natlex4.detail?p_lang=en&p_isn=107340).

4. Qatar Government Communications Office, "Labour Reform" (www.gco.gov.qa/en/focus/labour-reform/).

5. Abdoulaye Diop and others, "Welfare Index of Migrant Workers in the Gulf: the Case of Qatar," *International Migration* 58, no. 4 (August 2020), pp. 140–53 (https://doi.org/10.1111/imig.12667).

6. ILO, "Law No. 15 of 2017 concerning Domestic Workers," August 22, 2017 (www.ilo.org/dyn/natlex/natlex4.detail?p_lang=en&p_isn=105099&p_count=8&p_classification=22).

7. ILO, "Law No. 13 of 2017 which amends several provisions of the Labour Law promulgated by Law No. 14 of 2004 and Law No. 13 of 1990 which promulgates the Civil and Commercial Proceedings Law," August 16, 2017, (www.ilo.org/dyn/natlex/natlex4.detail?p_lang=en&p_isn=104948&p_count=1&p_classification=01.02).

8. On protecting wage payment: A Wage Protection System (WPS) was established in 2015, requiring employers to pay salaries directly into their employees' bank accounts, as opposed to in cash, in an effort to track failure to pay salaries. Problems remain, however. See ILO Project Office for the State of Qatar, "Assessment of the Wage Protection System in Qatar," June 2019 (www.ilo.org/wcmsp5/groups/public/—arabstates/—ro-beirut/documents/publication/wcms_726174.pdf); On introducing a non-discriminatory minimum wage, see: ILO, "Law No. 17 of 2020 Determining the National Minimum Wage for Workers and Domestic Workers," September 8, 2020 (www.ilo.org/beirut/projects/qatar-office/WCMS_754880/lang—en/index.htm). This law establishes a minimum wage of 1,000 Qatari riyals and requires employers to pay allowances of at least 300 riyals to cover food expenses and 500 riyals to cover housing costs, if neither are provided by employers. The minimum wage is 'non-discriminatory' in the sense that it applies to all workers of all nationalities and in all sectors, including domestic workers, who were previously excluded from labor laws; On the establishment of the Workers Support and Insurance Fund, see: ILO, "Law No. 17 of 2018 Establishing the Workers' Support and Insurance Fund," November 19, 2018 (www.ilo.org/dyn/natlex/natlex4.detail?p_lang=en&p_isn=107337&p_count=13&p_classification=01.02).

9. ILO, "Dismantling the kafala system and introducing a minimum wage mark new era for Qatar labour market," August 30, 2020 (https://www.ilo.org/global/about-the-ilo/newsroom/news/WCMS_754391/lang—en/index.htm).

10. Business and Human Rights Resource Centre, "Challenges to corporate accountability in the Gulf: Tracking labour abuse in a climate of near impunity," December 18, 2019 (https://www.business-humanrights.org/de/blog/challenges-to-corporate-accountability-in-the-gulf-tracking-labour-abuse-in-a-climate-of-near-impunity/).

11. Clara van Panhuys, Samia Kazi-Aoul, Geneviève Binette, "Migrant access to social protection under Bilateral Labour Agreements: A review of 120 countries and nine bilateral arrangements," ILO, Extension of Social Security Working Paper no. 57, 2017 (www.social-protection.org/gimi/gess/RessourcePDF.action?ressource.ressourceId=54405).

12. See Omer Karasapan, "Pandemic highlights the vulnerability of migrant workers in the Middle East," Brookings Institution, September 17, 2020 (www.brookings.edu/blog/future-development/2020/09/17/pandemic-highlights-the-vulnerability-of-migrant-workers-in-the-middle-east/) and Zahra Babar, "The COVID-19 Pandemic in the GCC: Underlying Vulnerabilities for Migrant Workers," Center for International and Regional Studies, Georgetown University in Qatar, April 22, 2020 (https://

cirs.georgetown.edu/news-analysis/COVID-19-pandemic-gcc-underlying-vulner
abilities-migrant-workers).

13. Babar, "The COVID-19 Pandemic in the GCC."

14. Ibid.

15. Qatar Government Communications Office, "Labour Reform"; see also ILO
and Ministry of Administrative Development, Labour and Social Affairs of Qatar,
"An Introduction to Joint Committees in Qatar," April 21, 2020 (www.ilo.org/beirut
/projects/qatar-office/WCMS_742257/lang—en/index.htm).

16. ILO, "Social Protection for Migrant Workers: A Necessary Response to the
Covid-10 Crisis," ILO Brief, June 23, 2020 (www.social-protection.org/gimi/Ressource
PDF.action?id=56783).

17. Mustafa Qadri, "The UAE's Kafala System: Harmless or Human Trafficking?,"
Carnegie Endowment for International Peace, July 7, 2020 (https://carnegieendowment
.org/2020/07/07/uae-s-kafala-system-harmless-or-human-trafficking-pub-82188).

18. Ibid.

19. Noha Aboueldahab, "Cultivating the Rule of Law in Qatar," *Middle East Insight* no. 151 National University of Singapore, Middle East Institute, October 12,
2016 (https://mei.nus.edu.sg/wp-content/uploads/2016/10/Download_Insight_151
_Aboueldahab.pdf).

20. Diop and others, "Welfare Index of Migrant Workers in the Gulf."

21. Confiscating passports of employees is also practiced in other Gulf countries.

22. Diop and others, "Welfare Index of Migrant Workers in the Gulf," p. 2 (emphasis added).

PART 4

STATE-SOCIETY RELATIONS

TWENTY

The Politics of Economic Reform

KRISTIAN COATES ULRICHSEN

RULERS IN ALL SIX Arab Gulf states have launched ambitious long-term "visions" for reform that are intended to diversify and prepare their economies for the eventual transition into a post-oil era. Whereas the language used to describe the reforms often portrays them as transformative, their results—to the extent that they can be measured as the plans unfold—have generally been more modest. One reason for the underperformance is that the visions have tended to prioritize the economic aspects of reform over the political and take as their starting point a blank slate, which does not in fact exist. Many, though not all, of the long-range visions have been drawn up by external consultants, but this does not alone explain why the politics of economic reform projects in Arab Gulf states have frequently been downplayed. A regionwide challenge that has defied easy resolution has been how to balance the demands of short-term political stability with the needs of longer-term economic sustainability.

Moreover, the impact of the COVID-19 pandemic, which started in China in late 2019 and spread rapidly worldwide, has hit Gulf economies hard in some of the sectors that had been among the priorities in many of their economic visions, such as tourism, hospitality, and aviation. This economic impact was magnified by a sharp drop in oil prices in 2020 when demand for oil fell sharply as economies around the world went into lockdown and supply initially (but temporarily) rose after the OPEC+ agreement foundered in March 2020.[1] As economies across the Gulf contracted by between 4 and 10 percent in 2020, the allocative practices of increasingly scarce state resources became more urgent public policy matters.[2]

Visions and Plans

The launch of Saudi Vision 2030 in April 2016 by then-Deputy Crown Prince Mohammad bin Salman focused worldwide attention onto the use of multiyear state-led plans as the drivers of economic diversification and development. Far from representing a new policy response to the prolonged slump in oil prices that began in 2014, these visions have featured prominently in regional policymaking since Oman launched its Vision 2020 in 1995. Usually covering several decades, the visions have focused on human and social capital development as well as the private and non-oil sectors and contain buzzwords designed to appeal to an international audience of potential investors and business partners. The visions and plans set out ambitious targets and objectives for diversifying and expanding Gulf economies to wean them gradually off oil rents.

Different policy motivations lay behind each of the national visions that appeared between 1995 and 2016. Bahrain and Oman face the most pressing need to diversify their economies as their already small oil reserves dwindle further. Decisionmakers in the United Arab Emirates (UAE) and Qatar lacked such urgency but launched strategic visions to underpin the growth of Dubai, Abu Dhabi, and Doha into global cities. Kuwait's vision was prepared at considerable public expense by Tony Blair Associates but was eventually scrapped and replaced by a "New Kuwait Vision 2035" that was more organic.[3] The Saudi plan was put together in response to the fall in world oil prices and the significant budgetary shortfalls that accumulated between 2014 and 2016 and led Mohammad bin Salman to order emergency cuts to government spending after he took control of the Council on Economic and Development Affairs in 2015.[4]

Certain features common to all the national plans and visions include a clear intent to create knowledge-based economies in which growth is driven by research, development, and innovation, as well as by the creation of internationally competitive value-added economic sectors. Heavy emphasis is placed on proposals to strengthen and expand the private sector to create the new jobs capable of absorbing the fast-growing and highly qualified cadres of young people entering the labor market. Most of the visions were drafted in part by teams of international consultants, and some of the language in Bahrain's Vision 2030 (in 2008) was strikingly similar to that in Saudi Vision 2030 (in 2016)—both of which were associated closely with the firm McKinsey despite being drawn up nearly a decade apart.[5]

Rhetoric and Reality

Arguably the most significant and consequential commonality of the visions and plans is the missing political aspect of economic reform processes. Most of the visions lack an appreciation for the sensitivity of the range of political and economic tradeoffs that may be required in any genuine transformation of political economies away from the redistributive models associated with the oil era. Such tradeoffs underpin the more intangible aspects of reform that cannot easily be obtained (or measured) by technocratic measures alone. Their absence, or their underestimation, makes it harder for policymakers to address issues such as the deep-rooted expectations, entitlements, and entrenched layers of vested interests within the context of the structural imbalances in many Gulf economies. This omission is problematic in part because of the presence of entrenched layers of vested economic and political interests able to block, or at least delay, reform initiatives.

In Saudi Arabia, for example, social insurance data indicate that fewer than 400,000 private sector jobs paid more than the 3,000 Saudi riyals per month, which is the figure often considered the minimum Saudi high school graduates will consider when seeking a job. Saudi Arabia did in fact create 417,000 new jobs in 2015, but 368,000 of them (88 percent) went to non-nationals in low-paying sectors, testifying to the continuing resilience of structural imbalances in regional economies.[6] Another example from Oman illustrates the tension between stability and sustainability, as well as political and economic considerations at moments of stress and uncertainty. In 2011, the Omani authorities raised public sector wages and created tens of thousands of new public sector jobs in the wake of socioeconomic unrest in February 2011 at the height of the uprisings in other Arab states. These measures undid years of patient and painstaking work to coax more Omanis into the private sector (a key pillar of Oman's Vision 2020) as an estimated 30,000 Omanis moved back into public sector work instead.[7]

Maintaining the political-economic equilibrium requires policymakers to perform a delicate balancing act, which limits their room for maneuver, especially on critical issues identified as prime targets for reform but that touch directly on aspects of the "social contract" in Gulf Cooperation Council (GCC) states. Attempts both in Bahrain and in Saudi Arabia to equalize the cost of hiring expatriates and nationals by imposing fees on expatriate hires ran into concerted opposition from business elites threatened by the potential loss of access to cheaper labor.[8] While the political influence of the Saudi business elite may have been tempered by Crown Prince Mohammad bin Salman since 2017, addressing the vested interest of the state-dependent middle class remains difficult, whether in Saudi Arabia or in other Gulf states. The trebling of the value-added tax (VAT) in Saudi Arabia in 2020 from 5 percent to 15 percent as part of the austerity measures in response to COVID-19, together with the suspension of the 1,000-riyal monthly cost-of-living allowance for public sector workers, constitutes one of the most direct attacks on the social contract in Saudi Arabia since it came into being in the 1950s.[9]

No Blank Slate

Rather than addressing competing and vested interests head on, government- and consultant-led visions for transition have too often taken for granted the existence of a blank slate that strips away the (need for) political aspects of economic reform. Although Gulf monarchies, with the partial exception of Kuwait, lack meaningful political pluralism, this does not mean that vested political and economic interests are insignificant. By contrast, the frequently opaque nature of politico-economic networks may be harder to dislodge than open or formal vested interests precisely because they lie beneath the surface of Gulf societies.

The challenge for decisionmakers in Arab Gulf (and other regional) states is how to reformulate a "ruling bargain" that was fashioned during a period of smaller populations and seemingly limitless oil revenues, but that no longer appears economically sustainable. Until the oil price collapse of 2014, there was a prevailing hope that painful but necessary changes could be made over the medium term rather than immediately. The regional upheaval in 2011 underscored that the instinctive policymaking response to signs of discontent was to intensify populist short-term measures in order to blunt or preempt the social and economic roots of public anger. Total state spending in all six GCC states rose by 20 percent in 2011 as governments responded to the Arab uprisings with new welfare packages and other benefits.[10]

While the measures taken in 2011 to quell the regional political unrest were largely successful, most were short term and had the unintended consequence, in the words of political economist Steffen Hertog, of creating "a ratchet effect that demands ever larger outlays during every political crisis" because expectations are easier to raise than they are to curb.[11] Sensitive cuts to salaries and benefits and some reform of subsidies did take place, but governments were reluctant and (in some cases) unable to make further, and more politically painful, reductions. Subsidy reform, in particular, remains a very sensitive issue that could rapidly become politicized, as evidenced by findings from a 2016 survey by Dubai-based ASDA'A Burson-Marsteller, which found that 93 percent of respondents in Bahrain, 92 percent in Oman and Qatar, and 86 percent in Saudi Arabia, were in favor of continuing subsidies.[12] A separate 2016 survey in Kuwait demonstrated the strength of attachment to the notion of the government as the provider of employment, as it found that 58 percent of unemployed Kuwaitis would rather wait for an opening in the public sector than take a job in the private sector.[13]

It is, perhaps, little surprise that the political sensitivity to tampering with mechanisms of wealth redistribution has been most evident in Kuwait and Bahrain, the two Gulf states with the most active parliamentary bodies. Bahrain softened the blow of higher meat prices in 2014 by compensating citizens for the additional cost incurred by the partial lifting of subsidies.[14] Four years later, Bahraini parliamentarians' vote to increase meat subsidies and other allowances led to a political standoff after the government rejected their proposal.[15] Months of debate and a political back-and-forth followed before the government abandoned plans to reform subsidies in May 2019, lest it trigger wider unrest.[16] In Kuwait, lawmakers amended a government proposal that would have raised the prices Kuwaiti citizens paid for water and electricity so that the measure would apply only to residents of apartment buildings (overwhelmingly populated by expatriates) and corporate users.[17] In addition, Kuwait was an outlier in 2020 as the only Gulf state not to impose significant austerity measures to address the economic impact of the pandemic.

Officials in Gulf capitals remain mindful of the violent backlashes in other regional states—such as Jordan in 2012 and Yemen in 2006—against attempts to scale back subsidies and raise the price of basic utilities and foodstuffs. Getting the political aspects of economic reform right will determine whether governments (and societies) in the Gulf can make the transition that the changes in their political economies will require, and sooner rather than later in some cases. However, shifting expectations and entitlements and taking on and dislodging vested interests cannot merely be wished into place by technocratic measures alone, and perhaps COVID-19 can provide the shock to the system that gives governments the political breathing space to move forward with structural economic reforms that can no longer be put off indefinitely. These vital social and political components of economic reform will need to be closely interlinked to have a chance of genuinely changing the relationship between citizen and state in eventual "post-rentier" polities.

Notes

1. Joshua Yaffa, "How the Russian-Saudi Oil War Went Awry—for Putin Most of All," *New Yorker*, April 15, 2020 (www.newyorker.com/news/dispatch/how-the-russian -saudi-oil-war-went-awry-for-putin-most-of-all).

2. Reuters, "IMF Revises Down Economic Forecasts for Most Gulf Countries," October 13, 2020 (www.reuters.com/article/imf-gulf-gdp/imf-revises-down-economic -forecasts-for-most-gulf-countries-idUSL8N2H44KV).

3. Sophie Olver-Ellis, "A New Vision for Kuwait," *London School of Economics Middle East Centre Blog* (blog), January 8, 2019 (https://blogs.lse.ac.uk/mec/2019/01 /08/a-new-vision-for-kuwait/).

4. Rick Gladstone, "Saudi Arabia, Squeezed by Low Oil Prices, Cuts Spending to Shrink Deficit," *New York Times*, December 28, 2015.

5. Salem Saif, "When Consultants Reign," *Jacobin*, May 9, 2016 (www.jacobinmag .com/2016/05/saudi-arabia-aramco-salman-mckinsey-privatization/).

6. "Saudis Shy Away from the Jobs Market," *Gulf States News* 40, no. 1011 (March 3, 2016), p. 8.

7. Steffen Hertog, "Arab Gulf States: An Assessment of Nationalisation Policies," Research Paper 1 (Gulf Labour Markets and Migration Programme, 2014), pp. 8–9 (http://hdl.handle.net/1814/32156).

8. Mary Sophia, "Saudi's Shoura Council Criticises Nitaqat System," *Gulf Business*, January 29, 2014 (https://gulfbusiness.com/saudis-shoura-council-criticises -nitaqat-system/); Hasan Tariq Al Hasan, "Bahrain Bids Its Economic Reform Farewell," openDemocracy, July 8, 2012 (www.opendemocracy.net/en/bahrain-bids-its -economic-reform-farewell/).

9. Tawfiq Naserallah, "Saudi Arabia to Increase VAT, Suspend Cost of Living Allowance," *Gulf News*, May 11, 2020 (https://gulfnews.com/world/gulf/saudi/saudi -arabia-to-increase-vat-suspend-cost-of-living-allowance-1.1589162480529).

10. Martin Dokoupil, "Gulf Arab States Should Cut State Spending Growth: IMF," Reuters, October 29, 2012 (www.reuters.com/article/us-imf-gulf/gulf-arab-states -should-cut-state-spending-growth-imf-idUKBRE89S0L020121029).

11. Steffen Hertog, "The Costs of Counter-Revolution in the GCC," *Foreign Policy*, May 31, 2011 (https://foreignpolicy.com/2011/05/31/the-costs-of-counter-revolution -in-the-gcc/).

12. Vivian Nereim, "Young Arabs Wedded to State Largess Pose Test for Gulf Leaders," Bloomberg, April 12, 2016 (www.bloomberg.com/news/articles/2016-04-12 /young-arabs-wedded-to-state-largess-pose-test-for-gulf-leaders).

13. Ahmad Jabr, "58 Percent Unemployed Kuwaitis Unwilling to Work in Private Sector" *Kuwait Times*, April 19, 2016 (www.zawya.com/mena/en/business/story/58

_percent_unemployed_Kuwaitis_unwilling_to_work_in_private_sector-ZAWYA 20160419051440/).

14. Stanley Carvalho, "Bahrain Planning More Subsidy Cuts, New Charges to Boost Revenues," Reuters, November 17, 2015 (www.zawya.com/mena/en/story /Bahrain_planning_more_subsidy_cuts_new_charges_to_boost_revenues_min -TR20151117nL8N13C2ABX4/).

15. Aziz El Yaakoubi, "Bahrain Government Rejects Parliament's Subsidy Reform Plan," Reuters, August 2, 2018 (www.reuters.com/article/bahrain-economy-subsidies /bahrain-government-rejects-parliaments-subsidy-reform-plan-idUSL5N1US66O).

16. Aziz El Yaakoubi, "Bahrain Ditches Subsidy Reform Plan as Political Tensions Simmer," Reuters, May 7, 2019 (https://fr.reuters.com/article/bahrain-economy -idINL5N22J6DF).

17. Zainab Fattah, "Untouched for Half a Century, Kuwait Utility Prices to Rise," Bloomberg, April 14, 2016 (www.bloomberg.com/news/articles/2016-04-14/untouched -for-half-a-century-kuwait-utility-prices-set-to-rise).

TWENTY ONE

Revisiting Late Rentierism

MATTHEW GRAY

MUCH IS MADE—QUITE rightly—of the social and economic reforms under-way in the Arab Gulf states. The Saudi Vision 2030 strategy attracts perhaps the most attention, but all Gulf states, and some cities or emirates within them, have a strategic development document promising varying degrees of economic, social, and other reform. These reform documents have led some observers to assume that the rentier bargain in these political economies, in which states use part of their oil revenues to buy the acquiescence of society, is on the way out.

But is this really the case? Is there any evidence that deep transformations are occurring in these systems? Or are the reforms more modest, tinkering with the existing system so as to sustain it rather than change it? The case made here is that while some genuine changes are underway in the Gulf, ultimately these are designed to maintain the existing political order, not to upset it.

Plus ça change . . .

The basic state-society dynamic in the Arab Gulf states is rentierism. This refers to a system in which the state receives a large part of its revenue from external "rents," or payments that are the result of natural endowment rather than economic production. Examples include fees (such as Suez Canal and Panama Canal transit fees), aid, transfers, and most commonly, oil and gas

Figure 21-1. Arab Gulf States: GDP and Oil Price Correlation, 2000–2019

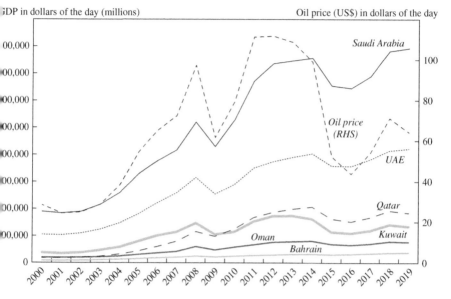

Source: Author's compilation, using statistics from World Bank, World Bank Development Indicators website (https://data
.worldbank.org/indicator/NY.GDP.MKTP.CD?view=chart); data from the *BP Statistical Review of World Energy 2020* (www
.bp.com/en/global/corporate/energy-economics/statistical-review-of-world-energy.html).
Note: RHS = right-hand side

royalties. In a rentier system, these rents are used by a state to avoid imposing taxes on society and, typically, to provide people with free services such
as healthcare and education. Rents also fund a repressive apparatus. This
means that the state does not have to make democratic concessions to society or permit much, if any, societal involvement in policymaking.[1]

Rentierism is not without its critics, but its basic features and mechanisms are widely accepted.[2] Rents remain the dominant source of state incomes in the Arab Gulf. As figure 21-1 shows, there is a stark correlation
between oil prices (and by extension, gas prices) and the gross domestic
product (GDP) of the Arab Gulf states. Even though these states have talked
about economic diversification for several decades now—since the late 1960s
in the case of Saudi Arabia, and the 1980s in most others—their economies
are no less vulnerable to changes in oil prices than they were a generation
or more ago.[3]

Figure 21-2 further illustrates the ongoing importance of rents. Keeping in mind that the years since 2014 have been a period of low oil prices,
the figure shows that the Arab Gulf states are fundamentally no less rentier

Figure 21-2. Rent Income as a Percentage of GDP, 1990–2018
Percent

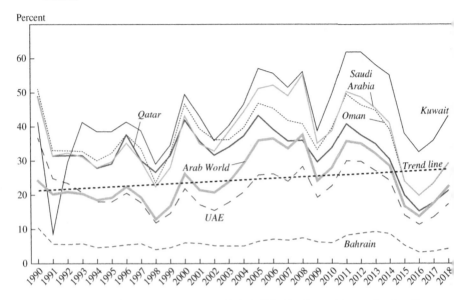

Source: Author's compilation, using statistics from World Bank, World Bank Development Indicators website (https://data
.worldbank.org/indicator).
Note: "Rent income" here includes both oil and gas receipts, but not other rent transfers.

than they were in the 1990s. Across all the Gulf states, and the Arab world
as a whole, rents have typically accounted for between 20 and 40 percent
of GDP, and higher still in a couple of especially oil-focused economies in
periods of very high prices. Importantly, also, the trend line for the region
has risen from 21 to 27 percent since 1990 and would have been even more
dramatic without the low oil prices after 2014.

This is not to say that the Gulf states are politically or economically
monolithic. The rents per capita vary markedly, along with the ways in which
they are spent, and state-society relations are still informed by other factors,
such as historical precedent, which can be a determinant of a regime's
potential legitimacy; societal structures, including the relative power of
merchants, tribes, clerics, and other societal actors; and external security perceptions, which account in part for the apparent paradox of Kuwait being
both the most rentier state in the Gulf while also possessing its most activist parliament. At their core, however, all six Gulf monarchies are fundamentally late rentier in their political uses of rents and the characteristics
that state-society dynamics subsequently exhibit.

But the Gulf States Are Now *Late* Rentier—and Still State-Dominated

This underlying feature of the Arab Gulf states dates back to the 1950s or 1960s, and there is scant evidence that rents have lost any of their political importance: in fact, rents are so dominant that they define the nature of these economies, permitting an absence of taxation, high state spending, and strong state involvement across the economy. Economic growth remains tied to oil and gas prices, as does the financial capacity of the state.

This does not preclude *any* reform—far from it—but reform is intended to adjust or modify the political economy rather than to reorder or restructure it. The political driver of reforms is regime and system maintenance, not transformation. This is most reforms so far have been in commercial processes and procedures or in regulation, such as the procedures required for starting, managing, or closing a business; legal institutional processes; import and export; government regulatory procedures; and, in some sectors, easier and more attractive foreign investment rules.[4] This is very different from neoliberal reforms, of which there have been considerably fewer. There have been some reductions to state subsidies, but only limited attempts to introduce taxation, only basic liberalization of stock markets, very little privatization of state-owned firms, and almost no substantive reforms to indigenous labor laws or toward floating currencies.

These are signs that the states have become "late" rentier.[5] By this, it is meant that these systems are still fundamentally rentier, with a share of rents distributed to society in exchange for political acquiescence. At the same time, however, the state has matured and developed, using rents in a more careful and nuanced fashion, and with greater responsiveness to society and more diverse development strategies. The late rentier state is more complex and active than early rentier ones, with greater room for more ambitious political-economy tactics, higher likelihood of (certain) reforms, and greater nuance in how the state interacts with society.

The late rentier states of the Gulf are also state capitalist. The state retains a strong ownership and regulatory role in the economy but allows market mechanisms to set most prices and lets the private sector operate in some parts of the economy. This is a much more dynamic form of state capitalism than the older ones of Egypt, Turkey, Syria, Iraq, and others in the mid- and late twentieth century. It is a "new" or "entrepreneurial" form that is more efficient, risk-tolerant, and internationally focused.[6] In a new state capitalist rentier system, the state retains ownership, or at least control, of key resources such as oil and gas, and owns major firms in telecommunications, aviation, education, and other key sectors (which constitute a large majority of most of the Gulf economies), while at the same time encouraging the private sector in other less strategic or less sensitive areas.

Any analysis of change in the Gulf states needs to keep in mind the dominance of these two dynamics—late rentierism and new state capitalism—in their political economies. It accounts for the presence of what otherwise might seem like paradoxes: the enduring importance of rents, despite decades of state promises to pursue economic diversification; the state's dominance of the economy but continued reference to private sector development; the significant—but selective—opening of these economies to competition and other aspects of globalization; and the fact that societal agency seems to have expanded in recent times but with little if any democratization or political reform following from this. There is substantial economic and social change occurring in the Gulf states, but states are deliberately managing this change, to ensure that it does not destabilize these economies or threaten the political and economic bases of incumbent regimes.

Policy Opportunities and Dilemmas

The structure of the Gulf political economies, especially late rentierism, is predicated on a stable and predictable economy and, above all, a steady flow of rents. This is a challenge because oil and gas rents are *anything but* steady: since the early 1970s, they have fluctuated dramatically, rising during periods of high demand or conflict, and falling during times of glut or recession—most recently, plummeting along with energy demand during the COVID-19 pandemic, and from a starting price that was already more modest than the average levels since the early 1970s. Late rentier leaders are tinkering with economic policy settings and pursuing diversification above all for this reason, hoping that less direct reliance on rents will stabilize and improve economic performance. However, there is a dilemma here: certainly, if reform imperatives are ignored, economic performance will suffer and bring political risks, but on the other hand, if reforms are done too quickly or carelessly, or cause societal groups to feel threatened, this can just as surely undermine a ruler's legitimacy and support. Far from rentierism being a simple matter of "buying off" society, in the longer-term it actually requires considerable care and tact from the ruling elite.

Thus far, the Gulf's rulers have managed this process reasonably well. They have proven durable, and some have enjoyed considerable popularity, despite the strains of sustained low oil prices from the mid-1980s to the early 2000s, the fluctuations in prices from 2008 to 2014, the low prices again after 2014, and the plummet in rents when the COVID-19 pandemic began in early 2020. They have used tools beyond rents and state capitalism too: elite relationships, economic statecraft, and historical claims to legitimacy have all added to their resilience. Even as their political economies became increasingly complex and globalized after the 1990s, rulers have largely avoided political concessions to society. Yet oil and gas are finite resources, and global demand is showing signs that oil demand is peaking. At some point in the future the rentier system will have run its course, and these regimes are already contemplating the post-oil era and beginning to gradually, cautiously reposition their economies for this. It is in the longer term, rather than the near future, that Gulf rulers and royal families will be most tested—and most at risk.

For these political economies to no longer be rentier but maintain current standards of living, far deeper and more dramatic reforms will be needed. As one example, a sophisticated and extensive taxation system is needed. At present, there are virtually no taxes on personal income, accrued wealth, or corporate profits; in 2015, states obtained only 6.3 percent of their revenue from taxes.[7] This is less than 2 percent of GDP; in the countries of the Organization for Economic Cooperation and Development (OECD) that same year, the average figure was 33.7 percent.[8] However, the introduction of much higher levels of taxation is impossible without a radical restructuring of the rentier arrangement, or even its dismantlement. This is why only simple and small taxes have been introduced or promised, such as a 5 percent sales tax. About more substantive taxation, as Saudi Crown Prince Mohammad bin Salman flatly stated in 2016: "There are going to be no income taxes, and no wealth taxes."[9]

Somewhat similarly, the other area where studied reform is needed is in labor markets. These are dual systems at present, with very low wages paid to unskilled foreign workers and very high ones to nationals. For nationals, there is little correlation between wages and productivity. Moreover, because nationals often lack the qualifications or experience needed for the most skilled positions, many of these jobs still go to expatriates. Rectifying this, so that the dual nature of the wage system is reduced or eliminated, and the skills and productivity of nationals are internationally competitive, is a mammoth task, but essential if genuine economic diversification is to be realized. While labor nationalization programs have been part of the political rhetoric in the region for several decades, there has been at best only very modest progress toward building an indigenous labor market that is globally competitive.

Much will come down to the individual dedication and skill of leaders. For the time being, major structural reforms can seem a distant imperative, and given their potential political cost, it can be tempting for a rentier leader to simply neglect them. Labor market reform is a clear case of this, with more substantial reforms entailing, in effect, an alteration of the rentier "bargain," which to date has constituted too great a political risk for incumbent leadership to hazard. In the nearer term, a focus on economic management, improved commercial practices and processes, and gradual broader reforms is likely to be the policy preference. This may appear to be more of the same; diversification has been a buzzword of development in the region for decades now. However, if oil prices remain suppressed, as they have been since 2014 and especially since the start of the 2020 global coronavirus pandemic, more significant reforms, such as investment in new sectors, privatization, and new competition policies, may increasingly be seen by leaders as worth the political risk. Eventually, as the end of the oil era comes increasingly into focus, profound reform will be essential if the Gulf economies are to thrive, and their ruling elites are to survive.

Notes

1. Hazem Beblawi, "The Rentier State in the Arab World," in *The Rentier State*, edited by Hazem Beblawi and Giacomo Luciani (London: Croom Helm, 1987), pp. 63–82; Michael L. Ross, "Does Oil Hinder Democracy?," *World Politics* 53, no. 3 (April 2001), pp. 325–61 (https://scholar.harvard.edu/files/levitsky/files/ross_world_politics.pdf).

2. Matthew Gray, "A Theory of 'Late Rentierism' in the Arab States of the Gulf," Occasional Paper 7 (Center for International and Regional Studies at Georgetown University School of Foreign Service in Qatar, 2011), p. 17 (https://repository.library.georgetown.edu/bitstream/handle/10822/558291/CIRSOccasionalPaper7Matthew Gray2011.pdf).

3. Ibid., pp. 28–30; Tim Niblock and Monica Malik, *The Political Economy of Saudi Arabia* (London: Routledge, 2007), pp. 52–82.

4. International Bank for Reconstruction and Development and the World Bank, "Doing Business 2019: Training for Reform," 16th edition (Washington, 2019) (www.doingbusiness.org/content/dam/doingBusiness/media/Annual-Reports/English/DB2019-report_web-version.pdf); passim.

5. As described in Gray, "A Theory of 'Late Rentierism.'"

6. Ian Bremmer, *The End of the Free Market: Who Wins the War between States and Corporations?* (New York: Portfolio, 2010); Matthew Gray, "Rentierism's Siblings: On the Linkages between Rents, Neopatrimonialism, and Entrepreneurial State Capitalism in the Persian Gulf Monarchies," *Journal of Arabian Studies* 8, supp. 1 (2018), pp. 29–33, 39–42 (https://doi.org/10.1080/21534764.2018.1546931).

7. Ali Alreshan and others, "Diversifying Government Revenue in the GCC: Next Steps," Paper prepared for the Annual Meeting of Ministers of Finance and Central Bank Governors, International Monetary Fund (IMF), October 26, 2016, p. 7 (www.imf.org/external/np/pp/eng/2016/102616.pdf).

8. Organization for Economic Cooperation and Development (OECD), *Revenue Statistics 2018* (Paris, 2018), p. 2 (www.oecd.org/publications/revenue-statistics-2522770x.htm).

9. "Transcript: Interview with Muhammad bin Salman," *The Economist*, January 6, 2016 (www.economist.com/middle-east-and-africa/2016/01/06/transcript-interview-with-muhammad-bin-salman).

TWENTY TWO

Why the GCC's Economic Diversification Challenges Are Unique

STEFFEN HERTOG

FEW OIL-RICH ECONOMIES HAVE more ambitious plans for economic diversification than those of the Gulf Cooperation Council (GCC). The Gulf monarchies bring along many assets in their quest for post-oil growth: fairly mature bureaucracies, good infrastructure, and solid public goods provision. They rank higher in all of these areas than most other hydrocarbon producers outside of the Organization for Economic Cooperation and Development (OECD). And yet the GCC also faces some obstacles to economic diversification that are unique to the region and not always well understood by policymakers or their advisers.

Most notably, the unusually generous unique social contract that provides for GCC citizens creates cost structures for private producers and disincentives on the private labor market that make conventional industrialization strategies difficult to implement. There is no clear blueprint or precedent for overcoming these constraints. Diversification will instead require cautious experimentation and a gradual reformulation of the social contract in a way that reduces distortions while maintaining living standards for GCC nationals.

How State Generosity Has Increased the Costs of Production

GCC governments have been successful in spreading middle class wealth fairly broadly among national populations that, by and large, were desperately poor just two generations ago. Yet the distribution of wealth through channels like generous state employment has also created fairly high costs for local producers; as in other high-income countries, operating a business in the GCC is not inexpensive, especially when firms are under pressure to employ nationals whose expectations for wages and working hours are informed by the generous packages available in government.

Different from conventional high-income countries, however, productivity levels in GCC private sectors have not kept pace with the rapid improvement in living standards and wages for citizens. As a result, there is a real disconnect between costs of production and efficiency of production. This does not affect the fortunes of the nontradables sector in the GCC very much, since it does not have to compete in international markets and is driven by government-generated demand. It does, however, impede the competitiveness of the tradables sector outside of oil and hydrocarbon-related products. A conventional industrialization path based on relatively low technology levels but cheap labor—which, as Dani Rodrik has shown, has become difficult under the best of circumstances—is not open to the GCC.[1] Even foreign workers, who on average are paid a fraction of citizens in the private sector, are considerably more expensive to employ in the GCC than in their countries of origin.

The relative weakness of national human resources is at the crux of the problem. GCC labor markets continue to be deeply distorted by expansive government employment, which accounts for about 70 percent of all jobs held by GCC citizens.[2] It undermines entrepreneurial incentives, raises wage expectations, and weakens the motivation to acquire skills relevant for the private sector. While this setup provides a middle-class lifestyle for a large share of nationals, the resulting labor market structures stymie privately driven diversification.

Different from non-oil economies, citizen wages in GCC economies tend to lie significantly above their marginal product, as evidenced by a striking scatterplot contained in a 2019 International Monetary Fund (IMF) report on Saudi Arabia (figure 22-1).[3]

Since productivity and practical skills remain relatively weak, the political pressure to provide more state employment in turn remains strong. At the same time, firms tend to focus on the nontradables sector serving the

Figure 22-1. Average Annual Wage and Productivity in Saudi Arabia and Other World Economies, 2019

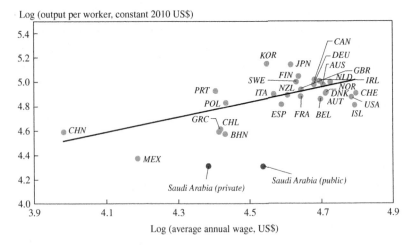

Source: International Monetary Fund, "Saudi Arabia: 2019 Article IV Consultation-Press Release and Staff Report," Country Report19/290 (Washington, September 9, 2019), p. 22.
Note: AUS = Australia; BEL = Belgium; BHN = Bahrain MEX = Mexico; CAN = Canada; CHL = Chile; CHN = China; DEU = Germany; ESP = Spain; FIN = Finland; FRA = France; GBR = Great Britain; GRC = Greece; IRL = Ireland; ISL = Iceland; ITA = Italy; JPN = Japan; KOR = Korea; NLD = Netherlands; NOR = Norway; NZL = New Zealand; POL = Poland; PRT = Portugal

local market, where they can rely on state-generated demand and can afford to incur higher production costs.

The GCC economies are a victim of their own success: unlike some oil-rich kleptocracies outside of the region, they have shared their riches relatively widely and greatly improved national living standards. As a result, however, production costs and real exchange rates are high, while productivity has been flatlining, as shown in IMF estimates of total factor productivity trends, as well as long-term productivity data from the Conference Board.

Competing on the cost of labor inputs is not feasible, so the GCC can only become internationally competitive by leapfrogging into advanced kinds of production. But few economies have managed to do so. Dubai has accomplished some of it through heavy use of skilled foreign manpower in its advanced service sectors, but the model is unlikely to be replicable for GCC countries with larger national populations. The experience of populous commodity-rich countries outside the region, like the oft-cited Malaysia, is not particularly relevant: Malaysia was not a rich, middle-class-based society *before* industrialization. Its per capita rents were limited, and it could therefore leverage ample cheap labor in the first stages of industrial growth.

That said, GCC economies have assets that other late industrializers do not have: ample capital, high penetration of consumer technology, well-run state-owned enterprises in critical sectors, and a geostrategic position between Europe, Asia, and Africa. Some economists see access to relatively cheap foreign labor as a further advantage, but the long-term evidence seems to be that reliance on such labor has pushed GCC economies onto a low productivity path—different from other industrializers, where growing supply constraints on national labor pushed firms into investing into skills and technology. GCC economies by and large remain organized around foreign labor that is cheap enough to maintain a convenient service economy for citizens—but not cheap enough to compete with truly low-cost producers in Asia, given that Asian foreign workers demand a hefty wage premium over what they can earn at home.

Is There a Solution?

The first conclusion from this discussion has to be that there is no ready blueprint for GCC diversification: both the assets and the constraints of GCC economies are unique. The best that policymakers can do is to alleviate the constraints in a targeted fashion while facilitating wide-ranging experimentation with new models of production that might leverage the GCC's specific assets.

The key binding constraint is low labor productivity. Although this can be said about almost every economy struggling to diversify, the factors depressing productivity of national labor are specific to the region. They include a labor market that is organized around public sector employment, in which nationals are deterred from seeking private sector jobs through competition with low-cost foreign workers and in which employers have few incentives to invest in skills or technology, given their barely constrained ability to import labor.

All these incentives need to change. This could happen by gradually converting excess public sector employment into a much less distortionary general cash grant for all citizens, subsidies for national labor in the private market (as already implemented in Kuwait), or migration management that reduces employers' incentives to rely on low-cost workers.[4] Gradual erosion of real public sector pay by not adjusting it to inflation might have to be part of the package too. We do not know the ideal policy mix, but we know which distortions need tackling, while recognizing the political need to maintain a middle-class lifestyle for citizens.

Local experience shows that labor market attitudes can change: in some hotels in Riyadh, Saudi citizens now provide room service—something that was socially unthinkable a decade ago. The willingness to take on private sector work is increasing. This needs to be accompanied by more targeted efforts at upskilling, moving away from the overproduction of university graduates in subjects of limited practical relevance. Saudi Arabia's university enrollment rate of around 70 percent might be the highest in the world, but few programs prepare graduates for the actual labor market; many of them instead merely serve to postpone unemployment by a few years, while increasing expectations of white-collar employment.

There is time to redefine the social contract while GCC countries, with the exception of Bahrain and potentially Oman, retain enough fiscal runway to smooth the transition to a new system. But if oil prices remain low, this will not be the case much longer, especially in the relatively less wealthy Saudi Arabia. Sticking to the current welfare system for too long increases the risk of a forced adjustment in which the social contract is forcibly dismantled through fiscal and currency crises—not unlike what Egypt has experienced since the mid-2010s.

Even if the incentive environment is reformed, the GCC's unique development constraints mean that there is no cookie-cutter recipe for diversification, and the international benchmarking that the region's public policy consultants are so fond of often is of limited relevance. The GCC instead has to find its own path toward leveraging its strengths in digital literacy, heavy industry, infrastructure, geography, and consumer tastes. Doing this will require a wide range of experimentation with new forms of production, a process of discovery that can be supported through the provision of credit, equity, and targeted training, and by building a specialized infrastructure. The process should involve private capital and be decentralized. It is less advisable to focus on a few large, state-engineered bets that could go wrong and end up as white elephants.

Before this writing in 2021, none of the GCC governments have done much to reform the core distributional bargain based on public employment. While there is investment in new sectors and infrastructures, the policy discussion about sustainability and reform of the GCC social contract remains limited. It is the hardest bit of the economic reform process, but also the one that will pay the highest long-term dividends.

Notes

This chapter is an updated version of an article on the London School of Economics (LSE) Middle East Centre's website: Steffen Hertog, "Why the GCC's Economic Diversification Challenges Are Unique," LSE Middle East Centre Blog (blog), August 7, 2020 (https://blogs.lse.ac.uk/mec/2020/08/07/why-the-gccs-economic-diversification -challenges-are-unique/).

1. Dani Rodrik, "Premature Deindustrialization," Working Paper 20935 (Cambridge, Mass.: National Bureau of Economic Research, February 2015) (www.nber.org /papers/w20935).

2. Steffen Hertog, "Arab Gulf States: An Assessment of Nationalisation Policies," Research Paper 1 (Gulf Labour Markets and Migration Programme, 2014) (http://hdl .handle.net/1814/32156).

3. International Monetary Fund, "Saudi Arabia: 2019 Article IV Consultation - Press Release and Staff Report," Country Report 19/290 (Washington, September 9, 2019), p. 22 (www.imf.org/en/Publications/CR/Issues/2019/09/09/Saudi-Arabia-2019 -Article-IV-Consultation-Press-Release-and-Staff-Report-48659).

4. Steffen Hertog, "Making Wealth Sharing More Efficient in High-Rent Countries: The Citizens' Income," *Energy Transitions* 1, no. 7 (2017), pp. 1–14 (https://doi .org/10.1007/s41825-017-0007-2).

TWENTY THREE

Gulf Representation and Parliaments in the Face of Austerity Measures

COURTNEY FREER

AUSTERITY MEASURES AND PROGRESS toward economic diversification are seriously needed in the states of the Gulf Cooperation Council (GCC), but compliance with past attempts to impose such measures has been inconsistent, despite substantial rhetorical support from political leaders. Legislative political structures are part of the problem. Indeed, there has been comparatively less progress toward the implementation of austerity in the GCC state with the most powerful elected parliament, Kuwait. Meanwhile, in Oman, Saudi Arabia, and the United Arab Emirates (UAE), where decisionmaking power is more centralized, there has been more movement toward consolidating austerity measures. Qatar is an outlier, since the blockade imposed against it in June 2017 by Bahrain, Egypt, Saudi Arabia, and the UAE has largely delayed the implementation of austerity measures that were previously discussed. Of course, all such diversification plans changed with the onset of the COVID-19 pandemic, which damaged global energy markets and made some areas of investment for diversification, like aviation and tourism, untenable.

The political leaders of all six GCC states have announced sweeping plans for economic reform: Bahrain 2030, New Kuwait or Vision 2035, Oman Vision 2040, Qatar National Vision 2030, Saudi Vision 2030, and UAE Vision 2021. These ambitious plans are meant to help ease the transition away from oil-dependent economies toward more diversified models with less state spending on disbursements to citizens through, for instance, public sector employment. The details of these visions have been examined elsewhere; this chapter describes the role of elected institutions in implementing such wide-ranging programs.

Parliaments in the GCC are often seen solely as means for members to secure material disbursements for their constituents or support from their governments. This understanding of elected bodies as distributive mechanisms, however simplistic and flawed it may be, appears to have informed policymakers when it comes to the implementation of austerity measures after 2014. Indeed, these elected bodies, though by no means the only mechanisms for voicing political opinion in the GCC, have been the site of important debates about proposed austerity measures pushed by Gulf governments after the fall in oil prices in 2014 and more urgently after the COVID-19 pandemic.

Further, it is worth noting that democratic political forms are not always those that achieve so-called liberal or democratic outcomes. For instance, in Kuwait, populist sentiment has become increasingly xenophobic in the face of the implementation of austerity measures. With Kuwaiti citizens worried about the effects of austerity measures on their own well-being, there has been increasing focus on taxing expatriates rather than citizens who are seen to have more of a claim to the Kuwaiti state; similar actions are emerging elsewhere in the Gulf as a means to avoid the consequences of austerity measures that governments insist they will implement. And in response to the COVID-19 pandemic many GCC governments drastically reduced their expatriate populations in order to protect their citizen populations from the effects of global recession.[1]

In this chapter I assess the means by which elected bodies in GCC states have effected plans for economic reform as a means to understand the role of these bodies in implementing broad-ranging economic visions.

Involvement of Elected Gulf Bodies

Although all of the GCC states have elected bodies of some form, only the parliaments of Bahrain, Kuwait, and Oman have legislative powers, and, although political blocs are formally banned in these states, they still contest elections; in other states, people run as individuals rather than as blocs. Qatar, Saudi Arabia, and the UAE have elected consultative assemblies with varying political influence.

In 2018, the Bahraini cabinet and parliament were tasked with putting together a comprehensive austerity plan as part of broader economic reforms, which are more urgent for Bahrain than its neighbors given its diminishing oil supply. In August 2018, the government rejected parliament's proposal to combine meat subsidies and cost-of-living allowances into a single package and to increase the size of that package for working and retired Bahrainis.[2] In May 2019, officials went further, announcing that they would not fully reform the subsidy system, despite International Monetary Fund (IMF) encouragement to implement direct taxes, reduce value-added taxation (VAT) exceptions, and gradually eliminate untargeted subsidies.[3] The Fiscal Balance Programme (FBP) had been announced in 2018 to help balance the budget by 2022 while continuing to provide assistance to citizens most in need and was expected to be rubber-stamped by the new parliament, which was elected in November 2018 and seen as an "excellent political buffer for a royal family-led government pressing greater economic austerity."[4] Ultimately, though, not even a loyalist parliament could assuage the government's fears about unrest due to the implementation of austerity measures, and plans to reform the country's subsidy system were abandoned in 2019.[5]

In Kuwait, which houses the most outspoken and powerful parliament in the region, the introduction of VAT has been delayed until 2021, but fuel subsidies, as well as water and electricity subsidies, were introduced in 2016.[6] Debates in the Kuwaiti parliament show a tendency to seek to shift responsibility for austerity onto the large expatriate population. Parliament member Safa al-Hashem is the most outspoken in her criticism of the expatriate population, having gone so far as to call the demographic imbalance (70 percent of the population is expatriate) "unnatural invasion"; she has also opined that expatriates should be charged for "the air they breathe" in Kuwait.[7] Some measures to shift the burden onto expatriates include the introduction of new healthcare costs for nonnationals, parliamentary approval to place fees on remittances, the introduction of fees on companies that employ "excess" foreigners (more than 50 percent of their total workforce), and an increase in work permit and transfer fees for expatriate workers.[8] Meanwhile, in 2017, parliament approved amendments to increase the number of holiday entitlements for both public and private sector employees, as well as the termination of thousands of expatriates from the public sector to hit Kuwaitization targets.[9]

In Oman, which faced localized protests during the Arab Spring, primarily surrounding issues related to rising costs of living, the parliament pledged to create 33,000 new jobs in 2015 despite calls for austerity.[10] Furthermore, in 2017, the Shura Council was accused of not urgently seeking to implement austerity measures.[11] Municipal elections in 2017 indicated discontent with austerity measures or plans and thus resulted in a surprisingly high turnover among elected officials.[12] In 2019, the National Fuel Subsidy System raised the system's minimum salary requirements, making some 69 percent of working Omanis eligible for an exemption; there is no such relief even for low-earning expatriates.[13] Having seen unwillingness in the Shura Council and in the municipal council to implement austerity measures, the government thus appears to have delayed their application, instead granting more support for the citizenry.

In 2016, as part of the introduction of austerity measures, Qatar raised gasoline prices and increased the price of residential electricity and water as well as the cost of postal services. The country's Central Municipal Council (CMC), an advisory body that has no binding decisionmaking power, actually recommended in 2018 that state support of expatriates be included in public distributions that currently go only to Qataris, since food prices increased after the blockade.[14] The blockade delayed the implementation of VAT and other proposed measures to further austerity beyond the removal of subsidies. There has, however, been considerable discussion of social issues, such as gender segregation, in the country's municipal council in the absence of concern about the immediate implementation of austerity measures.[15]

While Saudi Arabia lacks an elected parliament, it does house partially elected municipal councils, which have very limited decisionmaking power and focus on local issues such as street maintenance. These bodies have not been the site of public debate about austerity, although some measures were scaled back after their introduction proved unpopular, demonstrating their utility as indicators of public opinion. In April 2017, King Salman famously restored financial allowances to civil servants and military personnel that had previously been removed as part of austerity measures in September 2016 after a general outcry, particularly on social media.[16] Although elected bodies may not be the mechanism through which public opinion is filtered in the kingdom, popular sentiment has still been taken into account when it comes to the scaling back of austerity measures.

In the UAE, where VAT and subsidy reductions have been introduced, the elected Federal National Council (FNC) in 2015 asked for a reduction in fuel prices.[17] Even before the oil price drop in 2014, the FNC in 2013 asked the cabinet to exempt some citizens from water and electricity bills, likely because of the disparity in wealth across the seven constituent emirates.[18] Complaints about electricity shortages still arise from some of the smaller and poorer emirates, demonstrating the extent to which the effect of austerity measures is by no means uniform across the UAE.[19] Nonetheless, the FNC has at least provided a site for debate about the implementation of such measures

Conclusions

Four main policy-relevant conclusions can be drawn from this analysis. First, the elected bodies of the GCC are not just rubberstamp assemblies, particularly when it comes to control of the purse. And although they can protect disbursements, they do much more—such as seeking to scale back plans for austerity and, as I have discussed elsewhere, in some instances, to protect conservative social policies.[20]

Second, the necessary political reforms will not happen through the imposition of large-scale reforms. Large-scale plans are easy to implement, with or without politically powerful elected bodies. Piecemeal and slower change, such as the gradual reduction of subsidies, is more likely to succeed.

Third, the countries' large-scale economic reform visions would have broad-ranging effects on the citizen and expatriate residents of the GCC, yet expatriates remain largely unable to participate in these debates, despite the fact that they constitute substantial populations in these countries. If, for instance, the cost of living becomes too high with the lifting of subsidies, they could relocate, which would be problematic for states that rely on these populations, particularly in the construction sector. It is important, then, for austerity measures to take into account and protect the most economically vulnerable populations, whether citizen or expatriate. The forced departure of expatriates from the GCC in the wake of the pandemic and resultant economic contraction has made it clear how precarious their positions have been in these states, and some GCC nationals have been important in documenting problems with existing labor arrangements in their countries.[21]

Fourth, public opinion, of course, is not solely discerned through legislative or other elected bodies in the GCC, but rather through uninstitutionalized meetings like majlis and diwaniyat (information discussion groups) or through social media, as illustrated most clearly in Saudi Arabia. Looking at elected bodies in these states therefore gives us a limited, yet valuable, glimpse into the ongoing debates about government performance, particularly on the economy; the less institutionalized voices of public opinion about austerity should therefore also be sought.

Notes

1. Jamie Etheridge, Simeon Kerr, and Andrew England, "'They Want Us to Leave'—Foreign Workers under Pressure in the Gulf," *Financial Times*, July 28, 2020 (https://www.ft.com/content/77c2d7db-0ade-4665-9cb8-c82b72c2da66).

2. Reuters, "Bahrain Rejects Parliament's Subsidy Reform Plan," *Gulf News*, August 2, 2018 (https://gulfnews.com/world/gulf/bahrain/bahrain-rejects-parliaments-subsidy-reform-plan-1.2260846).

3. "Bahrain Scraps Subsidy Reforms Despite IMF Push to Introduce Austerity Measures," *Arabian Business*, May 8, 2019 (www.arabianbusiness.com/politics-economics/419563-bahrain-scraps-subsidy-reforms-despite-imf-push-to-introduce-austerity-measures).

4. Ibid.; Kristin Smith Diwan, "Bahrain's Carefully Managed Elections Remake Parliament," Arab Gulf States Institute in Washington (AGSIW) (blog), December 3, 2018 (https://agsiw.org/bahrains-carefully-managed-elections-remake-parliament/).

5. Aziz El Yaakoubi, "Bahrain Ditches Subsidy Reform Plan as Political Tensions Simmer," Reuters, May 7, 2019 (www.reuters.com/article/bahrain-economy/bahrain-ditches-subsidy-reform-plan-as-political-tensions-simmer-idUSL5N22J6DF).

6. Reuters, "Kuwait to Postpone VAT Implementation to 2021, Says Parliament Committee," May 15, 2018 (https://uk.reuters.com/article/us-kuwait-economy-tax/kuwait-to-postpone-vat-implementation-to-2021-says-parliament-committee-idUKKCN1IG0OW); The Economist Intelligence Unit, "Government Makes Subsidy Cuts," January 12, 2016 (www.eiu.com/industry/article/713847255/government-makes-subsidy-cuts/2016-01-12).

7. Ahmed Al-Naqeeb, "MP Safa Al Hashem Renews Call to Tax Expats Pockets, Tap Remittances," *Arab Times*, September 15, 2019 (www.arabtimesonline.com/news/mp-safa-al-hashem-renews-call-to-tax-expats-pockets-tap-remittances/); "Kuwaiti MP Reportedly Receives 'Death Threat' for Anti-Expat Remarks," *Gulf Business*, September 18, 2019 (https://gulfbusiness.com/kuwaiti-mp-reportedly-receives-death-threat-anti-expat-remarks/).

8. "Ministry Announces Expat Health Fees Increase Today," *Kuwait Times*, January 9, 2017 (https://news.kuwaittimes.net/website/ministry-announces-expat-health-fees-increase-today/); "Kuwait Parliament Committee Approves Fees on Remittance by Expatriates," *The Peninsula*, April 2, 2018 (https://thepeninsulaqatar.com/article/02/04/2018/Kuwait-parliament-committee-approves-fees-on-remittance-by-expatriates); "Kuwait Introduces New $830 Fee for Companies Employing 'Excess' Foreigners," *Gulf Business*, September 5, 2017 (https://gulfbusiness.com/kuwait-introduces-new-830-fee-companies-employing-excess-foreigners/); B. Izzak, "Work Permit, Transfer Fees Raised up to KD 50—All Kuwaitis, Farms, Industries Exempt from New Power Tariffs," *Kuwait Times*, April 19, 2016 (https://news.kuwaittimes.net/website/work-permit-transfer-fees-raised-kd-50/).

9. "Kuwait's Parliament Approves Expansion of Leave Allowance for Workers," *Gulf Business*, June 7, 2017 (https://gulfbusiness.com/kuwaits-parliament-approves -expansion-leave-allowance-workers/); "Kuwait: Around 5,600 Expats Terminated from Public Sector," *Gulf Insider*, May 3, 2019 (www.gulf-insider.com/kuwait-around -5600-expats-terminated-from-public-sector/).

10. "Oman Rejects Austerity Culture with Mass Job Creation," *New Arab*, December 29, 2015 (www.alaraby.co.uk/english/news/2015/12/29/oman-rejects-austerity -culture-with-mass-job-creation).

11. Robert Anderson, "Oman's Majlis Al Shura Accused of a Lack of Urgency for Austerity," *Gulf Business*, July 5, 2016 (https://gulfbusiness.com/omans-majlis-al-shura -accused-lack-urgency-austerity/).

12. Scott J. Weiner, "Oman's Municipal Elections Reveal Frustration with Austerity Program," AGSIW (blog), January 4, 2017 (https://agsiw.org/omans-municipal -elections-reveal-frustration-austerity-program/).

13. "Fuel Subsidies Net Widened for Omanis," *Times of Oman*, June 11, 2018 (https://timesofoman.com/article/136293/Oman/Oman-widens-fuel-subsidy-net-for -citizens).

14. "Include Expats on Public Distribution System: CMC," *Qatar Tribune*, January 31, 2018 (www.qatar-tribune.com/news-details/id/109470).

15. Courtney Freer, "Clients or Challengers?: Tribal Constituents in Kuwait, Qatar, and the UAE," *British Journal of Middle Eastern Studies* (2019): pp. 13–14 (https:// doi.org/10.1080/13530194.2019.1605881).

16. Reuters, "Saudi King Restores Civil Servant and Military Allowances Cut under Austerity: State TV," April 22, 2017 (https://uk.reuters.com/article/us-saudi -economy/saudi-king-restores-civil-servant-and-military-allowances-cut-under -austerity-state-tv-idUKKBN17O0MS).

17. Andy Staples, "Fuel Subsidies Cost UAE $2,378 per Person per Year," *Gulf News*, July 22, 2015 (https://gulfnews.com/business/energy/fuel-subsidies-cost-uae -2378-per-person-per-year-1.1554736).

18. Samir Salama, "Cabinet Turns Down FNC Requests for Utility Bill Exemption, Subsidies," *Gulf News*, November 12, 2013 (https://gulfnews.com/uae/govern ment/cabinet-turns-down-fnc-requests-for-utiltiy-bill-exemption-subsidies-1 .1254292).

19. Salam Al Amir, "Ajman Residents Plagued by Power Cuts Issue Plea for Help," *The National*, September 20, 2019 (www.thenational.ae/uae/ajman-residents-plagued -by-power-cuts-issue-plea-for-help-1.912356).

20. Freer, "Clients or Challengers?"

21. See, for instance, Mai Al-Nakib, "I Banish You: Reflections on Kuwait," *Los Angeles Review of Books* (blog), August 6, 2020 (https://blog.lareviewofbooks.org/essays /banish-reflections-kuwait/).

TWENTY FOUR

The True Jihad

Art and Social Change in Saudi Arabia

SEAN FOLEY

That is your role as an artist, to bring out the option that the politician can't say and that the religious man can't say . . . You bring out the solutions that people can't say.

—Abdulnasser Gharem

I'm an artist, and the artist's essential role is to reveal society's challenges. . . . Warning the people about ISIS is the true jihad, because we're fighting them with art not war.

—Nasser al-Qasabi

ON DECEMBER 23, 2019, Saudi Arabia's public prosecutor announced that five people had been sentenced to death and three others to jail for the murder of journalist Jamal Khashoggi in the Saudi consulate in Istanbul.[1] Among the prominent Saudis who had been linked to the murder but who was cleared by the state prosecutor was Saud al-Qahtani, a former adviser to Saudi Crown Prince Mohammad bin Salman (MBS). Later that day a lengthy poem—written in the nabati style of the Arabian peninsula—appeared on

Twitter attributed to Al-Qahtani; it declared his innocence, chastised his enemies, expressed his anger and outrage over his treatment over the past year, and praised MBS and King Salman.[2]

Entitled "Declared Innocent by He Who Judges Us All," Al-Qahtani's poem reminds us of the place of nabati poetry and the spoken word generally in Saudi society and the wider Gulf—a phenomenon that has received significant scholarly attention over the years.[3] Katrien Vanpee's work in particular demonstrates how nabati poetry has, in recent years, become a distinctly Khaleeji art form, especially since the inception of the Sha'ir al-Milyun television program.[4] By contrast, most scholars have overlooked other forms of cultural production in a country that has been dismissed as "despising" art.[5] While there are Saudis who have expressed similar views, MBS has not, and, ironically, Khashoggi did not.[6] These men, along with other key members of the kingdom's elite, have embraced the visual arts, comedy, film, and other artistic genres as critical drivers of social change. The country's creative class seeks to express the views of the Saudi masses while proposing new ways to discuss vexing challenges—a process that allows them to, in the words of Saudi artist Abdulnasser Gharem, "bring out solutions" in ways that clerics, politicians, and others cannot do in the twenty-first century.[7]

At the start of this century, Prince Khalid al-Faisal, governor of Asir in southern Saudi Arabia, sponsored new cultural institutions to combat what he saw as dangerous extremism in Saudi society while educating the people of the kingdom's south, four of whom participated in the September 11, 2001, terrorist attacks.[8] At one of those new institutions, the Al-Meftaha Arts Village, a group of young professionals were introduced by Jamal Khashoggi, then an editor of *Al-Watan*, (The Nation), a Saudi Arabic-language newspaper also sponsored by Prince Khalid.[9] These young men then started a majlis, a Saudi forum for group discussion, where they created a new Saudi model for creating art that discussed sensitive social issues.[10] Rather than utilizing the Western modern framework, in which an artist works in a studio as an individual and defines his or her works of art, they looked at artistic production as a group exercise where all of society could "have their own take" on a particular piece.[11]

Over time, this new approach allowed these artists to express the feelings and experiences of their society on key issues—from the dependence on oil exports to decaying infrastructure to the guardianship system—in ways that could not be replicated by academia, business, or the media. Collage and ambiguity were critical, for they allowed artists to include many (or even contradictory) viewpoints in their work and to explore sensitive topics while remaining effectively nonpartisan. But their refusal to take sides in key debates did not mean that they did not want their work to have an impact. Instead, they wanted to provoke a reaction, turning their art, to paraphrase Bertolt Brecht, into a "hammer with which to shape" their society.[12] As Gharem observed, art can be a "form of soft power" through which "you can change behavior."[13]

A decade after Gharem and his colleagues began their work in Asir, their movement had expanded across the country to include many additional men and women, including Khashoggi's two daughters. They also inspired a new generation of artists who were interested in stand-up comedy. These young Saudis believed that (a) existing Saudi modes of comedic self-expression failed to reflect the views of most of the country's society and (b) there was clear demand for cultural content that better reflected the values of Saudi society and could go beyond the limitations of their society's existing tools to voice social critique. They also used ambiguity to address multiple audiences simultaneously and saw their work as serving a higher purpose—namely, in the words of one comedian, encouraging "the viewer to critique and question, rather than passively receive."[14]

In the late 2000s, these comedians formed media companies that produced content for channels on YouTube—a platform that was then far less regulated than satellite or terrestrial television. Their videos often went viral and were extremely popular; one video got 59 million hits, a striking number for a country with a population of 30 million. Some of the comedic YouTube shows, such as "Lā Yektar" and "3al6ayer," became popular thanks to how they addressed corruption, religious extremism, terrorism, traffic problems, unemployment, and other important issues. "Al-Masāmīr," an adult comedic cartoon that addressed many of the same issues as the YouTube comedic shows, also earned a wide following. Notably, the comedians linked to these shows, such as Al-Masāmīr's Malik Nejer, became some of the most influential figures on Saudi social media.[15]

After YouTube's advertising policy changed in the late 2000s to allow the placement of ads within the videos posted on the site, these Saudi media companies became profitable thanks to partnerships with domestic and foreign companies to film commercials and to advertise in their videos. They used their newfound wealth to examine key social issues while transforming what was possible to discuss openly in society. A good example is "Hawājis" ("Concerns"), a satirical music video produced in late 2016 that starred a group of Saudi women singing in humorous sketches about the restrictions they faced in the kingdom.[16] The video, which has been viewed over

28 million times on YouTube, received extensive media coverage and was referenced when Saudi authorities announced in 2017 that they would lift the ban on women driving in the country. The announcement, which was made nine months to the day after Hawājis had been posted online, demonstrated that the Saudi creative class was a key barometer of the cultural and political winds in the country.

By that time, MBS had announced Vision 2030, his plan to reform the economy and end its dependence on oil exports. A central part of the reform program is to replace foreign workers with Saudis in the country's service industry, especially in culture and entertainment. Notably, the government wants Saudis to spend more of their entertainment money at home rather than abroad and to convince international investors that the country welcomes foreign investment.[17] The government created a Ministry of Culture and a General Entertainment Authority to publicize the arts and entertainment, and it has also promoted the country's creative class as a symbol of cultural openness and of a post-oil economy. Not only have Saudi media companies won significant new private investment, but private foundations and the government have funded prominent art exhibits and given prominent assignments to Saudi creatives.

Among the most important of the foundations that support the arts are Art Jameel, Mansouria Foundation for Culture and Creativity, the King Abdulaziz Center for World Culture (Ithra), and the Prince Mohammad bin Salman bin Abdulaziz Philanthropic Foundation (MiSK). Chaired by MBS, MiSK promotes goals that are analogous to those of leading creatives: encouraging creativity in society and promoting a new knowledge economy in keeping with Vision 2030.[18] And many of the country's leading creatives have formed close partnerships with MiSk and other similar organizations, including during the COVID-19 epidemic.

A good example is Ithra's initiative to train emerging Saudi and Saudi-based artists. As Laila al-Faddagh, the head of the Ithra Museum, told *Arab News* in August 2020, "One of our main pillars at Ithra is to support local talent, and now more than ever this kind of support is necessary. The world is going through a challenging time with the current crisis, and just like everyone else, artists and the cultural industry have been impacted by this pandemic."[19]

For his part, MBS has made clear that he personally supports Saudi artists and the vision they promote—even on projects not supported directly by Ithra, MiSK, or the Ministry of Culture. He had Ahmed Mater, one of the original artists in Asir, accompany him on a trip to China in 2016, where

Mater gave a painting of his celebrating Sino-Saudi ties to President Xi Jinping.[20] MBS has also weaved the messages of Saudi art into his speeches. In an address to an investment conference in Riyadh in late 2017, the crown prince referenced language from one of the central scenes of *Barakah Meets Barakah*—a Saudi romantic comedic movie that explores the challenges that young people face in a kingdom where there are limited opportunities for unrelated men and women to meet in person.[21]

The interest of MBS and other Saudi leaders in the country's creative class, however, has not stopped Saudi artists from building their institutions or producing works of art that speak on behalf of a changing society. In the feature-length 2020 cartoon movie, *Al-Masāmīr: The Film*, Nejer included Dana, a Saudi girl character, "who is passionate about robots and artificial intelligence," as one of the stars to augment Al-Masāmīr's overwhelmingly male cast.[22] As Nejer noted to the Saudi media, Dana allowed Al-Masāmīr "to keep pace with the changes witnessed by Saudi society," especially "the positive changes towards women that have occurred recently in the Kingdom."[23] Saudi comedian Nasser al-Qasabi has similarly kept pace with changes in Saudi society, including the rise of the Islamic State (IS) group and Saudi Arabia's dispute with Qatar. For their part, Gharem and Mater have founded studios and artistic incubators to "awaken" society while training a new generation of creatives.[24] Gharem and others have also continued to produce new works with potent messages. His *Prosperity without Growth* (2017) explores sectarianism through a pixelated piece that resembles a large ancient Greek mosaic at the center of which is a man on a throne wearing the clothing of a Sunni cleric and that of a Shīʿa cleric. In *The Safe*, Gharem uses a life-size white padded room to open a discussion about Khashoggi's murder. In September 2019, Gharem told Rebecca Anne Proctor that he had created *The Safe* to show that "dissident voices still exist" in Saudi Arabia and that modern art "could still come out of" the country.[25]

Even after the start of the COVID-19 epidemic in spring 2020, Saudi artists and other creatives continued to produce new works of art and strengthen their broader artistic community. *The Safe, Prosperity without Growth*, and other Gharem works appeared as part of *Smart Obedience*, his show in Berlin, Germany, which ran from September 2020 to November 2020.[26] As Mater told the Smithsonian's Carol Huh in an October 2020 interview, he is working on a new artistic project to document the history of Saudi Arabia.[27] He has also donated *Magnetism*, one of his most acclaimed works, to The Future Is Unwritten's Healing Arts Auction series—a joint initiative between Christie's, the World Health Organization (WHO)

Foundation, and UN75. The initiative, the *Arab News* noted in October 2020, "supports artist-led projects 'that directly facilitate community healing and healthcare messaging in the aftermath of the pandemic.'"[28]

As Bernard Haykel observed in 2019 in the *Middle East Journal*, Saudi Arabia's vibrant cultural scene and its influence on the country "cannot be reduced, nor properly understood" by the "hoary themes of royals, oil, and Islam."[29] Instead, it reflects the intersection of patronage networks along with technology and the desire of creative Saudis to voice a grass-roots social discourse—one that reflects Saudi public opinion, draws on foreign and domestic sources, and explores various present and possible futures of the kingdom. Their work illustrates the wisdom of Pascal Ménoret's insight that Saudis, "long believed to be monolithic and mute," can engage in meaningful public debates.[30] These dynamics have long been overlooked, since Western social science, as Saudi comedian Fahad Albutairi has noted, views Saudi Arabia as a totalitarian place where conventional politics cannot exist.[31] Ultimately, art allows us to better understand those politics and develop new policies to address them, but only if we, in Gharem's words, "listen to the artist."[32]

Notes

1. Reuters, "Saudi Sentences Five to Death, Three to Jail in Khashoggi Case," CNBC, December 23, 2019 (www.cnbc.com/2019/12/23/saudi-sentences-five-to-death -three-to-jail-in-khashoggi-case.html).

2. Nabati poetry is a genre of vernacular Arabic poetry from the Gulf whose idioms and rules differ markedly from those of classical Arabic poetry. The genre dates back centuries and is mentioned in Ibn Khaldun's *Muqadima*. ArabLit Contributor, "The Intersections of Poetry and Politics in Saudi Arabia," *ArabLit Quarterly*, January 16, 2020 (https://arablit.org/2020/01/16/the-intersections-of-poetry-and-politics-in -saudi-arabia/).

3. For example, see, Saad Abdullah Sowayan, *Nabati Poetry: The Oral Poetry of Arabia* (University of California Press, 1985); Robyn Cresswell and Bernard Haykel, "Poetry in Jihadi Culture," in *Jihadi Culture: The Art and Social Practices of Militant Islamists*, edited by Thomas Hegghammer (Cambridge University Press, 2017), pp. 22–41; and Hatem al-Zahrani, "The Poet's Self-Image versus Authority in Arabic Poetry: Between Classical and Modern" (PhD diss., Georgetown University, 2019) (http://hdl .handle.net/10822/1055995).

4. For more on this phenomenon, see Katrien Vanpee, "Allegiance Performed: Waṭaniyyah Poetry on the Stage of the Shāʿir al-Milyūn Competition," *Journal of Arabic Literature* 50, no. 2 (2019), pp. 173–96 (https://doi.org/10.1163/1570064x-12341384).

5. Noah Feldman, "Taking It to the Street," *Wall Street Journal*, October 25, 2012.

6. Abdulsalam al-Wayel, "'An ihtiqarna al-Fann . . . fauz Muhammad 'Asaf baina al-Hadif wa al-Gabaran," *As-Sharq*, June 29, 2013 (www.alsharq.net.sa/2013/06/29 /880540).

7. Sean Foley, *Changing Saudi Arabia: Art, Culture, and Society in the Kingdom* (Boulder, Colo.: Lynne Rienner, 2019); Ben Hubbard, "Artist Nurtures a Creative Oasis in Conservative Saudi Arabia," *New York Times*, April 15, 2016.

8. Foley, *Changing Saudi Arabia*, pp. 37–39.

9. Jasmine Bager, "I'm a Young Saudi Journalist. Jamal Khashoggi's Disappearance Will Not Silence Us," *Time*, October 19, 2018.

10. Author in conversation with Ahmed Mater, January 2014.

11. Author in conversation with Adnan Manjal, January 2014.

12. Douglas Schuler, *Liberating Voices: A Pattern Language for Communication Revolution* (MIT Press, 2008), p. 392.

13. Abdulnasser Gharem, interview by Ángeles Espinosa, "El arte es una forma de 'poder blando," *El Pais*, June 30, 2019 (https://elpais.com/cultura/2019/06/25/actuali dad/1561456615_432146.html?id_externo_rsoc=TW_CM_CUL).

14. Abir Musakkis, "'Ali al-Kalthami wa Komidiya al-Yutiyub fi as-Sa'udiya," *As-Sharq Al-Ausat*, June 17, 2003, (http://archive.aawsat.com/details.asp?section=54& article=732761&issueno=12620#.WeF2CmhSxPZ).

15. Dania Saadi, "Embracing Arab Animation," *New York Times*, October 26, 2011; William Bauer, "The Five Must-Follow Saudi Twitter Accounts," *Your Middle East*, April 29, 2013 (www.yourmiddleeast.com/columns/article/the-five-mustfollow-saudi -twitter-accounts_12624).

16. "*Hawajis*," posted by Majed Alesa (@Majedalesa), December 23, 2016 (https:// twitter.com/8iesS/status/812357839188586496).

17. Manish Pandey, "BTS: Why Saudi Arabia Wants High Profile Pop Stars," BBC, July 15, 2019 (www.bbc.com/news/newsbeat-48935232).

18. For more on MiSK, see Foley, *Changing Saudi Arabia*, pp. 165–73.

19. Rebecca Anne Proctor, "Saudi Artist Aziz Jamal Discusses Ithra's Aims to Support Local Saudi Talent," *Arab News*, August 23, 2020 (www.arabnews.com/node /1723416/lifestyle).

20. Sean Foley, "When Oil Is Not Enough: Sino-Saudi Relations and Vision 2030," *Asian Journal of Middle Eastern and Islamic Studies* 11, no. 1 (2017), p. 120 (https:// doi.org/10.1080/25765949.2017.12023296).

21. Sam Meredith, "Saudi Arabia Promises a Return to 'Moderate Islam,'" CNBC, October 25, 2017 (www.cnbc.com/2017/10/25/saudi-arabia-promises-a-return-to -moderate-islam.html).

22. "Film as-Su'ūdīya Al-*Masāmīr* yajtāḥu ṣalāt al-Ḵalījiya wa al-'Arabiya," *Al-mowaten*, January 5, 2020 (http://bit.ly/38xZtNj).

23. "Film as-Su'ūdīya."

24. Hubbard, "Artist Nurtures a Creative Oasis."

25. Rebecca Anne Proctor, "'We Have Our Own Individual Voices': Saudi Artists Debate Their Place in the Kingdom as the West Becomes Wary of Its Commitment

to Progress" *Artnet News,* September 12, 2019 (https://news.artnet.com/art-world/saudi-arabia-artists-1646848).

26. John Quin, "Stick Figures & Robotic Systems: At Berlin Gallery Weekend," *The Quietus,* September 19, 2020 (https://thequietus.com/articles/28949-berlin-gallery-weekend-review-ugo-rondinone-olafur-eliasson-philippe-parreno-nina-canell).

27. "Join the Curator: Ahmed Mater," posted by the Smithsonian's National Museum of Asian Art, October 5, 2020 (www.youtube.com/watch?v=4WYCW9DftFc&feature=youtu.be&fbclid=IwAR19ztk2WS3LLuqoo73JME_hU_3CJaXwS0vyZYfOmOasdJt_LKUDFRwN8GQ).

28. "Saudi Artist Ahmed Mater's 'Magnetism' to Go under the Hammer in COVID-19 auction," *Arab News,* October 7, 2020 (https://arab.news/n5da5).

29. Bernard Haykel, "*Changing Saudi Arabia: Art, Culture, and Society in the Kingdom* by Sean Foley (review)," *Middle East Journal* 73, no. 4 (Winter 2019), p. 679 (https://muse.jhu.edu/article/745788/pdf).

30. Pascal Ménoret, "Saudi TV's Dangerous Hit," translated by Pascale Ghazaleh, *Le Monde diplomatique,* September 2004 (http://kit.mondediplo.com/spip.php?article3990).

31. Erika Solomon, "Saudi's First Stand-up Comic Fahad Albutairi on Humour and His Homeland," *Financial Times,* February 16, 2017 (www.ft.com/content/ba279240-f2bb-11e6-8758-6876151821a6).

32. Gharem, "El arte es una forma de 'poder blando.'"

TWENTY FIVE

Sectarianism in the Gulf

GENEIVE ABDO

ACROSS THE MIDDLE EAST, sectarian conflict between Shi'a and Sunni Muslims has escalated over the past two decades. Sectarianism in Bahrain and Saudi Arabia, in the form of policy, often comes from the top down—government to people. However, there is also bottom-up, grassroots sectarianism that is perpetuated by Sunni extremist groups, Shi'a militias, and clerics on both sides of the religious divide. Leaders in these groups are often called "sectarian entrepreneurs," meaning that they create religious divisions for their own political purposes. The top feeds on the bottom, and vice versa. In modern Middle Eastern history, sectarian conflict escalates when there are seismic shifts due to wars, revolutions, or other major disruptions. The 1979 Islamic Revolution in Iran sparked polarization between Shi'a and Sunni communities and states, as did the Iran-Iraq War (1990–1998), the Gulf War, the US-led invasion of Iraq in 2003, and the war in Syria, which began as a national uprising in 2011 to oust President Bashar Assad and then evolved into sectarian conflict. The Iranian revolution, which resulted in the first theocratic Shi'a state, in particular challenged the Saudi claim to speak not only for Sunni Islam, but for all Muslims.

Political scientists and other academics are divided over how to explain the surge in conflict and whether it is on the decline, after years of escalation. Some scholars are committed to a school of thought that believes politicized conflict is the primary driver and that religious difference has little role to play. Such conflict can involve nonstate actors as well as states, which are often engaged in geopolitical rivalries. Iran and Saudi Arabia, for example, are the main drivers of sectarian identification within societies. Certainly the Saudi and Bahraini governments have perpetuated anti-Iran and anti-Shi'a propaganda that have influenced their respective populations. As a result, in Bahrain, society has become more polarized than ever, with Shi'a and Sunni eating in separate restaurants, attending separate universities, and self-segregating in general. In Saudi Arabia, because most Shi'a are isolated in the eastern province, there is less self-segregation but a deep degree of state discrimination against the Shi'a.

The second school of thought identifies religious difference within the Islamic tradition as a key driver of sectarian conflict. I have argued elsewhere in books and articles, as part of this minority view, that even if state competition were to cease, the bottom-up sectarian conflict would continue because religion has become a factor in how Muslims in the Middle East self-identify and, as a result, a driver of political mobilization.[1] In countries such as Iraq and Lebanon, where confessional forms of government were implemented, sect is of primary importance. In Iraq, religion plays an important role in society, even though the peak of the sectarian conflict between 2006 and 2008 has subsided. Scholars who do not believe religion plays an important role argue that sectarian conflict in fact is declining in the Middle East, even as state competition between Iran and Saudi Arabia intensifies.[2]

Saudi Arabia is a prime example of both top-down, institutionalized sectarianism and its bottom-up variant. For decades, the Saudi government has marginalized its minority Shi'a population. Their geographic seclusion has led to higher unemployment among the Shi'a than in the country at large, even though they live in an oil-rich province, a source of great wealth for the government. Because they are secluded, they have no access to Sunni businesses in the private sector. The mistreatment of Shi'a citizens in Saudi Arabia has continued unabated, even three years (at the time of this writing) after Crown Prince Mohammad bin Salman (MBS) vowed to depart from decades of state-sponsored sectarian discrimination against the country's minority Shi'a population. According to Human Rights Watch and US government studies, the Shi'a are restricted from practicing religious rituals, and the authorities even remove food stands during religious commemorations during Ashura, an annual ten-day mourning period when Shi'a mark the death of their imam.[3] Thus, while MBS publicly claims to pursue a nationalistic Saudi identity, he implements policies that marginalize the Shi'a population.

Anti-Shi'a depictions also still exist in Saudi textbooks. And more important, even though MBS restricted access on television and social media to Sunni preachers who spouted anti-Shi'a discourse, especially during the height of the Syrian civil war, many living outside the country continue to express their sectarian ideas online.[4]

In addition, many Shi'a activists were imprisoned or killed for participating in the uprising against the government in 2011. The case of Abbas al Hassan is one of many examples. On April 23, 2019, officials in Saudi Arabia executed al Hassan, a Shi'a activist, for allegedly spying for Iran. That same day, thirty-seven other Saudis were reportedly executed, some of whom were punished for protests against the government. Before al Hassan's execution, the United Nations working group on arbitrary detention in February 2018 noted al Hassan's case and that of fourteen others who faced similar charges of committing treason "by engaging with Iranian intelligence contacts . . . and supporting the spread of Shi'a doctrine." The United Nations concluded that the case did not meet fair trial and due process guarantees. Al Hassan's body still has not been returned to his family, and his murder is often compared to that of Jamal Khashoggi, the Saudi dissident whose body was dismembered on Saudi government orders in the Saudi consulate in Istanbul in 2018.[5] Both men were perceived to be critics of the government, and MBS has proven to have a zero-tolerance policy for his opponents.

In Bahrain, located sixteen kilometers from the eastern coast of Saudi Arabia, and linked by the King Fahd Causeway, the Sunni monarchy ruling over a majority Shi'a population also practices institutionalized discrimination against its Shi'a citizens.[6] According to some reliable estimates, the population there is 68 percent Shi'a, 32 percent Sunni.

Saudi Arabia has long considered Bahrain its protectorate, and Bahraini government policy is often subject to Saudi approval. Particularly since the 1979 Islamic Revolution, government top-down discrimination against the Shi'a and bottom-up sectarian conflict were intertwined. During the early 1980s, Iran backed a coup attempt by a Tehran-based Bahraini opposition group to assassinate members of Bahrain's royal family. In the 1990s, another coup was planned from Tehran by a group called Bahrain Hezbollah. This history has provided the government with some legitimacy in the eyes of the Sunnis that domestic threats from Shi'a oppositionists are perpetually on the horizon.

Among the many discriminatory policies against Bahrain's Shi'a is the revocation of their citizenship.[7] The most prominent case is that of Sheikh

Isa Qassim, who led the 2011 uprising against the government and is the spiritual leader of the country's religious Shi'a community. In June 2016, Qassim, 82 years old, was charged with money laundering and verbally accused of working for Iranian interests. He was stripped of his citizenship. Qassim now lives in Mashhad, Iran, and his move to the Islamic Republic has given credibility to accusations by the Bahraini government that he supports Velyat e-Faqih—guardianship of the Islamic jurist. This system of governance places the clergy above the state and was one of the foundations of the 1979 Islamic Revolution. The Bahraini government has argued that Qassim and other opposition figures wish to impose this form of theocratic governance in Bahrain and overthrow the current ruling family.

At the same time that the government revoked Qassim's citizenship, the authorities banned the moderate Shi'a Islamist opposition group he led, al-Wefaq. There was little reason for the government to ban al-Wefaq. It was a peaceful political movement, and some Shi'a leaders at times served as deputies in parliament. For years the group fought for a democratic form of governance to replace the dictatorial monarchy. Qassim eventually left for London for medical treatment, and then moved to the holy city of Mashhad in Iran, where he lives today.

More broadly, much like the empty attempts taken by Saudi Arabia to curb sectarianism, the Bahraini government also appears to be taking steps to address discrimination, but in practice the discrimination continues. According to the US Commission on International Religious Freedom, a 2019 study on Bahrain showed an increase in the number of Shi'a stripped of their citizenship as well as an increase in the Bahraini Ministry of Interior's crackdowns on dissent. The ministry announced an investigation into international social media accounts that "encourage sedition and harm civil peace, social fabric and stability." Government authorities also demolished the headquarters of the opposition newspaper *al-Wasat*, which it had forcibly closed in 2017 for "sowing divisions." *Al-Wasat* was considered an objective source of information, according to Western organizations.[8]

One of the few studies ever conducted on the socioeconomic disparity shows that Bahraini Shi'a are 42 percent less likely than Sunni citizens with similar attributes to be employed in the public sector. Shi'a citizens also have greater difficulty accessing medical care. During several field trips to Bahrain between 2011 and 2015, I observed different hospitals designated for Shi'a and Sunni; the latter were reportedly better equipped with more qualified medical personnel.[9]

Figure 25-1. Levels of Sectarian Division and Conflict in the Middle East (2018)

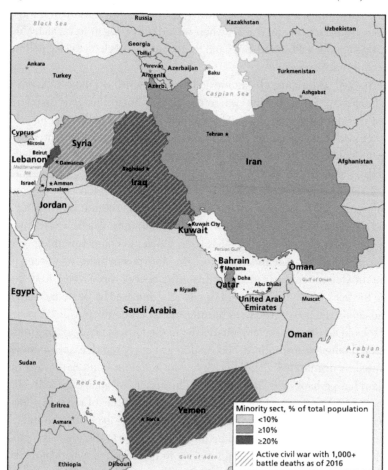

The measurements of whether sectarianism is declining or not are flawed. Absent the kind of bloody street fighting in Iraq and Syria between Shi'a and Sunni that occurred during the peak of wars in both countries, opinion surveys charting a decline must be viewed with caution for several reasons. Religious Muslims in the Middle East are often quick to deny religious differences, even though Islamists, such as Salafists, emphasize the difference between Shi'a and Sunni. Instead, ordinary people prefer to fall back on a narrative of many religions, including Muslims and Christians, coexisting peacefully. I have witnessed this first-hand while conducting interviews in the region since 2011, when sectarianism began to escalate. Yet surveys conducted by academics and think tank experts tend to take polling responses at face value.[10]

So, will sectarianism be an inevitable characteristic of the Middle East in the future? Probably. However, some studies point to changed conditions that could mitigate against it. A study by the RAND Corporation in 2019 concluded that geographic restructuring, civil society development, cross-sectarian interaction, and diminished gaps in socioeconomic disparity could all deescalate the conflict.[11]

Even if such monumental changes take place, the obstacle of religious difference will remain. Since the Revelation in the seventh century (CE) and the subsequent emergence of a distinct community of believers, Islam—its law, doctrine, and practice—has been subject to competing interpretations, adaptations, and understandings. In more recent times, beginning in the nineteenth century, much of this same energy was devoted to defining the faith within the context of "modernity" imposed by Western colonial and economic power. Today, in the aftermath of the Arab rebellions, many of the old constraints on religious debate in the form of dictatorial regimes, ossified religious institutions, and geopolitical proxy wars have been undermined or dismantled altogether. Space for religious contestation within Islam has perhaps never been greater. This has its advantages as well as its downside. What we might call the "democratization" of religion allows many more players—and particularly nonstate actors—to claim to be authorities at interpreting the faith. The downside is how to discern who is the religious authority. Is it the Sunni cleric in Saudi Arabia who claims the Shi'a are not *real* Muslims or the Shi'a militia commander leader in Iraq who is killing Sunnis?

Notes

1. Geneive Abdo, *The New Sectarianism: The Arab Uprisings and the Rebirth of the Shi'a-Sunni Divide* (Oxford University Press, 2017).

2. Justin Gengler, "Sectarianism from the Top Down or Bottom Up? Explaining the Middle East's Unlikely De-sectarianization after the Arab Spring," *Review of Faith & International Affairs* 18, no.1 (2020), pp. 109–13 (https://doi.org/10.1080/15570274 .2020.1729526).

3. Adam Coogle, "Saudi Arabia's 'Reforms' Don't Include Tolerance of Shia Community," Human Rights Watch, Dispatch, September 21, 2018 (www.hrw.org/news /2018/09/21/saudi-arabias-reforms-dont-include-tolerance-shia-community).

4. Geneive Abdo, and Abdallah Hendawy, "Saudi Arabia Is Trying to Contain the Spread of Salafism. It Won't work," *Washington Post*, December 20, 2017.

5. Agnes Callamard and others, "Mandates of the Special Rapporteur on extra-judicial, summary or arbitrary executions; the Working Group on Arbitrary Detention; the Special Rapporteur on the promotion and protection of the right to freedom of opinion and expression; the Special Rapporteur on the right of everyone to the en-joyment of the highest attainable standard of physical and mental health; the Spe-cial Rapporteur on the independence of judges and lawyers; the special rapporteur on freedom of religion or belief; the Special Rapporteur on the promotion and pro-tection of human rights and fundamental freedoms while countering terrorism and the Special Rapporteur on torture and other cruel, inhuman or degrading treatment or punishment," United Nations Human Rights Office of the High Commissioner, UA SAU 1/2018, February 8, 2018 (https://spcommreports.ohchr.org/TMResultsBase/DownLoadPublicCommunicationFile?gId=23639).

6. Scott Weiner, "Religious Freedom Conditions in Bahrain in 2019," United States Commission on International Religious Freedom, February 2020 (www.uscirf.gov/sites/default/files/2020%20Bahrain%20Country%20Update.pdf).

7. United Nations, Office of the High Commissioner for Human Rights, "Bah-rain Should Stop Persecution of Shi'a Muslims and Return Its Citizenship to Their Spiritual Leader," April 24, 2014, (www.ohchr.org/en/NewsEvents/Pages/DisplayNews.aspx?NewsID=14533&LangI%20D=E).

8. Human Rights Watch, "Bahrain: Only Independent Newspaper Shut Down," June 18, 2017, (www.hrw.org/news/2017/06/18/bahrain-only-independent-newspaper-shut-down); Weiner, "Religious Freedom Conditions in Bahrain in 2019."

9. Jeffrey Martini, Dalia Dassa Kaye, and Becca Wasser, eds., "Countering Sec-tarianism in the Middle East," RAND Corporation, Research Report, 2019 (www.rand.org/pubs/research_reports/RR2799.html).

10. David Pollock, "Sunnis and Shia in Bahrain: New Survey Shows Both Conflict and Consensus," Fikra Forum Policy Analysis (Washington Institute for Near East Policy, November 20, 2017), (www.washingtoninstitute.org/fikraforum/view/sunnis-and-shia-in-bahrain-new-survey-shows-both-conflict-and-consensus).

11. Jeffrey Martini, Dalia Dassa Kaye, and Becca Wasser, eds., "Countering Sec-tarianism in the Middle East: Lessons from Lebanon, Bahrain, Syria, and Iraq," RAND Corporation, Research Brief, 2019 (www.rand.org/pubs/research_briefs/RB10052.html).

PART 5

GEOSTRATEGIC CONCERNS

TWENTY SIX

A New Chapter for Intraregional Relations?

Cohesion, Crises, and Clashes in the GCC

YASMINA ABOUZZOHOUR

FORTY YEARS AFTER ITS founding, the Gulf Cooperation Council (GCC) is still reeling from the consequences of the Saudi and Emirati-led blockade against Qatar, and it may soon face an existential crisis as major challenges overrun member states' initial shared security perceptions, cultural and structural similarities, and security ties. Three main challenges threaten GCC cohesion and have led to disputes and crises over the past few decades: (1) Gulf monarchies' clashing ideologies and interests; (2) their reluctance to deepen ties owing to economic incompatibilities and political differences; and (3) their lack of structural integration. Yet the partial resolution of the 2017–2021 Gulf crisis offers these monarchies the opportunity not only to mend fences and improve bilateral ties, but also to address foreign policy differences and enact reforms to maximize their economic cohesion.

As a first step, Gulf decisionmakers must agree on the threat posed by major Middle East players such as Iran and Turkey. Neutral GCC members may also mediate a rapprochement between some of their neighbors and these major players. Failing this, GCC states could still salvage their economic relationship and promote deeper integration if they separate political ideology from economic cooperation. Finally, the GCC as an organization urgently requires structural reform, starting with the creation of an independent and authoritative supranational body in charge of overseeing coordination and refereeing intraregional conflicts. This would allow the organization to avoid full-blown diplomatic crises and would appease decisionmakers in neutral states who have expressed fear of retaliation from Gulf hegemons over disagreements.

Major Challenges

Within the GCC, ideological differences, conflicting interests, and economic incompatibility have slowed economic progress, stalled security cooperation, and led to major diplomatic crises. In fact, the organization never managed to establish a single currency or develop a customs union, despite years of planning.[1] Meanwhile, security cooperation has been undermined by disagreements between GCC states on major regional conflicts—including those in Yemen, Libya, and Syria—as well as by differing views on Iran and Turkey.

Foreign policy differences have also led to major crises between member states, such as in 2014, when Saudi Arabia, the United Arab Emirates (UAE), and Bahrain suspended ties with Qatar, which they accused of supporting the Muslim Brotherhood and promoting hostile media.[2] A more intense and long-lasting crisis took place from 2017 to 2021, triggered by similar drivers. The Saudi-Emirati axis suspended ties with and led a blockade against Qatar due to the latter's supposed interference in other GCC states' domestic politics, support of radical groups in the region, and close ties to regional rivals—all charges that Qatar denies.[3]

THREAT PERCEPTION

Clashing interests and ideologies between the Gulf monarchies have hindered intraregional cooperation, strained bilateral ties, and triggered clashes. Disagreements on Iran are generally linked to the different threat perceptions of GCC states, as well as their economic interests. On one side, Saudi Arabia, Bahrain, and to a lesser extent the UAE (one of Iran's largest trade partners) have maintained a hostile stance toward Tehran, which they view as a major threat to traditional monarchism and Sunni Islam in the region. This perceived threat is especially relevant to Bahrain, where the majority

Shi'a population has often clashed with the Sunni ruling family, and where the latter fears potential Iranian interference in its domestic affairs (although Iranian policymakers have not expressed formal support for Bahraini Shi'as so far).[4]

On the other side, Oman and Qatar enjoy cordial relations with Iran, while Kuwait has adopted a neutral stance. In fact, Oman—which has maintained strong economic ties with Iran since the Pahlavi era—played a major role in facilitating the Joint Comprehensive Plan of Action in 2015.[5] Qatar and Iran boast close economic ties, especially with respect to oil, gas, and shipping, and have established security agreements. Their relationship was further strengthened by the Gulf crisis, during which Iran provided Qatar with diplomatic and economic support and kept its airspace open to Qatari aircraft.

Despite a minor territorial dispute over the Al-Durra gas field and tensions related to Kuwait's support of Iraq during the Iran-Iraq War (1980–1988), Kuwait has sought to improve relations with Tehran while ensuring that it does not alienate its Gulf neighbors. In fact, unlike Riyadh and Abu Dhabi, Kuwait maintained formal ties with Iran after the breakdown of the Iran nuclear deal in 2017. This can be attributed to Kuwaiti decisionmakers' plan to boost the country's economy through the development of a megaproject that would border the Shatt al-Arab waterway (partially claimed by Iran). The urban center, Madinat al-Hareer, would potentially join China's Belt and Road Initiative. Once completed, it would connect the Silk Road's routes through Asia all the way to Iran. As a result, Kuwaiti decisionmakers seek Iran's support for the project.[6]

IDEOLOGICAL DIFFERENCES

The Arab uprisings further complicated intra-GCC relations, as Qatar generally favored revolutionary movements across the region, while Saudi Arabia and the UAE did not. This was perhaps most apparent in Libya, where Doha supported the United Nations–backed Government of National Accord, while the UAE supported Field Marshal Khalifa Hifter. In another example, Oman did not join the Saudi-led coalition in Yemen, while Qatar, which had joined at the onset of the war, left after the blockade was declared in 2017.

These differences triggered major clashes within the GCC, including the recent Gulf crisis, which was resolved by the signing of the Al-Ula declaration in January 2021. The Gulf crisis had far-reaching impacts on the

GCC as an organization. It led to the breakdown of ties between the involved states, stalled economic and security agreements, undermined the bloc's organizational structure, and stoked fear among neutral states such as Oman and Kuwait that they might suffer a similar fate as Qatar if they failed to fall in line with the Saudi-Emirati regional agenda.[7] These fears were exacerbated by the intensification of military coordination between Saudi Arabia and the UAE in 2018.[8]

DIVERGING INTERESTS

The GCC has strengthened economic cooperation between member states through common economic, energy, and infrastructure projects, as well as the creation in 2008 of a common internal market.[9] In the leadup to the 2017–2021 blockade, trade within the bloc increased significantly—from $48.6 billion in 2008 to $74.3 billion in 2017.[10] Yet several factors have hindered deeper intra-GCC integration, including some member states' reluctance to join an upgraded political and monetary union, share a common currency, or adopt a unionwide foreign policy.

Indeed, Oman, which had advocated for closer military cooperation in the 1990s, repeatedly vowed to leave any upgraded union after the 2011 uprisings, presumably to avoid straying from its neutral foreign policy—especially on Iran.[11] Similarly, Kuwait's neutral position on Iran and Turkey and its commitment to the Palestinian question puts its foreign policy at odds with that of Saudi Arabia and the UAE. Oman and Kuwait's refusal to cut ties with Qatar during the Gulf crisis was also a point of contention among GCC states.

Plans for a monetary union have highlighted intra-GCC divergences. Oman and the UAE refused to join the long-planned monetary union in 2006 and 2009, respectively. Although Kuwait remained committed to the plan—and formed a joint monetary council along with Saudi Arabia, Qatar, and Bahrain in 2010—it preemptively de-pegged its currency from the dollar in 2007, putting it at odds with its neighbors.[12] While the monetary union had been years in the making by 2010, the GCC had not yet addressed major problems related to common statistical measures and mobility of capital, trade, and workers.[13]

Furthermore, economic incompatibility and wealth inequality within the GCC may lead to tensions within the bloc. Major structural issues make Oman and Bahrain more economically vulnerable than the other Gulf monarchies; in fact, they have required financial aid from the GCC several times in the past decade.[14] This has presented a challenge to the union as wealthier members repeatedly bailed them out, most memorably through development packages during the 2011 uprisings. It also creates pressure on Omani policymakers who worry that aid will come with strings attached, especially after the death of Sultan Qaboos bin Said, who spearheaded Oman's neutral foreign policy.[15]

Finally, Saudi Arabia's role as a growing regional hegemon—given its large economy, population, and military—may strain its relationship with other GCC states, chief among them the UAE. While the two states are strong allies in foreign policy and have similar interests, they sometimes adopt slightly or moderately different stances on various geopolitical issues, such as normalization with Israel, the war in Yemen, and the Syrian civil war. Where they will most likely collide, however, is in business competition, as both attempt to reduce their overreliance on hydrocarbons through economic diversification. Saudi Arabia and the UAE are bound to compete for expertise and investment as they aim to develop similar sectors, including tourism, petrochemicals, and financial services. In February 2021, Riyadh announced that, starting in 2024, it would only give state contracts to companies based in the kingdom, thereby challenging Dubai's dominance as the Middle East and North Africa (MENA) region's financial capital.[16]

Outlook and Recommendations

Although partially resolved, the Gulf crisis will have far-reaching impacts on the GCC as an organization. The crisis has both shaken GCC members and threatened the bloc's credibility on the world stage. It has revealed the bloc's structural flaws and raised fears within certain member states that stronger neighbors may try to control them or sway their foreign policies. It has also highlighted major economic incompatibilities and different foreign policy goals within the organization. If the Gulf monarchies want to salvage the organization, they must prioritize major reforms.

First, the end of the blockade on Qatar presents an opportunity for GCC members to reconsider their foreign policy differences. Qatar can now join Oman as an apt mediator between its Gulf neighbors and Tehran. Failing successful mediation, the Gulf states must agree (to disagree) on the threat that the Iranian regime represents to them as an organization and as part of the broader MENA region. The Al-Ula declaration can also open the door for a rapprochement between Turkey, on one side, and Saudi Arabia and the UAE on the other.

Second, the GCC urgently requires major structural reform. It is highly problematic that there is no permanent judicial entity with the authority to resolve intraregional disputes or protect existing agreements in the event of an internal crisis. When the blockade cut off Qatar's land border, prior economic agreements such as the common market were affected. Despite the gravity of the situation, no existing structure was able to resolve the dispute, including the Supreme Council—the GCC's highest authority, which is composed of the monarchs of the six member states. In fact, the GCC's charter stipulates that the Supreme Council may refer such issues to the Commission of Settlement and Disputes, a nonpermanent body attached to the council that attempts to settle political and diplomatic disputes between member states.[17]

One major issue, however, is the extemporaneous nature of the process whereby the Supreme Council may establish "the composition of the Commission for every case on an 'ad hoc' basis."[18] Nonetheless, the process is not legally binding. The Commission does not have the authority to impose a ruling; it can merely submit recommendations to the Supreme Council. Member states can then follow these recommendations, ignore them, or move the case to the international level.

Importantly, despite the legal provision for the formation of a dispute settlement body, no such entity was established to resolve the Gulf crisis. In fact, there is no evidence that the provision has ever been implemented.[19] Instead of resolving intraregional conflict through formal processes at the organizational level, GCC states have tended to pursue individual initiatives—another major structural issue that must be addressed. Member states' unwillingness to rely on organizational processes, combined with the absence of a credible, independent, and authoritative conflict resolution mechanism, has created a need for individual or external efforts that bypass the GCC altogether. Oman and Kuwait's attempt to mediate between clashing parties during the Gulf crisis exemplifies this problem.

The Gulf crisis has also shed light on the problem of GCC-related decisionmaking taking place between some members. For example, Oman and Kuwait were not consulted by their neighbors before the blockade on Qatar was announced; the way in which the decision was reached, as well as the blockade itself, thus undermined the GCC's organizational structure.

These issues can be resolved through major structural change, driven by an independent and permanent supranational body within the GCC with the authority to oversee the organization's dealings, create or reform its structural mechanisms, referee intraregional conflicts before they turn into full-blown diplomatic crises, and check the influence of strong states. Importantly, this entity's decisions and recommendations must be legally binding. In addition to minimizing crises and increasing cohesion, the creation of such a body would appease Omani and Kuwaiti decisionmakers, who have worried about retaliation from the Saudi-Emirati bloc over their differences during the Gulf crisis.

Finally, and perhaps most important in a post-coronavirus era, intra-GCC relations can thrive under a model driven by economic interests, wherein member states would separate political ideology from economic cooperation. As a first step, the Gulf monarchies could refocus their efforts on creating the long-sought monetary union. Instead of focusing solely on establishing a unified currency, they also need to develop common monetary and fiscal policies (which could be facilitated through the creation of a regional system of central banks similar to the European system); achieve further economic convergence; increase intraregional trade; improve mobility of capital, trade, and workers; and take concrete steps to diversify their economies away from hydrocarbons. For these attempts to be successful, GCC member states would have to prioritize economic interests over political ideology. If this were achieved, deeper integration would take place despite political crises and independently of foreign policy. This option, however, is highly dependent on the will of Gulf leadership.

Notes

1. Angie Abdel Zaher, Dipasri Ghosh, and Dilip K. Ghosh, "Common Currency Unit for Gulf Cooperation Council: Is It Feasible?," *Review of Economics and Finance* 15 (2019), pp. 67–80 (www.bapress.ca/ref/ref-article/Common%20Currency%20Unit%20for%20Gulf%20Cooperation%20Council_Is%20it%20Feasible.pdf).

2. Yahya Mofreh Alzahrani, "Gulf Union: Imperative or Elective?," Al Jazeera Centre for Studies, March 2015 (https://studies.aljazeera.net/en/dossiers/2015/03/201533165858954762.html).

3. Matthias Sailer and Stephan Roll, "Three Scenarios for the Qatar Crisis: Regime Change, Resolution or Cold War in the Gulf," SWP Comments 25 (Stiftung Wissenschaft und Politik / German Institute for International and Security Affairs, July 2017) (https://nbn-resolving.org/urn:nbn:de:0168-ssoar-53553-8).

4. Nader Habibi, "The Impact of Sanctions on Iran-GCC Economic Relations," Middle East Brief 45 (Brandeis University Crown Center for Middle East Studies, November 2010) (www.brandeis.edu/crown/publications/middle-east-briefs/pdfs/1-100/meb45.pdf).

5. Cinzia Bianco, "The GCC Monarchies: Perceptions of the Iranian Threat amid Shifting Geopolitics," *International Spectator* 55, no. 2 (2020), pp. 92–107 (https://doi.org/10.1080/03932729.2020.1742505).

6. Habibi, "The Impact of Sanctions."

7. Jonathan Schanzer and Varsha Koduvayur, "Kuwait and Oman Are Stuck in Arab No Man's Land," *Foreign Policy*, June 14, 2018 (https://foreignpolicy.com/2018/06/14/kuwait-and-oman-are-stuck-in-the-arab-no-mans-land/).

8. United Arab Emirates Ministry of Energy and Infrastructure, "Saudi-Emirati Coordination Council" (www.moei.gov.ae/en/about-ministry/saudi-emirati-coordination-council.aspx?DisableResponsive=1).

9. Ashraf Mishrif and Salma Al-Naamani, "Regional Integration, the Private Sector and Diversification in the GCC Countries," in *Economic Diversification in The Gulf Region*, edited by Ashraf Mishrif and Yousuf Al Balushi (Singapore: Palgrave Macmillan, 2018), Volume 1, pp. 209–33.

10. United Nations Conference on Trade and Development, "Merchandise: Intra-Trade and Extra-Trade of Country Groups by Product, Annual" (https://unctadstat.unctad.org/wds/TableViewer/tableView.aspx?ReportId=24397).

11. Jeffrey Martini and others, "The Outlook for Arab Gulf Cooperation" Research Report (RAND Corporation, 2016) (https://doi.org/10.7249/RR1429); Joseph A. Kechichian, "The Gulf Security Pact: Another GCC Dilemma," *Al Jazeera*, February 24, 2014 (www.aljazeera.com/opinions/2014/2/24/the-gulf-security-pact-another-gcc-dilemma).

12. Robin Wigglesworth, "UAE Quits Gulf Monetary Union," *Financial Times*, May 20, 2009 (www.ft.com/content/822cab2e-4534-11de-b6c8-00144feabdc0).

13. Samir Salama and Zaher Bitar, "GCC Monetary Union Plan Will Not Fly," *Gulf News*, December 7, 2010 (https://gulfnews.com/world/gulf/gcc-monetary-union-plan-will-not-fly-1.724443).

14. Silvia Colombo, "The GCC and the Arab Spring: A Tale of Double Standards," *International Spectator* 47, no. 4 (2012), pp. 110–26 (https://doi.org/10.1080/03932729.2012.733199); Simeon Kerr, "Oman Gets $1bn in Aid from Qatar," *Financial Times*, October 28, 2020 (www.ft.com/content/8ba9e58f-3c66-45f3-8417-0cb39f3a9083); Oxford Analytica, "Oman and Bahrain Are the Most Vulnerable Gulf States," *Daily Brief*, May 6, 2020 (https://dailybrief.oxan.com/Analysis/DB252404/Oman-and-Bahrain-are-the-most-vulnerable-Gulf-states).

15. Fiona MacDonald, Turki Al Balushi, and Sylvia Westall, "Oman Weighs Seeking Financial Aid from Gulf Countries," Bloomberg, June 11, 2020 (www.bloomberg.com/news/articles/2020-06-11/oman-said-to-test-waters-for-aid-from-gulf-neighbors-amid-crisis?sref=GlDWwUQu); "Oman Looks for Aid in a Fraught GCC Where Strings Are Attached," *TRT World*, June 13, 2020 (www.trtworld.com/magazine/oman-looks-for-aid-in-a-fraught-gcc-where-strings-are-attached-37251).

16. Marwa Rashad, Davide Barbuscia, and Hadeel Al Sayegh, "Analysis: Saudi Arabia Eyes Dubai's Crown with HQ Ultimatum," Reuters, February 16, 2021 (www.reuters.com/article/us-saudi-economy-emirates-analysis-idUSKBN2AG1I5).

17. Secretariat General of the Gulf Cooperation Council, "The Charter: Article Ten" (www.gcc-sg.org/en-us/AboutGCC/Pages/Primarylaw.aspx).

18. Ibid.

19. Marco Pinfari, "Nothing but Failure? The Arab League and the Gulf Cooperation Council as Mediators in Middle Eastern Conflicts," Working Paper 45 (Crisis States Research Centre, March 2009) (www.files.ethz.ch/isn/98212/WP45.2.pdf).

TWENTY SEVEN

Rivalry for Export

The Gulf Crisis Goes to Africa

ZACH VERTIN

THE RUPTURE OF THE Gulf Cooperation Council (GCC) in 2017 polarized the Arabian Peninsula and forced difficult choices on antagonists and neutral parties alike. But the political, economic, and security impacts of the feud also extend well beyond the immediate region. In the wake of the crisis, as dueling states looked beyond the Gulf to advance their claims, affirm their legitimacy, or marginalize their adversaries, the feud was promptly exported abroad—most consequentially to the Horn of Africa. The Gulf Arab crisis catalyzed new geopolitical competition astride the Red Sea and has shaped events on its western shores, where African states have both welcomed new attention and struggled to manage the accompanying strife.

When the so-called Arab Quartet—Saudi Arabia, the United Arab Emirates (UAE), Egypt, and Bahrain—cut ties with neighboring Qatar in June 2017 and imposed an economic blockade, the opposing camps, which soon included Turkey, moved to secure friends, loyalties, and land on Africa's Red Sea coast.[1] In addition to pledging cash and investments, the antagonists snapped up rights to new commercial ports and military outposts on both sides of the Red Sea, keen to secure prized coastline in Djibouti, Eritrea, Somalia, and Sudan, as well as in Yemen.

The surge of new engagement in the Horn of Africa is most notably a product of the Gulf feud, but it is not the only motivating factor; nor did the trend begin in 2017. Recent Gulf interest dates to the Arab Spring, and especially the crisis in Egypt, as the tumultuous events of 2011 to 2013 deepened concerns about regime security at home. Gulf leaders responded by projecting influence beyond their immediate near-abroad, as the bounds of a perceived security complex expanded.[2] Soon thereafter, in 2014, Saudi and Emirati monarchies looked to buy influence in Sudan and Eritrea, concerned that Iran might establish a toehold in the Red Sea and leave them vulnerable on their western flank. A year later, the Saudi and Emirati sheikhs secured military perches on the African coast from which to launch assaults into Yemen, where the fight with Iranian-backed Houthis was intensifying.

Geoeconomics have also driven new engagement astride the Red Sea. The network of waterways connecting the Red Sea and Gulf of Aden to the Indian Ocean and the Mediterranean represents one of the most important shipping passages in the world. Each year tens of thousands of ships pass through the Bab al Mandab, the narrow strait separating the Horn and the Arabian Peninsula. Growing Chinese trade volume, born of China's Belt and Road Initiative, further raises the stakes for Gulf players, as do new opportunities to access consumer classes in Africa. The UAE, a global leader in port development and operation, hopes new port acquisitions and developments in the Horn, coupled with port stakes in Yemen, Jeddah, and Suez, will allow it not only to remain a relevant player in the years to come, but also to play a leading role in shaping the future of maritime trade across the region.

While the rush of Gulf engagement in the Horn of Africa has demonstrated huge potential for political integration and economic development among Red Sea states, it has also revealed how vulnerable the Horn—long beset by its own instability and proxy conflicts—is to external shocks. Some governments in the region have managed to manipulate external rivalries to serve their own domestic agendas, but most have suffered consequences. Amid a season of extraordinary political change in the Horn, the larger, more populous, and less-developed countries must find a way to capitalize on opportunities presented by new Gulf engagement without "surrendering their sovereignty or getting drawn into rivalries that offer little reward."[3]

Around the Horn

A tour around the Horn of Africa sheds light on the real, and perceived, effects of the Gulf feud to date, as well as on the potential implications for domestic and regional politics in the near future.

Nowhere did recent Gulf engagement cause more turbulence than in Somalia, a fragmented state that has long struggled to stand up a stable central government. Saudi Arabia, Turkey, Qatar, and the UAE have all been active in Somalia, hoping to secure political alliances, commercial contracts, and influence over Africa's longest coastline.[4] Somali politicians have proven adept at manipulating foreign interest to serve their individual agendas, but the Gulf rivalry has also introduced extraordinary stress and exacerbated tensions between Somalia's federal capital and its peripheries.

Turkey has been active in Somalia since 2011, well before the Gulf states showed interest, and its approach has won broad support among Somali citizens. Ankara began sending humanitarian aid during the country's 2011 famine, and Turkish businesses, goods, and schools soon followed. The Turkish government opened its largest foreign embassy in Mogadishu in 2016, and the doors of a new Turkish military training facility opened a year later. Regional rivals—including Egypt, Saudi Arabia, and the UAE—have signaled unease about Turkey's reach in Somalia, concerned that President Recep Tayyip Erdogan's investments reflect a wider effort to project "neo-Ottoman" influence across the empire's former territories.[5]

The UAE also invested in Somalia before the Gulf crisis, launching counterpiracy initiatives, training security forces, and making inroads with political elites. But the relationship soured in 2017 when President Mohamed Abdullahi Farmajo refused to sever ties with his Qatari backers or come out in support of the quartet's blockade. When he later accused UAE officials of interfering in the country's domestic affairs, Abu Dhabi promptly turned on the president and shifted its attention to Somalia's federal states.[6] Among other moves, it negotiated deals for an Emirati military base and seaports in the semi-autonomous regions of Somaliland and Puntland. The breakaway regions pledged public support for the quartet while Mogadishu condemned the UAE for violating its sovereignty.[7]

Critics complain that Farmajo has staked too much on his relationship to Doha, not least in elevating Fahad Yassin, a close Qatari confidant, to head the national intelligence and security agency. Fair or not, opponents suspect Qatari support for the duo's campaign to consolidate power—including by undermining rivals, weakening federal states, stacking government agencies with loyalists, and corrupting state institutions.[8]

In recent years, foreign observers have expressed hopes that Somalia, after decades of instability, might finally turn the corner. But as national elections approach, and institutional power struggles intensify, Somali candidates are again looking to external benefactors to help strengthen their positions at home; another poll marred by foreign influence and dueling financiers may well be in the offing.

ETHIOPIA

One stop to the west, Gulf states have put great personal faith in Abiy Ahmed, Ethiopia's 44-year-old prime minister. The charismatic leader ushered out the country's old guard in 2018 before ushering in a raft of sweeping reforms. Abiy won support around the globe for ending Ethiopia's state of emergency, opening space for journalists, appointing women to senior government positions, and pledging to privatize major industries. He also declared an end to two decades of conflict with neighboring Eritrea—for which he was awarded the Nobel Peace Prize. Abiy has initiated one of the world's most important political transitions, but also its most fragile, and both his vision and his tactics are the subject of intense debate.[9]

In Abiy, Gulf actors saw a partner who might bring stability to Ethiopia—the heavyweight of the region and the linchpin of politics and economics in the Horn. They also saw an opportunity to develop the country's infrastructure, link its 110 million landlocked consumers to Red Sea ports, and gain access to newly privatized industry contracts. The UAE pledged $3 billion in aid and investment in 2018, when Abiy needed it most, and later helped grease the rapprochement with Eritrea. Ceremonies marking the historic pact followed in Abu Dhabi and Jeddah in September 2018, and discussion of revitalized seaports, oil pipelines, and other investments ensued.[10]

Despite the new courtship, Abiy has taken deliberate steps to demonstrate his independence from dueling Gulf camps. Though he steered clear of Qatari engagement while fortifying ties with the UAE, Abiy later made an official visit to Qatar, in the spring of 2019, to discuss regional politics and investment promotion with the Qatari emir. Meanwhile, though Turkey's engagement in Ethiopia often garners less attention, Turkish business in the country not only exceeds its investments in neighboring Sudan and Somalia but is greater than in any other state in Africa.[11]

Abiy knows he must maneuver carefully to avoid being seen as reliant on, or beholden to, Gulf benefactors—especially given Ethiopia's Orthodox Christian establishment and long-standing concern about Muslim influence from abroad. This dynamic manifests in both domestic and foreign policy, as Ethiopian elites are wary of any Gulf state involvement in their ongoing dispute with Egypt—itself a benefactor of Saudi and Emirati largesse, over the erection of the Grand Ethiopian Renaissance Dam. Negotiations over the Nile River, and the $4 billion hydropower dam, touch core questions of politics, economics, and national identity in each state and, by extension, the countries of the entire Nile River basin.

More immediately, while Abiy's ascendance was accompanied by a sense optimism, the changing of the guard has also yielded ethnic violence, political turmoil, mass displacement, and a spike in ethno-nationalist rhetoric.[12] Despite high hopes for Abiy and his reformist rhetoric, opponents now argue that the much-acclaimed prime minister is relapsing into the heavy-handed governance of old. Ethiopia's transition is only beginning, and the road ahead will be rocky. Continued investment from wealthy Arab partners can aid the country's historic transition, but the long-term interests of both the Gulf states and Ethiopia will be best served if those investments are not focused on Abiy alone but are broadly distributed and account for the country's complex ethno-regional politics.[13]

ERITREA

President Isaias Afwerki's regime may have benefited most from Gulf engagement to date, and in serendipitous fashion. When Saudi Arabia and the UAE joined Yemen's war in 2015, the two coalition partners sought to establish a military facility in Djibouti, from which they could launch missions against Houthi fighters. But after a spectacular falling-out with Djiboutian authorities scuttled that plan, Riyadh and Abu Dhabi instead struck a basing deal with Isaias to use Eritrea's nearby port of Assab, from which UAE fighter jets and warships soon began launching attacks toward Yemen's port city of Aden—just 150 miles to the east.[14]

UAE officials also hope to redevelop Assab's defunct commercial port and make it the primary lifeline for its larger, and landlocked, neighbor, Ethiopia.[15] Asmara was reportedly offered cash, fuel, and infrastructure improvements in exchange.[16] More importantly, the partnership with Riyadh and Abu Dhabi helped bring Isaias in from the cold—including by legitimizing the peace pact with Ethiopia and supporting rescindment of UN sanctions against his long-ostracized regime.[17]

While détente between Ethiopia and Eritrea is cause for optimism, a host of thorny issues stand in the way of full normalization, and domestic politics in both countries are sure to complicate the best-laid plans. Meanwhile, Saudi and Emirati officials report having found Isaias a difficult and confusing ally. He stunned Emirati officials by refusing their offer to establish an embassy in Asmara and frustrated Saudi patrons by complicating Riyadh's effort to establish a Red Sea Council.[18] As elsewhere in the Horn, Gulf leaders should be cautious of investing too heavily in individuals: Isaias has long been the most unpredictable figure in the region, and without an external enemy in Ethiopia to justify his authoritarianism his grip on power may finally be loosening.[19]

SUDAN

Before succumbing to popular protests in 2019, President Omar al-Bashir had proved deft in courting foreign suitors. Having traded ideology and a political platform for a policy of survival, his opportunistic regime accepted paychecks from anyone offering. What he promised in exchange, however, was reliable only until a better offer presented itself. In the years preceding its eventual demise, Bashir's government courted Iran, Saudi Arabia, the UAE, Qatar, and Turkey—sometimes accepting concurrent financial support from dueling rivals.

Despite benefiting from crucial financial injections from Saudi Arabia and the UAE, Bashir's government opted not to support the blockade in 2017. He later fortified ties with Qatar and Turkey and infuriated neighbors by granting the Turks and Qataris port concessions on Sudan's Red Sea Coast. Saudi and Egyptian officials cried foul, again angered by the prospect of President Erdogan asserting influence on their borders.[20]

When Bashir's regime came under unprecedented pressure from protesters late in 2018, Riyadh and Abu Dhabi cut off their financial lifeline, hastened his demise, and moved quickly to pull Khartoum into their orbit. Emirati and Saudi leaders employed resources and muscle to engineer a new dispensation—one with a cooperative client committed to stabilizing the situation, suppressing Sudanese Islamists, and marginalizing Doha and Ankara.

But their heavy-handed interventions did not go down well on the streets of Khartoum, where popular protesters saw their movement for democratic change being hijacked.[21] Saudi and UAE officials eventually adjusted course, and Sudanese stakeholders agreed to appoint a hybrid civil-military government to guide the country through a three-year political transition.

After thirty years of corruption, violence, and misrule, Sudan's caretaker government faces a task both delicate and Herculean. Its success or failure will be hugely dependent on continued political and financial aid from all quarters, not least from the Gulf.[22] Gulf states can and should be part of shaping a positive outcome, but they must also be careful not to overplay their hands.

DJIBOUTI

The tiny state of Djibouti has also struggled to balance foreign relationships amid the Gulf feud and broader geopolitical changes across the Red Sea region—including the development of competing seaports, historic changes in neighboring Ethiopia and Eritrea, the war in Yemen, and great-power competition.[23] Djibouti has emerged as a centerpiece of new Red Sea competition, not only because of its existing deep-water ports complex, but because of its prime real estate at the nexus of the Red Sea and the Gulf of Aden, where billions of dollars of seaborne trade passes each day. In addition to hosting US, French, and Japanese military bases, Djiboutian officials welcomed China's establishment of its first overseas base in 2017; India, Russia, and Saudi Arabia have also signaled interest.

Djibouti puts a premium on its relationship with Saudi Arabia and, though it voiced public support for the Saudi-led quartet in 2017, and downgraded relations with Doha, Djiboutian officials later expressed private regret over that decision.[24] In addition to a subsequent row with the UAE and the expulsion of Emirati port operator DP World, Djibouti's public pronouncement prompted Qatar to withdraw 400 military observers it had stationed on Djibouti's border with Eritrea, the product of a 2010 ceasefire pact Doha negotiated between the two.

China's supplanting the UAE as Djibouti's main port partner also reflects the interplay between regional actors and global powers in the Red Sea and the wider Indian Ocean region. As Beijing drives an economic and infrastructure agenda—note its bankrolling of Djibouti's new multi-purpose port, a revamped rail link to Addis Ababa, free trade zones, and talk of hydrocarbon exploitation—Gulf states are variously cooperating and competing with China as they look to shape their own geoeconomic relationships with Beijing.[25]

Cooperation over Competition?

In 2017 and 2018, regional diplomats initiated a series of consultations toward creation of a so-called Red Sea forum—a collective through which Red Sea states might come together to discuss shared interests, identify emergent threats, and fashion common solutions.[26] Competing visions precipitated both collaboration and tension, as regional states felt each other out, testing different ideas about the ideal design for a forum, its membership, and its objectives.[27]

Then, in January 2020, officials in Riyadh announced the establishment of the Council of the Arab and African countries of the Red Sea and the Gulf of Aden, a collective comprising nine members: Djibouti, Egypt, Eritrea, Jordan, Saudi Arabia, Somalia, Sudan, Somalia, and Yemen. The inauguration of the council and its founding charter followed months of wrangling over differing visions. And while its creation is an important development, the nascent council exists largely on paper, which means opportunities remain to shape its character, composition, and agenda. Further development of the forum has since been curtailed by the COVID-19 pandemic; no meetings have been convened, and parallel work by interested institutions—including the African Union and Intergovernmental Authority on Development (IGAD)—to foster Red Sea multilateralism has stalled.

In the ideal Red Sea forum, African and Gulf states (and other partners, where appropriate) could together confront issues such as trade and infrastructure development, maritime security, mixed migration, labor and financial flows, and conflict management.[28] At a minimum, such a forum could raise the costs of destabilizing activity—including those resulting from Gulf rivalries—and provide African countries a platform to engage Gulf states on a more equal footing. Such a multilateral forum will not cure all ills, but it could offer this diverse group of stakeholders a venue to maximize opportunity and minimize risk in what might otherwise become a dangerously chaotic arena.[29] This best-case scenario for the Red Sea region is unlikely to be realized, however, as long as Middle Eastern rivalries and zero-sum posturing prevail.

Toward a New Transregional Order

The flurry of foreign activity in the Horn of Africa began to slow in late 2019, when newly engaged Gulf states (and Turkey) began reflecting on their interventions to date and on an altered geopolitical landscape. The onset of the COVID-19 pandemic then upended the foreign policy context altogether, as dual health and economic crises forced governments on both sides of the Red Sea to turn inward—and to reallocate resources. For the fragile governments of the Horn, several of which are navigating periods of profound political change, the pandemic is further testing what their already stretched societies can bear.

It is too soon to accurately appraise the long-term effects of the coronavirus on GCC engagement in the Horn of Africa and the wider Red Sea region, except to say that it will be shaped by a host of near-term challenges, including strains on public health capacity, fluctuations in global production and trade, intensified debt burdens, increased social pressure, diminished discretionary budgets and dwindling foreign direct investment, and limits on policymaking bandwidth.

Regardless of the pandemic's influence, the surge of new foreign engagement in the Horn of Africa—from feuding Gulf states, Turkey, and a wider field of foreign actors—has infused the region, and the adjacent seas, with greater geopolitical import. A new transregional order is in the making, though whether the Red Sea region becomes a zone of contest, or of cooperation, remains to be determined.[30] The prospects for political integration, economic development, and security cooperation astride this corridor are cause for optimism, and Gulf actors have a role to play in each. But if left unresolved, the GCC feud could undermine these aspirations and render this land and seascape dangerous for Gulf and Horn states alike.

Notes

This chapter was drafted in 2019. It draws on a body of research and analysis set forth by the author in a series of reports, opinions, and essays on Red Sea dynamics published from 2018 to 2019. It draws substantially, and in some cases directly, on the following works by the author: "Red Sea Rivalries: The Gulf States Are Playing a Dangerous Game in the Horn of Africa." Foreign Affairs, January 15, 2019 (www.foreignaffairs .com/articles/east-africa/2019-01-15/ red-sea-rivalries); "Red Sea Blueprints: Designing a Forum for Gulf and Horn States," Order from Chaos (blog), March 12, 2019 (www.brookings.edu/blog/order-from-chaos/2019/03/12/red-sea-blueprints/); "Turkey and the New Scramble for Africa: Ottoman Designs or Unfounded Fears?" Lawfare (blog),

May 19, 2019 (*www.lawfareblog.com/turkey-and-new-scramble-africa-ottoman-designs-or-unfounded-fears*); "*Red Sea Rivalries: The Gulf, the Horn, and the New Geopolitics of the Red Sea*," Report (Brookings Doha Center, June 2019) (*www.brookings.edu/wp-content/uploads/2019/06/Red-Sea-Rivalries.-The-Gulf-The-Horn-and-the-New-Geopolitics-of-the-Red-Sea-English-pdf.pdf*); "*Toward a Red Sea Forum: The Gulf, the Horn of Africa, and Architecture for a New Regional Order*," Analysis Paper 27 (Brookings Doha Center, November 2019) (*www.brookings.edu/wp-content/uploads/2019/11/Red_Sea_Forum_English_Web.pdf*); and "*Red Sea Geopolitics: Six Plotlines to Watch*," Lawfare (*blog*), December 15, 2019 (*www.lawfareblog.com/red-sea-geopolitics-six-plotlines-watch*).

The author would like to extend special thanks to Rebecca Lim, whose collaboration and contributions to this chapter were essential to its completion.

1. Turkey initially sought to remain neutral in the intra-Gulf row, but eventually came to Qatar's aid, providing food, water, supplies, and troops in the wake of the blockade. Willing or not, it has since been seen as an antagonist by the quartet countries. See Gulsen Solaker and Tom Finn, "Turkey Throws Support behind Qatar in Rift with Gulf Arabs," Reuters, June 7, 2017 (https://fr.reuters.com/article/us-gulf-qatar-turkey-idUSKBN18Y1E9); Vertin, "Red Sea Geopolitics."

2. Harry Verhoeven, "The Gulf and the Horn: Changing Geographies of Security Interdependence and Competing Visions of Regional Order," *Civil Wars* 3 (June 12, 2018), p. 349 (doi: 10.1080/13698249.2018.1483125).

3. Vertin, "Red Sea Rivalries."

4. Ibid.

5. Ibid.

6. In 2018, Somali security officials seized nearly $10 million in cash from an Emirati plane on the tarmac at Mogadishu airport and accused the UAE of intending to use the money to fund the federal government's political rivals. Alexander Cornwell and Noah Browning, "UAE Denounces Seizure of Cash and Plane in Somalia," Reuters, April 10, 2018 (www.zawya.com/uae/en/economy/story/UAE_denounces_seizure_of_cash_and_plane_in_Somalia-TR20180410nL8N1RN4OKX1/).

7. Jacqulyn Meyer Kantack, "The Gulf Contest for the Horn of Africa," *Critical Threats*, September 26, 2017 (www.criticalthreats.org/analysis/the-gulf-contest-for-the-horn-of-africa).

8. For example, see Abdulallahi Mohamed Ali, "Somalia Must Save Itself from Qatar," *National Interest*, June 22, 2020 (https://nationalinterest.org/feature/somalia-must-save-itself-qatar-163233).

9. Zach Vertin, "Alfred Nobel Catches 'Abiy-Mania': Praise and Caution for Ethiopia's Prize Winner," *Order from Chaos* (blog), October 15, 2019 (https://www.brookings.edu/blog/order-from-chaos/2019/10/15/alfred-nobel-catches-abiy-mania/).

10. Vertin, "Red Sea Geopolitics."

11. Figures as of 2018. Bilal Derso, "Africa: Ethiopia Tops Turkish Investment Destinations of Africa - EIC," *Ethiopian Herald*, January 31, 2018 (https://allafrica.com/stories/201801310663.html).

12. Vertin, "Red Sea Geopolitics."

13. Ibid.

14. Ibid.

15. Ibid.

16. Alex Mello and Michael Knights, "West of Suez for the United Arab Emirates," *War on the Rocks*, September 2, 2016 (https://warontherocks.com/2016/09/west-of-suez-for-the-united-arab-emirates/).

17. Vertin, "Red Sea Rivalries:."

18. Senior diplomats, interviews with the author, Riyadh, Saudi Arabia, and Dubai, UAE, October 2019.

19. Vertin, "Red Sea Rivalries."

20. Vertin, "Turkey and the New Scramble for Africa."

21. Vertin, "Red Sea Geopolitics."

22. Ibid.

23. Vertin, "Toward a Red Sea Forum," p. 26.

24. Interviews with author, Djibouti, April 2018.

25. Vertin, "Toward a Red Sea Forum," p. 6.

26. Ibid., p. 1.

27. Ibid.

28. Vertin, "Red Sea Geopolitics."

29. Vertin, "Toward a Red Sea Forum," p. 2.

30. Ibid., p. 32.

TWENTY EIGHT

Is the Iran-Saudi Conflict Resolvable?

IBRAHIM FRAIHAT

AS THE MIDDLE EAST continues to fall deeper into political instability, the conflict between Iran and Saudi Arabia remains at the heart of most of the region's conflicts. Iran and Saudi Arabia are engaged in a zero-sum conflict with no clear way out of the chaos. Furthermore, the Trump administration played a significant role in pushing this conflict to the brink by imposing harsher sanctions on Iran and increasing arms sales to Saudi Arabia, making it difficult for the Biden administration to undo the damage.

This chapter argues that three factors are driving escalation of the conflict: security, sectarianism, and the involvement of the US administration. Nevertheless, the conflict remains resolvable despite its complexity. Addressing the security needs of both parties and reforming their conflict strategies, particularly on sectarianism and the balance between hard and soft power, is at the core of any prospective resolution of the conflict.

Security has been cited as a primary motivator of this conflict. Iran and Saudi Arabia are both caught up in a perception of encirclement.[1] Iran sees itself encircled by American bases from all sides, while Saudi Arabia perceives itself encircled by armed Iranian militias in Iraq, Syria, Lebanon, and Yemen. Iran responds with what Ali Vaez describes as a forward defense policy, based on deterring its enemies through the use of proxies.[2] However, said proxies clash with Saudi security needs, reinforcing the Saudis' perception of encirclement. Iran's foreign policy of arming militias in the Middle

East has undermined security in the region as Saudi Arabia fights to counter the Iranian encirclement.

The security dilemma was deepened by the US invasion of Iraq in 2003, which facilitated what Riyadh calls Iran's "expansionist policy" in the region by removing the Sunni-dominated government in Iran's arch enemy, Iraq, thereby allowing Iran's hegemon aspirations to guide its foreign policy. The shift of Iraq's position created an unbalanced regional order that Saudi Arabia hoped to balance again by overthrowing the Assad regime in Syria.

Another key aspect of security for Riyadh and Tehran is regime security, which Curtis R. Ryan argues is the key driver of alliance politics in the Middle East.[3] Both regimes need domestic and regional legitimacy to hold power. The Iranian revolution in 1979 brought to power Ayatollah Ruhollah Khomeini, who argued that Islam and hereditary kingship are incompatible and declared an intent to export the revolution outside Iran.[4] These actions serve the Saudi regime and give it legitimacy in fighting an external threat, thus consolidating internal unity. The Iranian regime, on the other hand, also linked its legitimacy within its own constituency to the fight against American hegemony in the region.

While security is the major cause of this conflict, sectarianism has been used as a convenient tool by both parties to advance their political agendas. The heavy manipulation of sectarianism has turned it from a tool into a cause for further conflict escalation and reinforcement of conflict drivers. Fanar Haddad states that both parties use sectarian divides as an instrument to mobilize domestic and regional support against the other.[5] While the debate over whether sectarianism's role is causal or merely instrumental may be unresolved, increased politicization of sectarianism reinforces Iranian-Saudi animosity. Regardless, sectarianism has caused structural rifts in societies where the Shi'a community enjoys a sizable presence, as in Iraq, Syria, and Bahrain. In Yemen, for example, sectarianism was hardly noticed before the Houthi rebellion in 2014. However, it will take Yemen years, or even decades, to undo the sectarian divide caused by the war between Saudi Arabia and the Houthis, Iran's proxy in Yemen.

The US intervention has severely affected this already tense situation, further escalating the conflict. Nothing has had a more escalatory impact on the conflict between Iran and Saudi Arabia in recent years than the 2015 Joint Comprehensive Plan of Action (JCPOA), also known the Iran nuclear deal, between Iran and the US-led 5 + 1 group. The Saudis felt excluded from the process and betrayed by their main security guarantor, the United States, which refused to consider Iran's foreign policy behavior in the negotiations. As a result, Iran gained more leverage and resources to keep meddling in affairs throughout the region.[6]

President Donald Trump withdrew from the nuclear deal, imposed the harshest sanctions ever on Iran, inflamed the arms race, and clashed with Iran on a number of occasions. Trump withdrew from the nuclear deal but failed miserably to bring Iran back to a new deal under his terms or curtail Tehran's nuclear activities.

Will President Joe Biden be able to undo the damage that Trump created? Not necessarily. First, the withdrawal from the deal raises serious trust issues; Iran has no guarantee that Biden or other future presidents will not back out of any new deal.[7] Second, it is difficult for Iran to compromise after the assassination in 2020 of national figures like Qassim Soleimani, commander of the Quds Forces, and Mohsen Fakhrizadeh, the head of Iran's nuclear project. Iranian officials have repeatedly vowed revenge, warning that these men's killers would "not be safe on earth."[8] Third, the removal of some of the sanctions that Trump imposed on Iran requires congressional approval, something that Biden cannot always rely on. The fact of the matter is that US involvement has exacerbated the conflict by creating additional layers of complexity with respect to security and sectarianism.

Insights for a Lasting Resolution

Although the conflict is complex, it is resolvable. This can be seen in at least two major areas: addressing security needs and reforming conflict strategies.

ADDRESSING SECURITY NEEDS

The US invasion of Iraq in 2003 and the subsequent shift in Baghdad's position toward Iran created a structural imbalance in the Middle East's regional order that must be addressed. The problem started in Iraq and can be solved in Iraq. Iran scholar Fatima al-Smadi argues that Saudi Arabia needs to take Iraq back to the "Arab side" because no rapprochement is possible without Iraq.[9] At the same time, Iran considers maintaining influence in Iraq to be an essential part of its national security strategy.

In fact, to restore the regional balance of power, Iraq needs to be independent from the influence of Iran and Saudi Arabia, as well as the United

States. Iraq must be for the Iraqis. A democratic, nonsectarian, and prosperous Iraq will address a key security dilemma. Given its geography and demographics (including its Sunni and Shi'a populations), Iraq is strongly positioned to play a bridging role between Iran and the wider region. Otherwise, Baghdad will continue to be a battleground for regional rivalry.

The United States' heavy presence in the Gulf and its role as the region's sole security vendor has led Saudi Arabia to a high level of "security dependency," making it vulnerable to political changes and developments in Washington. The Obama, Trump, and Biden administrations have each brought a distinct set of implications for Saudi Arabia's foreign policy, conflict with Iran, and security strategy. Saudi Arabia should develop its own security strategy and thus remain independent of changes brought about by US presidential elections.

Another aspect of rebalancing the regional order may be to expand the order itself. The inclusion of Turkey and Pakistan in the West Asia and North Africa (WANA) region could be beneficial. Jane Kinninmont explains that, with the rising interest of Asian powers, it is perhaps time to reconceptualize Gulf security not as the burden or asset of a superpower, but as a "global public good" that should be governed multilaterally.[10] Incorporating Turkey and Pakistan could create a new venue for building political alliances and potentially ending the polarization between Arabs and Iranians or Sunnis and Shi'as. Furthermore, integrating Iran, rather than confronting it, may have a better chance of rebalancing the regional order. Concessions of equal value from both sides—the inclusion of Iran in the region's political and economic structure, and Iran's scaling back its arming of militias—could reduce the existing tensions.

REFORMING CONFLICT STRATEGIES

Iran and Saudi Arabia rely on strategies characterized by security competition in the traditional form of an arms race, building up alliances, maximizing hard power, and overwhelming the other rival. By relying solely on hard power, each party is locking itself into a vicious cycle that will ultimately lead to a protracted stalemate. Both Iran and Saudi Arabia should seek to substantially revise their conflict strategies. This can be done in two areas: soft power strategy reform and sectarian policy reform.

SOFT POWER STRATEGY REFORM

Both parties need to invest in developing soft power in order to decrease their dependence on classic conflict strategies (for example, arms races). Iran's image in the region has seriously deteriorated, especially after its support of Assad in Syria.[11] Once a victim of chemical weapons during the Iran-Iraq War (1980–1988), Iran became a victimizer, finding itself in the same camp as the Assad regime, which allegedly used chemical weapons against its own people. The Iranian model and image are not appealing in the Arab world today, and the loss of soft power has been severe, particularly with respect to regional legitimacy. Building armed militias in the region is not the way for Iran to win the hearts and minds of the region's people. Rather than spreading instability in the region, Iran should seek to unite its rhetoric and build partnerships.

Saudi Arabia needs to rebrand itself in a way that advances transparency and good governance. Crown Prince Mohammad Bin Salman (MBS) engaged in reform in 2017 on several levels; however, this has been seen as merely a step to consolidate his power. MBS also arrested moderate popular clerics, a decision that Human Rights Watch called "politically motivated."[12] Since the September 11 attacks in the United States, nothing has damaged Saudi Arabia's image and undermined its soft power more than the murder of Saudi journalist Jamal Khashoggi. It will take Saudi Arabia's soft power years, if not decades, to recover from the damage that crime caused.

SECTARIAN POLICY REFORM

Iran needs to remove the sectarian components of its foreign policy, such as the idea that it "supports the oppressed," which may be seen as hypocritical given its support of the oppressor in Syria. The politicization of sectarianism causes the wider public in the Arab world to reject Iran's integration into the region. Iran should refrain from presenting itself as the guardian of the region's Shi'a communities, which only further strains the relationship between these communities and their fellow Sunni citizens, raising questions about their loyalty to their states. For example, many question whether Hezbollah's first loyalty is to Lebanon or Iran and whether the Houthis serve Yemen's national interest or *Velayat-e Faqih* (the rule of the Faqih).[13]

Saudi Arabia and other regional governments, on the other hand, should stop doubting the loyalties of their Shi'a communities, as doing so could become a self-fulfilling prophecy. Treating Saudi Shi'as as if they were loyal to Iran might actually lead them to become so. According to Jamal Khashoggi, the Wahhabi clergy in Saudi Arabia had been increasingly alienating the Shi'as with their rhetoric.[14] Saudi authorities need to engage with Shi'a communities in a genuine dialogue that addresses their social, political, economic, and religious grievances. Only by doing so can Saudi Arabia guarantee the full loyalty of Saudi Shi'as. A solidly built internal front is as important for Riyadh's conflict strategy as the arms race is for Iran's. As Simon Mabon states, "increasing tolerance will reduce the severity of internal security dilemmas driven by religious indifferences" and "remove an important degree of competition from the rivalry."[15]

Conclusion

Many factors affect this conflict, but security remains the major driving force behind its constant escalation over the past decade. Sectarianism is an intervening variable that the parties have manipulated to serve their own political agendas. The United States, and particularly the radical different approaches of the Obama, Trump, and Biden administrations, has put the conflict on a roller coaster, pushing it to high levels of chaos and uncertainty.

Despite the bleak prospects for resolving the conflict between Iran and Saudi Arabia, rapprochement remains a possibility. A starting point would be for the parties to finally acknowledge that their traditional conflict strategies—armed militias and arms races—have only escalated the conflict. They need to engage in serious policy reform that involves both investing in soft power and eliminating the politicization of sectarianism. Finally, the security dilemma cannot be resolved by an arms race or new leadership in the White House. A regional security strategy to fix the imbalance that the US invasion of Iraq created in 2003 will have to evolve from within the region.

Notes

This chapter is based on the author's most recent book, Iran and Saudi Arabia: Taming a Chaotic Conflict *(Edinburgh University Press, 2020)*

1. Imad Mansour, "Iran and Instability in the Middle East: How Preferences Influence the Regional Order," *International Journal* 63, no. 4 (Autumn 2008), pp. 941–64, 943 (www.jstor.org/stable/40204430).

2. Ali Vaez, interview, discussion, and email correspondence with the author, February 2016.

3. Curtis R. Ryan, "Regime Security and Shifting Alliances in the Middle East," in "The Qatar Crisis," Briefing 31 (Project on Middle East Political Science, October 2017), p. 35 (https://pomeps.org/wp-content/uploads/2017/10/POMEPS_GCC _Qatar-Crisis.pdf).

4. Raymond Hinnebusch, *International Politics of the Middle East* (Manchester University Press, 2015).

5. Fanar Haddad, *Sectarianism in Iraq: Antagonistic Visions of Unity* (Columbia University Press, 2011).

6. Shahram Akbarzadeh, "The Sectarian Divide in Iran-Saudi Relations," in *Foreign Policy of Iran under President Hassan Rouhani's First Term (2013–2017)*, edited by Luciano Zaccara (Singapore: Palgrave Macmillan, 2020).

7. Saheb Sadeghi, "How Biden Can Stop Iran's Conservatives from Undermining the Nuclear Deal," *Foreign Policy*, December 21, 2020 (https://foreignpolicy.com /2020/12/21/how-biden-can-stop-irans-conservatives-from-undermining-the-nuclear -deal/).

8. Robin Wright, "Biden Faces a Minefield in New Diplomacy with Iran," *New Yorker*, January 4, 2021 (https://www.newyorker.com/news/our-columnists/biden-faces -a-minefield-in-new-diplomacy-with-iran).

9. Fatima al-Smadi, interview and discussion with the author, Doha, Qatar, June 2015.

10. Jane Kinninmont, "Iran and the GCC: Unnecessary Insecurity," Research Paper (London: Chatham House, July 2015) (www.chathamhouse.org/sites/default /files/field/field_document/20150703IranGCCKinninmont.pdf).

11. Jessica Watkins, "Iran in Iraq: Soft Power after Soleimani," London School of Economics and Political Science (blog), January 8, 2020 (https://blogs.lse.ac.uk/mec /2020/01/08/iran-in-iraq-soft-power-after-soleimani/).

12. Human Rights Watch, "Saudi Arabia: Prominent Clerics Arrested," September 15, 2017 (www.hrw.org/news/2017/09/15/saudi-arabia-prominent-clerics-arrested).

13. Henner Fürtig, "Conflict and Cooperation in the Persian Gulf: The Interregional Order and US Policy," *Middle East Journal* 61, no. 4 (Autumn 2007), pp. 627–40 (www.jstor.org/stable/4330451).

14. Jamal Khashoggi, interview and discussion with author, Doha, Qatar, November 2015.

15. Simon Mabon, *Saudi Arabia and Iran: Soft Power Rivalry in the Middle East* (London: I. B. Tauris, 2013), pp. 219–21.

TWENTY NINE

GCC-Arab Relations

RAMI GEORGE KHOURI

FROM 2010 THROUGH 2019, the Gulf Cooperation Council (GCC) members pursued much bolder policies than usual. Saudi Arabia and the United Arab Emirates (UAE) in particular embraced unusually dynamic, often militarized, foreign policies, notably in Syria, Yemen, Qatar, Lebanon, Israel-Palestine, and Libya, which ranged from embarrassing failures to strategic innovations. The new, activist GCC foreign policies that project soft and hard power into other people's lands are also a trial-and-error learning process in how to conduct statecraft abroad.

The evolving foreign relations between the GCC and other Arab states are driven mainly by two countries—Saudi Arabia and the UAE—and four forces: (1) strong and lingering fears about domestic transitions toward democratic elections in Arab countries following the 2011–2013 and 2019–2020 uprisings; (2) a determination to do what is necessary to push back on expanding Iranian influence in the region (whether real, imagined, or exaggerated); (3) reactions to the UN Security Council (P5 + 1) nuclear agreement with Iran, and concerns that the United States was shifting its strategic focus to Asia and may no longer be as willing to protect GCC states; and (4) a realization that current GCC economic development policies, which are based on energy exports, are unsustainable in the medium to long term and that new strategic opportunities and relationships are required to create stable societies.

The GCC drive to preserve traditional Arab monarchic or autocratic governance systems and curtail Iranian ties across the region was initially a response to the 2011–2013 uprisings, in the wake of which Muslim Brotherhood parties won elections and assumed political leadership in Egypt and Tunisia. This trend became too close for comfort when large-scale demonstrations erupted in GCC member state Bahrain, which had to call in Saudi and Emirati military and financial assistance to quell the popular rebellion against the government.

The new Saudi-Emirati foreign policy was characterized by much dynamism, along with some militarism and adventurism, with Bahrain usually in tow; Qatar also experimented with a few economic, strategic, and infrastructural engagements abroad, including, reportedly, military assistance in Libya and Syria, while Oman and Kuwait pursued their traditionally cautious and conciliatory policies.

These new trends developed at a time when the Saudi and Emirati monarchies' leaders-in-waiting—Mohammad bin Salman and Mohammad bin Zayed Al Nahyan—were positioning themselves to assume power and assert that power more widely in the region. They were determined to show the world and their own people that they were neither helpless nor totally reliant on foreign protection, and could muster their significant financial, strategic, and military assets to take care of their own security needs. They would do this through dramatic foreign policy changes that instantly transformed their countries into strategic players in the region.

Saudi Arabia, the UAE, and some supportive Arab states like Egypt sought to preserve the prevailing monarchic political order that had defined the GCC for half a century, and to use whatever means they could to prevent Islamists or allies of Iran from assuming power through elections, rebellions, or other means. The Arab uprisings in the years 2012–2019 indicated, however, that the old political order they sought to preserve was widely rejected by many, and perhaps most, Arabs. The continuing popular uprisings in Sudan, Algeria, Lebanon, Iraq, and, to a lesser extent, Jordan and Morocco, suggest that the majority of Arab citizens do not aspire to the same top-heavy governance systems that some GCC countries work actively to preserve.

The Saudi-Emirati efforts to prevent the emergence of populist governance through protests and uprisings have been most evident in Egypt, Libya, Jordan, Bahrain, and Syria. This strategy, however, risks generating big new challenges for GCC leaders and the region as a whole. Preserving the old authoritarian bargain may only exacerbate the discontent and determination of citizenries agitating in the streets to change it, as witnessed in Algeria, Sudan, Lebanon, and Iraq; it could backfire by sparking even more turbulent uprisings or revolutions that favor more populist and democratic governance systems.

The Saudi-UAE-led war on Yemen has been the most dramatic use of military force in the Arab region—as well as the most glaring failure. By the end of 2019, political signs and troop redeployments indicated that the Saudis and Emiratis had recognized their unsuccessful attempt to showcase their military capabilities and had begun to explore how to end the war and reach a political agreement that would see the Ansarullah movement (Houthis) play a role in governance—precisely the outcome the war was supposed to prevent. Saudi-Emirati militarism also significantly strengthened Iran's military and political links with the Houthis, while leading the United States to sanction and criticize the Saudis for their destructive role in Yemen.

These events followed equally unsuccessful attempts by Saudi Arabia, the UAE, and Qatar, along with other private parties in other GCC states, to support the anti-Assad rebels in Syria. Alongside failed policies by the United States, European states, and other Arab states, these policies only stoked a much greater concentration of Islamist militants in Syria, expanded Hezbollah's military presence and prowess outside Lebanon, opened the door for a greater Russian and Iranian political and military presence in Syria and Iraq, and unleashed one of the most sorrowful refugee flows in modern Arab history. The UAE has now revived its diplomatic presence in Damascus and supports the government it had tried to topple.

The Saudi attempt to pressure the Lebanese government and people to marginalize Hezbollah included making promises of financial and military support to the government and backing the Sunni factions headed by Prime Minister Saad Hariri. In one bizarre episode the Saudis appear to have held Hariri in their country against his will and forced him to make a televised statement resigning his position and criticizing Hezbollah. This amateurish and impulsive Saudi policy backfired when Hariri returned to head a Hezbollah-backed government.

Some GCC states exported and militarized feuds that had lingered within the Gulf region, like the Qatar-UAE-Saudi tensions that erupted in the June 2017 embargo of Qatar by Saudi Arabia, the UAE, Bahrain, and Egypt. Qatari support for Libya's internationally recognized government and Saudi-UAE support for Khalifa Hifter's military drive to control the entire country represent a dramatic projection of GCC power abroad, irresponsibly fueling a faraway war that could expand into a bigger confrontation, given the involvement of Russia, France, and Turkey on opposing sides. One of the few GCC foreign interventions that worked was the Saudi-Emirati support for Egypt's field marshal-turned-president Abdel-Fattah el-Sissi in summer 2013, when he overthrew the elected government of President Mohamed Morsi. By 2015, this evolved into a joint regional strategy through which the UAE and Saudi Arabia sought the participation of Arab, Islamic, and other countries in various attempts to create a joint military force or to coordinate political and economic pressures against Iran and Islamist movements like the Muslim Brotherhood. By late 2019, perhaps owing to the wake-up call of the attack on the Abqaiq oil facility on September 14, Riyadh had toned down its failed and counterproductive anti-Iran rhetoric, and, along with the UAE leadership, seemed to be quietly exploring dialogue opportunities with Tehran.

A more positive dimension of GCC Arab policies has been the persistence of Saudi Arabia, the UAE, Qatar, Kuwait, and Oman in their traditional role as mediators and peacemakers. They have variously helped to launch negotiations and seal conflict-ending agreements in Lebanon, Eritrea, Ethiopia, Djibouti, Palestine, Sudan, Afghanistan, and elsewhere. Such mediation creates goodwill toward the GCC, a more stable neighborhood, and new opportunities for investments in trade and economic development.

The long-term impact of some GCC states' innovative and more muscular foreign policy moves remain unclear, because most of the dramatic initiatives have either failed or are still playing themselves out, often in fast-changing circumstances. One example of ongoing on-the-job-learning has been the unusual situation of some GCC states finding themselves supporting parties in other lands that are fighting each other, as happened in northern Syria and southern Yemen in 2019. Similarly, GCC leaders are learning that agreements that seem to offer them clear long-term strategic gains can be revoked quickly when other GCC states step in and offer their new partners better terms. This has happened several times in the Horn of Africa, where GCC states continue to offer local parties financial aid, infrastructural investments, training, and port management.

The direct involvement of three GCC states in several Arab and African countries in the Horn of Africa and Red Sea regions has been perhaps their most complex and multisectoral new foreign policy direction. Some analysts see these developments as reflecting competition between two broad camps for leverage in these regions: Turkey and Qatar in one camp, and Saudi Arabia, the UAE, and Egypt in the other. Most of these Arab/Middle Eastern states seek to promote their own long-term strategic, logistical, and economic interests, at a time when they see China actively promoting long-term economic expansion that they can benefit from.

The UAE, Qatar, and Saudi Arabia are the most active in this realm, often alongside or in competition with Turkey. Among the most important examples of these new foreign policy moves are:

- The UAE's on-and-off agreements to develop ports, free zones, military bases, and other facilities in Djibouti, Somalia, Puntland, Eritrea, and Somaliland.

- Qatar's on-and-off military observers in Djibouti; its long-term agreements in Sudan to develop ports, military, and utilities facilities, as well as mining, agricultural, and banking projects; and its agreement to develop ports and job-creation projects in Somalia.

- Saudi Arabia's financial aid and joint military exercises with Somalia and Sudan, military cooperation with Eritrea, access to a Djibouti military camp, and pledge to build a base in Djibouti.

Some GCC states, such as the UAE and Saudi Arabia, ventured further afield to gain allies in their disputes with Iran, including governments in Chad, Senegal, and Mauritania. The GCC states have had limited involvement or impact in North Africa beyond the war in Libya, though both Qatar and Saudi Arabia tried to woo the new Tunisian government after the 2011 regime was overthrown, and the UAE and Saudi Arabia offered significant financial aid to support the Sudanese regime of Omar al-Bashir and the generals who remained in power after his fall.

Simultaneously, GCC states that develop strategic ties with other Arab or African countries often try to win their new partners' support in their own GCC feuds, as happened after the 2017 blockade of Qatar. Some GCC states entered into complex relationships with other states, such as Turkey, which has also expanded into the Horn of Africa, opening embassies, military bases, and ports while increasing trade ties. As Turkey, Iran, and Israel pursue their regional policies in ways that they feel best serve their interests, some GCC states have indicated over the past decade that they wish to pursue similar paths and are now in the process of learning how through trial-and-error.

One other issue that led a few GCC states to explore foreign policy innovations was the obvious desire of Saudi Arabia, the UAE, and Bahrain to forge closer and more public ties with Israel. This was largely driven by the desire to support the long-promised but mysterious US "deal of the century" plan to resolve the Israeli-Palestinian conflict within the wider frame of Israeli-Arab relations. In 2019, Bahrain hosted a preliminary workshop involving Arabs, Israelis, and foreign states on promoting economic development in Palestine and the wider region as a first step toward a political process; the effort received only minor public support in the Arab region and internationally because it so obviously neglected the core political problems that had to be resolved before economic ties could be developed. It is unclear if this effort to forge more open ties between some GCC societies and Israel will be any more successful than formal contacts between GCC governments and Israel. The regional water research facility in Oman that includes Arab and Israeli experts continues to operate, however, suggesting the Arabs' willingness to resolve the conflict with Israel in a just and permanent manner that is anchored in international law and United Nations resolutions. To date, they have been less receptive to the US approach.

THIRTY

EU-GCC Relations

PERLA SROUR-GANDON

FOR CENTURIES, THE COUNTRIES of the European Union (EU) have enjoyed a natural relationship with their southern Mediterranean neighbors, with whom they share geographic and cultural ties. The relationship between the EU and the Gulf Cooperation Council (GCC) was established more recently, in the 1980s, a couple of years after the creation of the GCC organization in 1981. From the EU point of view, the GCC states were often referred to as "the neighbors of our neighbors," but this geographic distance is shrinking. GCC states and other regional players are increasing their influence in the EU's neighborhood directly to the south and on the African continent, where the European presence used to dominate. After 2011, this was the case in Egypt, Syria, Libya, and more recently in Somalia and Sudan. The EU is progressively revising its strategy toward the "wider Middle East," and more specifically toward the GCC, to allow for better engagement and cooperation. It will be materialized soon with the upcoming EU Joint Communication, announced by European Commission President Ursula von der Leyen and paving the way for reinforcing the strategic partnership.[1]

Initial exchanges between the EU and GCC began in 1983, but relations were formalized with the signature of the EU-GCC Cooperation Agreement in 1988.[2] The first articles of the Cooperation Agreement set the tone: it is aimed at enhancing economic cooperation. As mentioned in article 1, the agreement intends "to broaden and consolidate their economic and technical cooperation relations and also cooperation in energy, industry, trade and services, agriculture, fisheries, investment, science, technology and environment" and "to help strengthen the process of economic development and diversification of the GCC countries and so reinforce the role of the GCC in contributing to peace and stability in the region." Since then, GCC relations with the EU have always been tailored by region, with the intention both to facilitate economic and political relations and to strengthen stability in a region of strategic importance. It is important to note that the EU has inspired the GCC as a model of economic integration and cooperation among member states. However, attempts to form a "Gulf Union" that includes a common market, a common currency, and a customs union remain limited so far.

Before and despite the intra-GCC crisis, the EU and the GCC developed and have maintained a close relationship. On the political side, the EU and the GCC used to hold regular dialogues at the ministerial or senior official level. The last EU-GCC 26th Session of the Joint Council and Ministerial Meeting took place in Brussels, on February 21, 2022, and was cochaired by Josep Borrell, the EU High Representative/Vice President and His Highness Prince Faisal bin Farhan Al Saud, Minister of Foreign Affairs of the Kingdom of Saudi Arabia and chairman of the current session of the Ministerial Council of the GCC.[3] The previous Ministerial Meeting was held in May 2015 and was followed with the EU-GCC Joint Cooperation Committee meeting on April 4, 2016, in Riyadh. A senior officials meeting is also held annually to discuss EU-GCC relations and regional issues.

In other areas, relations have been intense, particularly in trade: the EU was still the primary trading partner of the six GCC states in 2017, and China was second. This circumstance might change in the near future as China is strongly positioning itself. To illustrate, one of the recent examples is the strengthening of China-United Arab Emirates (UAE) cooperation.[4] Although there are strong EU-GCC trade relations, it is important to note that a free trade agreement (FTA) between the two regions was initiated in 1990, but the GCC unilaterally suspended the FTA negotiations with the EU on December 29, 2008, mainly owing to the absence of a customs union within the GCC. In parallel with the political dialogue and the trade relationship, the EU and the GCC have developed strong technical cooperation through Joint Cooperation Committee meetings. In recent years, several projects and initiatives were launched, such as the former EU-GCC INCONET (scientific cooperation in research and innovation), the EU-GCC Macroeconomic Dialogue, and the EU-GCC Clean Energy Network. Further initiatives are being developed on economic diversification, climate change, business, cooperation in the security field, and public diplomacy.

The crisis among the GCC states began during a diplomatic rift in March 2014 between Qatar, on the one hand, and the Kingdom of Saudi Arabia, the UAE, Bahrain, and Egypt on the other. The three countries had withdrawn their ambassadors from Qatar on March 6, 2014, in response to Qatar's open support of the Muslim Brotherhood and criticism of Egypt's interim government. During the Riyadh Extraordinary GCC Summit of November 16, 2014, a reconciliation took place between Qatar and its neighbors (Saudi Arabia, Bahrain, and the UAE), putting a formal end to the dispute that had affected the GCC and allowing for the return of all three ambassadors to Doha. However, a more violent crisis exploded a couple of years later, in June 2017. Since then, the EU has adopted a neutral position. As indicated in several statements issued by the European External Action Service (EEAS), the EU supported the Kuwaiti mediation efforts, trusts that the crisis will be solved internally, and supports an intra-Gulf negotiated solution.[5] During the visit of the European Parliament Committee on Foreign Affairs to the GCC headquarters in Riyadh in February 2018, the chair praised the EU-GCC relationship.[6] The crisis could have contributed to a further destabilization of the whole Middle East region, as it is now combined with new challenges such as the coronavirus pandemic. The crisis also affected stability in several countries of the Horn of Africa, such as Somalia, Eritrea, and Sudan.[7] Libya is an additional example: France, the UAE, and Egypt supported Khalifa Hifter in the eastern parts of the country, Qatar and Turkey supported the internationally recognized government in the west. The risk of confrontation was real following Turkish military intervention in Libya in 2020.[8] The EU welcomed the full normalization of relations among themselves, signed at the GCC summit in the Saudi city of AlUla (Al-Ula) on January 5, 2021.[9]

Also, the COVID-19 crisis exacerbated further political and security challenges that have long prevented the effectiveness of the GCC. Therefore, GCC cohesion is more important than ever to fostering regional cooperation; unity within the GCC helps to promote regional cooperation, peace, and stability. Furthermore, deescalation in the region is vital, and cohesion will contribute to investor confidence, which can promote prosperity and additional investments.

Today, EU-GCC relations are at a crossroads, and the future of the relationship is evolving. Initially, relations were based on economic and trade engagement, but recent developments suggest that they will become more strategic, particularly on the security aspects. With this in mind, the EU has developed its diplomatic presence in the area. For many years, Saudi Arabia hosted the only EU delegation in Riyadh, covering diplomatic relations with Saudi Arabia, the GCC Secretariat, and the five other GCC countries. Aiming to increase its diplomatic presence in the region, the EU opened a delegation in Abu Dhabi in 2015; in Kuwait in July 2019; and the signing for a future diplomatic presence in Qatar took place in the margin of the EU-GCC 26th Session of the Joint Council and Ministerial Meeting in February 2022.[10] The diplomatic presence includes the reinforcement of staff within the EU delegations in specific fields of expertise (human rights, humanitarian aid/GCC donors, green transition, regional maritime security).

The EU is also developing bilateral ties with individual GCC states while maintaining multilateral relations in the framework of the GCC organization itself. To expand these bilateral relationships, the EU has signed several cooperation arrangements with Kuwait, the UAE, Qatar, and Oman. One strong aspect of this cooperation is to develop further economic diversification. As a result, all GCC countries have established, with different methods and different timeframes, diversification plans and visions. These reforms are crucial in order to reduce the heavy dependence of their economies on hydrocarbon revenues. The EU is keen to cooperate further with GCC countries in that field as highlighted during the recent ministerial meeting. GCC states hope to develop and modernize other sectors of their economies, such as tourism, healthcare, finance, infrastructure, and the green transition.

China continues to invest progressively in these fields and is proposing to assist the GCC. The EU should react quickly, as it could offer its strong knowledge and is well positioned to share its "lessons learned" experience in the area of economic diversification. Another crucial field in which the EU and the GCC should build cooperation is through the establishment of a regular dialogue on key human rights issues (such as the status of foreign workers, who constitute a large part of the population in GCC countries). Relatedly, EU-GCC relations need to account for the future aspirations of the growing GCC youth population; more than half of the population of the GCC is under the age of 30. However, the GCC youth population varies from country to country. The youth bulge (the population that is under the age of 25) ranges from 25 percent in Qatar to 50 percent in Oman. In the UAE it is 34 percent, 35 percent in Bahrain, 40 percent in Kuwait, and 46 percent in Saudi Arabia.[11] In addition, the GCC youth population is highly connected to social media and the digital world. On this future important challenge, the EU and the GCC could see an opportunity to cooperate further in supporting the region's youth population through economic empowerment, education, and job creation.

Notes

The information and views in this chapter are those of the author and do not necessarily reflect the official opinion of the European Union.

1. European Commission, "Joint Communication on the Partnership with the Gulf" (https://www.europarl.europa.eu/legislative-train/theme-a-stronger-europe-in-the-world/file-partnership-with-the-gulf).

2. European Economic Community and Countries Party to the Charter of the Cooperation Council for the Arab States of the Gulf, "EU-GCC Cooperation Agreement," 1988 (https://eeas.europa.eu/sites/eeas/files/tradoc_140300.pdf).

3. Council of the EU, "Co-Chairs' Statement - 26th EU-GCC Joint Council and Ministerial Meeting" (https://www.consilium.europa.eu/en/press/press-releases/2022/02/22/co-chairs-statement-26th-eu-gcc-joint-council-and-ministerial-meeting/).

4. Samir Salama, "UAE-China Cooperation Leads to Pioneering Partnerships in Various Fields: Mohamed Bin Zayed," *Gulf News*, July 22, 2019 (https://gulfnews.com/uae/uae-china-cooperation-leads-to-pioneering-partnerships-in-various-fields-mohamed-bin-zayed-1.65372834).

5. European External Action Service (EEAS), "EU Backs Mediation Efforts to Resolve Gulf Crisis," News Story, July 4, 2017 (https://eeas.europa.eu/headquarters/headquarters-homepage/29255/eu-backs-mediation-efforts-resolve-gulf-crisis_en).

6. European Parliament, "Committee on Foreign Affairs (AFET) of the European Parliament and the Subcommittee on Human Rights (DROI): Delegation to the Kingdom of Saudi Arabia, the State of Kuwait and the Islamic Republic of Iran on 11–15 February," Press Statement, February 15, 2018 (http://www.europarl.europa.eu/cmsdata/138863/Press%20release%20AFET%20-%2015Feb2018.pdf).

7. Ronen Bergman and David D. Kirkpatrick, "With Guns, Cash and Terrorism, Gulf States Vie for Power in Somalia," *New York Times*, July 22, 2019 (www.nytimes.com/2019/07/22/world/africa/somalia-qatar-uae.html).

8. Andrew England, Laura Pitel, and Simeon Kerr, "UAE vs. Turkey: The Regional Rivalries Pitting MBZ against Erdogan," *Financial Times*, October 26, 2020 (www.ft.com/content/990f13cf-613f-48a5-ac02-c8c73741a786).

9. EEAS, "GCC, Statement by the High Representative Josep Borrell on the Normalisation of Relations Among Gulf Countries," June 1, 2021 (https://eeas.europa.eu/headquarters/headquarters-homepage_en/91184/GCC:%20Statement%20by%20the%20High%20Representative%20Josep%20Borrell%20on%20the%20normalisation%20of%20relations%20among%20Gulf%20countries).

10. EEAS, "European Union Opens a New Delegation in Kuwait City," Press Release, July 14, 2019 (https://eeas.europa.eu/diplomatic-network/gulf-cooperation-council-gcc/65425/european-union-opens-new-delegation-kuwait-city_en). EEAS,

"Qatar: Establishment Agreement signed for opening of the EU Delegation in Doha," press release, February 21, 2022 (https://eeas.europa.eu/headquarters/headquarters -homepage/111210/qatar-establishment-agreement-signed-opening-eu-delegation -doha_en).

11. Oxford Business Group, "Dubai Seeking to Meet Needs of GCC Youth Population," Analysis, 2016 (https://oxfordbusinessgroup.com/analysis/young-heart -meeting-needs-region%E2%80%99s-growing-youth-population).

THIRTY ONE

The Emergence of GCC-Israel Relations Is a Fixture of the New Middle East

OMAR H. RAHMAN

THE DEVELOPMENT OF OPEN, friendly relations between Israel and some Gulf Arab states has emerged as a significant new dynamic of the twenty-first-century Middle East. In a region beset by widespread upheaval and civil war, shifting geopolitical alignments, and the competition between rival coalitions seeking to expand their spheres of influence and determine outcomes in other weak and fractured states, this dynamic has taken on a powerful strategic imperative for the Gulf side, in particular. While a formal relationship with Israel has long been held in check by the intractability of the Israeli-Palestinian conflict, the Palestinian national movement's diminished capacity to influence regional politics has given the Gulf states wider latitude to prioritize their national interests over "Arab" ones.

The lines of communication and cooperation between the Gulf states and Israel are not new, however. Multiple countries in the region, including Qatar, Bahrain, and Oman, established connections with Israel in the 1990s after the Palestine Liberation Organization (PLO) and Israel signed the Oslo Accords.[1] Although peace between Israelis and Palestinians was

This chapter was previously published as Omar H. Rahman, "The Emergence of GCC-Israel Relations in a Changing Middle East," Brookings Institution, July 28, 2021 (https://www.brookings.edu/research/the-emergence-of-gcc-israel-relations-in-a-changing-middle-east/).

never consummated, the red line prohibiting a liaison with Israel among the Arab states was blurred. Since then, ties have developed informally and clandestinely, largely kept under wraps because of the persistent objection among Arab publics to normalizing relations with Israel while the Palestinian people remain under Israeli occupation. In 2002, the sequencing of proposed Arab relations with Israel was codified in the Saudi-led Arab Peace Initiative: first a Palestinian state on the 1967 borders, then normalization with the entire Arab world.

As the two sides have expanded their cooperation in recent years, these back-channel links have inevitably become more visible. So too has publicity become an increasing part of the objective for the Gulf states as they have sought the approval of Washington, which led, in part, to the breakthrough diplomatic accords signed by the United Arab Emirates (UAE) and Bahrain with Israel at the White House on September 15, 2020.

Still, the Gulf Cooperation Council (GCC) is far from a unanimous bloc, and the nature and scope of relations with Israel vary between the Gulf states. The closest to Israel among them are undoubtedly the UAE and Bahrain, both of which established contacts over many years and now have taken the step toward full normalization as part of the so-called Abraham Accords.[2]

Saudi Arabia, as part of this axis of like-minded states pursuing coordinated foreign policy objectives, shares strategic motivations with the UAE and Bahrain regarding Israel. Indeed, Riyadh and Tel Aviv have cooperated covertly for years, mostly around security issues and intelligence sharing, but the Gulf kingdom has its own calculus in considering formal relations.[3] This includes its unique status in the Islamic world as the custodian of the two holiest places in Islam, and the legitimacy the House of Saud must protect in that role. The country is also much larger and more diverse than its counterparts, with powerful contingencies that do not perceive Israel favorably.[4] Still, the signaling from the political establishment, especially the younger generation led by Crown Prince Mohammad bin Salman, is clearly trending toward a different approach to Israel that does not preclude normalizing ties ahead of an Israeli-Palestinian peace deal.[5]

Although Oman has yet to normalize ties with Israel, the Gulf state has long had an outlier's approach among the GCC members, publicly backing Egypt in its 1979 peace agreement with Israel and hosting senior Israeli officials as early as the mid-1990s, including Prime Minister Yitzhak Rabin in 1994.[6] Moreover, unlike its compatriots in the region, Oman's relationship with Israel does not stem from a desire to confront adversarial regional forces, but from Oman's long-standing posture of neutrality and diplomacy, and the desire to maintain positive relations with all nations in the region, including Israel and Iran.[7] This foreign policy was developed by the late Sultan Qaboos bin Said, and his successor, Sultan Haitham bin Tariq Al Said, has appeared ready to maintain it, if possible.[8] However, doing so could be contingent on Oman's ability to preserve independence from the Saudi-UAE axis for its economic stability, a bloc that has shown few reservations over pressuring other countries to adopt its positions.

Qatar, for example, was subjected to a regional blockade by the Saudi-UAE axis over its discrete foreign policy from 2017 to 2021. Like Oman, Qatar prioritizes an independent foreign policy from its GCC neighbors while developing a working relationship with Israel, which it has done since the mid-1990s. Doha has leveraged this relationship to play an active role on the Israeli-Palestinian scene, particularly in Gaza as an intermediary between Israel and Hamas and as a financial stabilizer.[9] Given Qatar's broader regional posture and rivalry with the Saudi-UAE axis, it is unlikely that it will formalize relations with Israel in the near term. In fact, it may be able to capitalize on its clear, but unstated, opposition to abandoning the Palestinians in favor of Israel within the GCC. Conceivably, however, Qatar could follow its rivals on the path to normalization if the payoff becomes too large to ignore.

Finally, Kuwait is distinguished in the GCC as being publicly opposed to having relations with Israel while the latter continues to rule over the Palestinians. Not long before his death in September 2020, the late Sheikh Sabah Al Ahmad Al Sabah said Kuwait had no desire to change its regional policies and would be the last to normalize ties.[10] This continued fidelity to the Palestinians could be a result of Kuwait's more representative politics than that of its peers; it has an empowered parliament and a fairly well developed intellectual elite with historic ties to Arab nationalist movements, including the once large and influential Palestinian expatriate community in Kuwait.[11]

Drivers of a New Approach

Among all the Gulf states pursuing relations with Israel, perhaps the UAE's motivations best encapsulate the changing regional dynamics. Contrary to the historically normative view of Israel in the Arab world, the UAE holds Israel to be neither an enemy nor a threat to regional stability. According to the worldview of Abu Dhabi's Crown Prince Sheikh Mohammed bin Zayed

Al Nahyan, the principal threats to the UAE and its allies are an expansionist Iran and transnational political Islamists.[12] In this panorama, both of these malign actors have been willing and able to take advantage of regional instability to advance their positions through foreign meddling or intervention—in the case of Iran, and through the democratic process—in the case of the Muslim Brotherhood and its affiliates, who are backed by a rival coalition headed by Turkey and Qatar. In contrast, the UAE views Israel as a formidable regional power that shares these views and is willing to act to counter regional adversaries. A formal alliance with Israel, therefore, makes strategic sense. So, while the normalization agreements were billed by the Trump administration, which brokered them, as peace accords, they were clearly driven by coalition building rather than peace building.

Moreover, amid the threat posed by the spread of popular uprisings in the region, the Gulf states have become eager purchasers of sophisticated surveillance technology in order to more effectively police their populations.[13] For its part, Israel has been a willing purveyor of this technology with few reservations about possible human rights abuses.[14] This dimension has offered new commercial pathways that dovetail with the UAE's own ambitions of becoming a regional technology and innovation hub. Since normalization, the sides have moved swiftly to establish robust bilateral trade and investments, including in the oil and gas sector.[15]

But most significant of all, the Saudi-UAE axis views a closer relationship with Israel as an indirect means of preserving its partnership with Washington. This motivation is largely shared across the GCC because of the importance of the decades-old US-backed security architecture in the region. However, in recent years the Gulf states have had ample reason for concern about America's long-term commitment. In particular, lengthy and costly US military engagements in the Middle East have generated fatigue at home. And while energy security was once the bonding agent of the US-Gulf alliance, a resurgence in American energy production over the past decade has created the perception of its coming unglued. These and other factors have led successive US administrations to signal a desire to modify, and perhaps reduce, America's posture and presence in the region—a sentiment that may only deepen as the economic costs of the COVID-19 pandemic rise.[16] For the Gulf states, however, which are highly anxious about the regional outlook, retaining America's commitment to their security is paramount.[17]

Given America's dedication to Israel's security, the Gulf states may reasonably assume that creating links with Israel will help shore up their own security ties with the United States. Rightly or wrongly, the Gulf states perceive US foreign policy as exceedingly sensitive to Israeli interests and concerns. What the Gulf states also know from experience is that being Israel's ostensible enemy has not aided their relationship with the United States, has not endeared them to certain quarters of the American political and diplomatic establishment, and has obstructed their acquisition of advanced military hardware and technology reserved for Israel and other close allies outside the region.[18]

So, could a different relationship with Israel salvage the Gulf states' fading importance in the US strategic assessment and neutralize officials who wish to "rethink" Saudi ties?[19] The Saudi-UAE axis appears to believe so and is betting that a new regional security alliance with Israel can be the bonding agent of the future.

Moreover, Israel and the Gulf axis have found common cause in trying to steer America's Middle East policy in a mutually beneficial direction.[20] In particular, the two sides viewed the Obama administration's pursuit of a nuclear agreement with Iran, and subsequently an end to Iranian isolation, as troubling and dangerous. Finding ways to counter the Obama administration's agenda became an opportunity for the two sides to work together without US involvement—a significant step in the development of this relationship—and the eventual basis for working with the incoming Trump administration.[21]

Indeed, this strategy proved quite successful as the Trump administration made forging a deeper Gulf-Israel alliance the anchor of its Middle East foreign policy. In doing so, the administration offered virtually unqualified support to both sides, including exiting Obama's signature Joint Comprehensive Plan of Action (JCPOA) nuclear agreement and implementing a "maximum pressure" campaign against Iran.

Nonetheless, the UAE's decision to formalize relations with Israel in September 2020 should not be viewed solely through the lens of its relations with the Trump administration. The potential for Trump to lose the presidency in the November 2020 election was almost certainly a motivating factor, as well, with an expectation that Democrats would also look favorably on the UAE for normalizing ties with Israel. Indeed, at the time the normalization agreements were signed, both sides of the political aisle welcomed the breakthrough despite the growing politicization of US-Gulf relations under the Trump administration and the increasingly negative view of Saudi-UAE policies inside progressive Democratic circles.[22] In point of fact, the Biden campaign lambasted America's Gulf allies prior to the election, yet Biden has refrained from initiating a major recalibration of US-Saudi or US-UAE relations since taking office, a sign that the normalization agreements may have had the desired effect in Washington.[23]

Risks and Costs

While public relations in Washington are an important component of Gulf-Israel ties, so too is the perception in the Middle East, where the risks of having this relationship have long been prohibitive. Yet among regional governments the reaction to the advancement of Gulf-Israel relations in general, and the UAE-Israel normalization agreement in particular, has ranged from neutral to positive. The exceptions were, unsurprisingly, Iran and, ironically, Turkey, which maintains extensive ties with Israel in spite of its estrangement under the presidency of Recep Tayyip Erdogan.[24]

This reception to normalization is a dramatic departure from the past. Egypt, for example, was suspended from the Arab League for a decade after signing a peace deal with Israel in 1979, despite its capital city hosting the institution. This difference between then and now likely attests to the growing influence of the Gulf states over other countries in the region; to the erosion of Palestinian political leverage; and to the diminished zeal attached to their cause. For their part, Palestinians largely viewed the normalization agreement as an act of "betrayal" and denounced it in strong terms. Nonetheless, the Mahmoud Abbas-led Palestinian leadership failed in its attempt to have the agreement condemned by the Arab League.

Among Arab publics the reaction has been relatively muted. Certainly, public opinion in the Middle East, especially in the Gulf, is difficult to gauge given the general suppression of free speech, undemocratic rule, and a lack of polling or independent media. There have been some notable signs of opposition, including in Bahrain, where more than fifteen civil society groups released a statement objecting to the normalization deal.[25] And the regional opinion polling that exists, such as the Arab Opinion Index, has shown overwhelming opposition to recognizing Israel.[26] Nonetheless, popular backlash in the streets has not been a factor.

In assessing risk, however, it is important to understand the context in which processes occur and how likely that context is to change over time. Gulf-Israel ties were initiated after the signing of the Oslo Accords, when the peace process with the PLO opened the doors for others to engage with Israel. Importantly, the persistence of the Oslo process well past its mandate continued to provide political cover to the relationship in spite of

Israel's ongoing occupation and oppression of Palestinians. After nearly three decades, however, the Oslo framework is exhausted. If the post-Oslo stage is marked by popular mobilization against Israeli annexation and permanent rule, it could cast the relationship between the Gulf states and Israel in a harsher light. Indeed, it is even possible for the Gulf states to be drawn into direct support of Israel's occupation.[27]

In addition to risk, the relationship comes with a cost. One of the last remaining issues of consensus and unity among Arab states is support for the Palestinian cause—a valuable commodity for a region increasingly fractured and at odds. The Arab Peace Initiative remains a signature achievement in bringing together the commitment of the entire Arab world to normalize relations with Israel in exchange for peace with the Palestinians. Abandoning this initiative is a great loss, even if it failed to gain traction over the past two decades. So too is the forfeiture of unified backing for the Palestinian people, as securing their freedom and rights remains a moral imperative for the region and the world.

To conclude, relations between most Gulf states and Israel are not new or uniform, but changes in regional dynamics have given some GCC members a new strategic imperative for drawing closer to their former adversary. Animated by a host of regional threats and the need to keep the United States engaged in their security, the Saudi-UAE axis has broken with the Arab world's longstanding Palestine-first policy in pursuit of an alliance with Israel. Although these states have deemed normalization more of an asset than a liability at this juncture, an open relationship is not without risks and costs that may become more apparent down the road.

Notes

1. Kristian Coates Ulrichsen, "Israel and the Arab Gulf States: Drivers and Directions of Change," Rice University, Baker Institute for Policy, September 2016, pp. 3–4 (https://www.bakerinstitute.org/media/files/research_document/13eaaa71/CME-pub-GCCIsrael-090716.pdf); Simon Henderson, "Israeli-GCC Ties Twenty-Five Years after the First Gulf War," inFocus Quarterly Policy Analysis (Washington Institute for Near East Policy, October 14, 2015) (www.washingtoninstitute.org/policy-analysis/view/israel-gcc-ties-twenty-five-years-after-the-first-gulf-war).

2. US Department of State, "The Abraham Accords" (www.state.gov/the-abraham-accords/).

3. Ulrichsen, "Israel and the Arab Gulf States," pp. 2, 6–9; Asher Orkaby, "Rivals with Benefits: Israel and Saudi Arabia's Secret History of Cooperation," Foreign Affairs, March 13, 2015 (www.foreignaffairs.com/articles/middle-east/2015-03-13/rivals-benefits).

4. Hussein Ibish, "After the UAE, Who Will and Won't Be Next to Normalize with Israel?," Arab Gulf States Institute in Washington (AGSIW) (blog), August 24, 2020 (https://agsiw.org/after-the-uae-who-will-and-wont-be-next-to-normalize-with -israel/).

5. Yasmine Farouk, "What Would Happen if Israel and Saudi Arabia Established Official Relations?," Commentary, Carnegie Endowment for International Peace, October 15, 2020 (https://carnegieendowment.org/2020/10/15/what-would-happen-if -israel-and-saudi-arabia-established-official-relations-pub-82964).

6. Ulrichsen, "Israel and the Arab Gulf States," pp. 3–4; Oman also hosted Prime Minister Benjamin Netanyahu in 2018.

7. Abdullah Baabood, "Oman and the Gulf Diplomatic Crisis," *Gulf Affairs* (Autumn 2017), pp. 30–31 (www.oxgaps.org/files/commentary_-_baabood.pdf).

8. Kristian Coates Ulrichsen and Giorgio Cafiero, "Oman Plays It Safe on Israel," Middle East Institute (MEI), October 27, 2020 (www.mei.edu/publications/oman-plays -it-safe-israel).

9. Adnan Abu Amer, "Qatar Boosts Its Influence in Gaza," *Al-Monitor*, April 14, 2019 (www.al-monitor.com/pulse/originals/2019/04/qatar-support-hamas-gaza-pa -abbas-israel-us-humanitarian.html); Jonathan Spyer, "Israel and Qatar Have an Unlikely Partnership for Dealing with Gaza," *Jerusalem Post*, September 10, 2020 (www .jpost.com/arab-israeli-conflict/israel-and-qatar-have-an-unlikely-partnership-for -dealing-with-gaza-641878).

10. "Kuwait Says It'll Be 'Last to Normalize' with Israel, Will Stand by Palestinians," *Times of Israel*, August 16, 2020 (www.timesofisrael.com/kuwaiti-officials-reject -israel-normalization-reaffirm-support-for-palestinians/).

11. Normalization with Israel is clearly a policy driven from the top down.

12. This is the author's opinion, however other accounts back this view up, including Robert F. Worth, "Mohammed bin Zayed's Dark Vision of the Middle East's Future," *New York Times Magazine*, January 9, 2020.

13. Laura Mackenzie, "Surveillance State: How Gulf Governments Keep Watch on Us," *Wired*, January 21, 2020 (https://wired.me/technology/privacy/surveillance-gulf -states/).

14. Neri Zilber, "Gulf Cyber Cooperation with Israel: Balancing Threats and Rights," Policy Watch 3066, Washington Institute for Near East Policy, January 17, 2019 (www.washingtoninstitute.org/policy-analysis/view/gulf-cyber-cooperation-with -israel-balancing-threats-and-rights); Chaim Levinson, "With Israel's Encouragement, NSO Sold Spyware to UAE and Other Gulf States," *Haaretz*, August 25, 2020 (www .haaretz.com/middle-east-news/.premium-with-israel-s-encouragement-nso-sold -spyware-to-uae-and-other-gulf-states-1.9093465).

15. Yousef Saba, "UAE Seeks $1Trillion in Economic Activity with Israel by 2031," Reuters, September 14, 2021 (https://www.reuters.com/world/middle-east/uae-aims -1-trillion-activity-with-israel-by-2031-2021-09-14/).

16. Daniel Benaim, "A Progressive Course Correction for US-Saudi Relations," Report, Century Foundation, June 25, 2020 (https://tcf.org/content/report/progressive -course-correction-u-s-saudi-relations/); Benaim describes "rethinkers" of American

policy on US-Saudi relations as those who advocate for fundamental changes to the relationship altogether.

17. Omar H. Rahman, "What's behind the Relationship between Israel and Arab Gulf States?," *Order from Chaos* (blog), January 28, 2019 (www.brookings.edu/blog /order-from-chaos/2019/01/28/whats-behind-the-relationship-between-israel-and -arab-gulf-states/).

18. Indeed, following the signing of the normalization agreements, the UAE believed it would be granted access to the coveted F-35 fighter aircraft that Israel also receives. After this led to controversy, US congressional representatives introduced a bipartisan bill that would give Israel a quasi-veto over US arms sales to regional partners, an astounding measure of sovereignty to cede to a foreign power, and one more justification for seeing Israel as the key to a better partnership with the United States. Ultimately, Israel gave its consent to the United States to sell the F-35 jets to the UAE, and on December 9, 2020, the Senate voted against resolutions that would block the sale to the UAE. See JTA and Ron Kampeas, "Bipartisan Bill Would Give Israel a Veto on Middle East Arms Sales," *Haaretz*, October 4, 2020 (www.haaretz.com/us -news/bipartisan-bill-would-give-israel-a-veto-on-middle-east-arms-sales-1.9206918); Barak Ravid, "Israel Drops Opposition to F-35 Deal between US and UAE," *Axios*, October 23, 2020 (www.axios.com/israel-drops-opposition-to-f-35-deal-uae-trump -d393d6ee-b50a-49e5-845b-edb11438295e.html).

19. Benaim, "A Progressive Course Correction for US-Saudi Relations."

20. Adam Entous, "Donald Trump's New World Order," *New Yorker*, June 11, 2018, (www.newyorker.com/magazine/2018/06/18/donald-trumps-new-world-order);   Entous describes secret cooperation between Israeli and Emirati officials to oppose Obama's foreign policy on Iran and to persuade the Trump campaign and administration to adopt its own foreign policy perspective. Benaim also describes Saudi and Emirati efforts to interfere with Obama's foreign policy in the Middle East, as well as to "undermine the policies of a US administration within the US system."

21. Ibid.

22. Marc Rod, "Congressional Democrats Offer Subdued Praise on Abraham Accords," *Jewish Insider*, September 17, 2020 (https://jewishinsider.com/2020/09 /congressional-democrats-offer-subdued-praise-on-abraham-accords/); Alex Emmons, Aida Chavez, and Akela Levy, "Joe Biden, in Departure from Obama, Says He Would Make Saudi Arabia a Pariah," *The Intercept*, November 21, 2019 (https://theintercept .com/2019/11/21/democratic-debate-joe-biden-saudi-arabia/).

23. Robin Wright, "The Sweeping Impact of a Broken Campaign Promise," *The New Yorker*, March 1, 2021 (https://www.newyorker.com/news/our-columnists/biden -betrayed-his-promise-to-defend-human-rights-and-jamal-khashoggi).

24. "Turkey Denounces Bahrain-Israel Normalization Deal," *Daily Sabah*, September 12, 2020 (www.dailysabah.com/politics/diplomacy/turkey-denounces-bahrain -israel-normalization-deal).

25. Merissa Khurman and others, "News Roundup: UAE, Bahrain Normalize Relations with Israel," Viewpoint Series, Wilson Center, September 16, 2020 (www .wilsoncenter.org/article/news-roundup-uae-bahrain-normalize-relations-israel).

26. "The 2017–2018 Arab Opinion Index: Main Results in Brief," Arab Center for Research and Policy Studies, May 9, 2018, pp. 31–32 (www.dohainstitute.org/en/News/Pages/ACRPS-Releases-Arab-Index-2017-2018.aspx).

27. And in fact, a joint $3 billion fund announced by Israel, the UAE, and the United States was described by one US official as intended to modernize Israeli checkpoints in the territories, among other things. In order to make this palatable, they are waging a campaign to reframe the Palestinians in a negative light. See Stephen Farrell and Dan Williams, "Israel Says UAE Visit 'Making History' - Palestinians Call It 'Shameful,'" Reuters, October 20, 2020 (www.reuters.com/article/us-emirates-israel/uae-government-delegation-heads-to-israel-for-first-official-visit-idUSKBN2750PI).

THIRTY TWO

Conclusion
The GCC Looks to the Future

TARIK M. YOUSEF
ADEL ABDEL GHAFAR

IN 2020 AND 2021, GCC countries endured multiple, simultaneous shocks, the effects of which are likely to persist long into the future. Economically, states had to deal with a dual crisis: the collapse in energy prices and the public health impact of the COVID-19 pandemic. Together, these shocks put public finances under enormous strain and pushed economies into recession. Politically, it was a year of significant changes both domestically and internationally. First, the baton of leadership passed to a younger generation in Oman and Kuwait. Second, after having established close relations with the Trump administration, the fragile Saudi-Emirati alliance moved into uncharted waters with the new Biden administration. With the failure of Trump's "maximum pressure" Iran policy and Biden's intent to resurrect the Iran nuclear deal, regional security concerns have increased, especially considering multiple attacks on Saudi Arabia's oil infrastructure and facilities.

The chapters in this volume analyze these common, intertwined challenges in the GCC and outline pathways forward. Crucial to providing collective solutions to these pressing challenges, the authors argue, will be the degree of cooperation between the member states. However, as a supranational body, the GCC came under extreme pressure during the 2017 crisis, when deep disagreements between countries over regional security and politics led to an economic and political blockade of Qatar that threatened the survival of the bloc. Lacking effective internal mechanisms for dispute settlement and reluctant to engage with external efforts at mediation, the fractured GCC was unable to prevent an escalation of the rift that engulfed neighbors, divided allies, and ripped at the Gulf's social fabric and communal trust for over four years.[1] Moreover, months after the 2021 Al-Ula breakthrough agreement, progress toward resolving the underlying disagreements between member states has been limited, and the long-term outlook for the GCC as a body remains uncertain.

Security Cooperation and Threat Perceptions

Some areas of policy will be easier to tackle in the future through GCC collective action than others, where individual member state preferences and choices will prevail. Security is one area where numerous challenges will hinder cooperation among member states. Although the bloc does have a mutual defense agreement, a nominal joint force, and numerous security cooperation protocols, member states have increasingly organized for their security independently through agreements with external partners and strategic alliances, weapons purchases and manufacturing investments, and the arming and use of proxy forces abroad when needed. Crucial differences prevail regarding relations with and threat perceptions from regional powers such as Iran and Turkey, as well as Israel, since the signing of the Abraham Accords with Bahrain and the United Arab Emirates (UAE) in 2020.[2]

First, a collective GCC approach to Iran is lacking. Saudi Arabia perceives Iranian encirclement through proxies in Yemen, Syria, Iraq, and Lebanon, as well as the direct threat from Iran itself, as the key national security concern facing the kingdom. On the opposite end of the spectrum, Oman and Qatar's friendlier relations with Iran have been a source of concern for Saudi Arabia and the UAE, which would prefer a more unified and aggressive posture toward Iran. Growing security and military cooperation between Israel, Bahrain, and the UAE has added another layer of division and complexity to regional security arrangements within the GCC and toward Iran. As the Biden administration attempts to resurrect the JCPOA, it will likely face objections from Gulf and Israeli allies who are united in their opposition to a deal that does not confront Iran's regional ambitions. Russia's invasion of Ukraine in 2022 may encourage the United States to push aside these concerns and focus on a deal limiting nuclear enrichment so that Iranian oil production can help offset disturbances in global energy supplies.

Relations with another regional power, Turkey, also remain a sticking point. Since President Erdogan assumed power, Turkey has used the global stage to position itself as the leader of the Muslim world, putting Ankara at odds with the historical positioning of the Saudi monarchy. Since the 2011 Arab uprisings, Turkey on the one hand, and Saudi Arabia and the UAE on the other, have found themselves on opposite sides of the political transitions and conflicts in Egypt, Libya, and Tunisia, and more recently in Syria, the Horn of Africa, and the eastern Mediterranean. The stationing of Turkish military forces in Qatar during the 2017 Gulf crisis placed Ankara at the heart of the crisis and enables it to influence future GCC security arrangements.[3] Not to be outdone, the UAE has sought to increase its leverage in the eastern Mediterranean, including, among other actions, signing a mutual defense agreement with Greece in 2020.[4]

Another key issue that has led to a divergence of views and policies within the GCC is the role of political Islam in the Middle East. The Muslim Brotherhood remains the primary ideological challenge to Saudi Arabia's dynasty and leadership aspirations abroad, a threat perception that it shares with the UAE.[5] The emergence of parties affiliated with the Muslim Brotherhood in Egypt, Libya, Morocco, Tunisia, and Yemen following the Arab Spring protests triggered open conflict with Qatar, which has been more sympathetic to Islamist political parties. The ensuing geopolitical competition, fought using soft and hard power, destabilized the wider Middle East and pushed the GCC to the brink of war in 2017. Whether Islamist parties, which have suffered blanket repression and political setbacks in recent years, will continue to serve as a source of regional and domestic polarization remains an open question.[6]

Since President Biden took office in 2021, there have been numerous signs of a deescalation of tensions within the GCC and the wider region. There are growing perceptions that the United States is downsizing its GCC security commitments and signaling to allies the need for conflict resolution.[7] Deescalation may also be the consequence of strategic exhaustion among GCC actors after close to a decade of rivalry and the inability of any one side to achieve clear victory in various theaters of geopolitical competition. The economic toll of the COVID-19 pandemic recession also has contributed to shifting the policy focus to economic recovery, including through resuming trade and investment cooperation abroad. Signs of reduced tensions are promising, but it remains to be seen whether they reflect longer-term trends or shorter-term strategic calculations among the actors in the region.

Economic Integration and National Competition

At the core of the GCC's mission lies the ambition of economic integration. In the early 2000s, integration efforts gained serious momentum following the signing of the customs union agreement in 2003 and the adoption of the common market agreement in 2008.[8] The bloc went further by briefly considering the adoption of a common currency managed by a GCC monetary authority in 2008. These efforts continued in the face of the global financial crisis and after the Arab Spring protests, when fiscally strained members Bahrain and Oman received financial support from stronger economies. Economic integration efforts slowed, however, after the collapse of international oil prices in 2014, and they were dealt a severe blow after the economic blockade of Qatar in 2017. Not only did the blockade rupture political trust within the bloc, but it also disrupted trade and financial flows and gave rise to broader fears about economic security among smaller member states.

As many of the chapters in this volume emphasize, there are significant gains to be made from pursuing deeper economic integration within the GCC, especially given the normalization of diplomatic relations between Qatar and Saudi Arabia in 2021 and the gradual restoration of economic links with Qatar by the blockading countries.[9] Incentives for a renewed emphasis on integration have been further bolstered by the economic dislocation in GCC countries caused by COVID-19 and the oil price shock, including supply chain bottlenecks and worries about adequate food imports from abroad. This acute vulnerability to external policy developments and adverse market conditions has heightened the sense of economic insecurity among all members, has reenforced the need for income and production diversification, and has revived the interest in economic cooperation among Gulf leaders.

At the same time, the return of diplomatic normalization and the 2021 recovery in international oil prices appear to have ushered in a new trend of rising economic nationalism and competition between Gulf states.[10] This was seen in 2021 in efforts by Riyadh to dislodge Dubai's long-held position as the financial and trading hub of international firms in the GCC. This followed a rare public display of disunity between Saudi Arabia and the UAE within OPEC over oil production quotas. Initial cooperation efforts on taxation policy within the GCC have faltered, and Saudi Arabia's decision to increase its value-added tax by 200 percent in 2020 and exclude free trade zones in member countries from the customs agreement opens the door for further divergence in economic policy within the bloc, breeding mistrust among other GCC countries and ultimately weakening prospects for deeper integration.[11]

Within this fragile context, the Gulf states are entering a period that will require greater economic cooperation as a means of addressing their common, long-term economic challenges. Independent of whether current oil price increases persist (or are a temporal reflection of the global post-pandemic economic rebound), long-term prospects for Gulf oil are being shaped by the acceleration of investments in alternative energy in Western countries as they seek to counter climate change. Declining international demand for oil means that Gulf governments will continue to face fiscal constraints within a rentier economic model.[12] A short- to mid-term return to high oil prices suggests a last opportunity for Gulf governments to channel oil revenues into further investments in large-scale economic diversification projects and incentives for small and medium-sized enterprise development.

New approaches to private sector development and economic diversification will be needed to meet the challenge that all Gulf states face to create jobs for their national youth populations. They also face a shared demographic challenge related to continuing dependence on guest workers, increasingly seen by policymakers as a barrier to the employment of nationals and a threat to traditional social and cultural norms in the Gulf. Moreover, with their ongoing dependence on food imports, each of the Gulf states faces growing concerns about food security. Underlying these long-term socioeconomic concerns is how Gulf states will address multiple threats related to climate change, given high local carbon footprints, increasingly intolerable summer heats, and their position in a wider region struggling with water shortages and rising economic vulnerability related to climate.[13]

Reforming the GCC Union

The long-term security and economic challenges facing the Gulf states during a period of growing global threats and policy uncertainty are daunting. They require policy coordination and deeper integration among member states in ways not seen before in the GCC's four-decade history. Without such policy adjustments, political disagreements are bound to trigger another major crisis, and economic competition between members will likely lead to a race to the bottom. Moreover, the GCC structure, as it stands today, which favors national governments over supranational bodies in decisionmaking, is increasingly ill-equipped to deal with future challenges. Revitalizing it to strengthen collective action will require reforms that rely on Gulf leaders' political commitment to the GCC organization.

There is no easy fix for the GCC structure, which remains, according to one observer, "hostage to both imbalance of geographical size and political power between Saudi Arabia and the five smaller countries, and the tension between personalization and institutionalization in decision making structures."[14] Absent a "grand vision" that embraces integration to overcome these impediments, leaders could focus on more realistic objectives and incremental reforms.[15] Institutionally, this would involve some devolution of decisionmaking powers to the GCC Secretariat to improve organizational effectiveness. It remains to be seen whether today's Gulf leaders are ready to take the necessary steps or if the GCC will eventually succumb to the familiar pattern of failed regional integration projects observed throughout the Middle East.

Notes

1. Abdulmalik M. Altamimi, "An Appraisal of the Gulf Cooperation Council's Mechanisms for Co-Operation and the Settlement of Disputes," *Asian Journal of International Law* 10, no. 2 (July 2020): 321–45.

2. Samuel Ramani, "The Qatar Blockade Is Over, but the Gulf Crisis Lives On," *Foreign Policy*, January 27, 2021 (https://foreignpolicy.com/2021/01/27/qatar-blockade -gcc-divisions-turkey-libya-palestine/).

3. Dalay Galip, "Turkey's Libra Policy: New Flexibility, New Goals," ISPI, May 27, 2021 (https://www.ispionline.it/en/pubblicazione/turkeys-libya-policy-new-flexibility -new-goals-30609); Andrew Wilks, "Turkey, Saudi Arabia Eye Improved Ties after Gulf Crisis Ends," Recep Tayyip Erdogan News, Al Jazeera, *Al Jazeera*, January 25, 2021 (https://www.aljazeera.com/news/2021/1/25/turkey-and-saudi-arabia-on-the-verge -of-a-return-to-cordiality).

4. Sean Mathews, "UAE Joins Greek, Egyptian Naval Exercise in Eastern Mediterranean," *Al-Monitor*, December 1, 2020 (https://www.al-monitor.com/originals /2020/12/uae-greece-defense-agreement-turkey-eastern-mediterranean.html).

5. Adel Abdel Ghafar, "Between Geopolitics and Geoeconomics: The Growing Role of Gulf States in the Eastern Mediterranean," Istituto Affari Internazionali, 2021 (https://www.iai.it/sites/default/files/iaip2106.pdf).

6. "Across the Arab World, Islamists' Brief Stints in Power Have Failed," *The Economist*, August 24, 2021 (https://www.economist.com/special-report/2021/08/24/across -the-arab-world-islamists-brief-stints-in-power-have-failed).

7. David Ignatius, "How Regional Realignments Are Helping Depressurize the Middle East," *Washington Post*, October 5, 2021.

8. World Bank, *Economic Integration in the GCC* (Washington, 2010) (https://doi.org/10.1596/27898).

9. Tim Fox, "Region's Economies Will Benefit from Gulf-Qatar Deal" (blog), Atlantic Council, January 25, 2021 (https://www.atlanticcouncil.org/blogs/menasource/regions-economies-will-benefit-from-gulf-qatar-deal/).

10. Andrew England and Simeon Kerr, Gulf Tensions: Saudi Arabia Flexes Its Economic Muscles," *Financial Times*, October 24, 2021.

11. Karen Young, "Have Taxes Killed GCC "Economic Integration?," *Al-Monitor*, May 14, 2020 (https://www.al-monitor.com/originals/2020/05/tax-hikes-kill-gulf-gcc-economic-integration-saudi-arabia.html).

12. Irfan Aleem Qureshi, "Structural Reforms, Fiscal Sustainability, and Inter-generational Wealth as the GCC Transitions to a Post-Oil Future," January 2021 (https://www.researchgate.net/publication/348741270_Structural_Reforms_Fiscal_Sustainability_and_Inter-generational_Wealth_as_the_GCC_transitions_to_a_post-oil_future).

13. Jack Sargent, "Climate Change and the Rentier States of the Gulf Cooperation Council," (blog) Middle East Centre, September 8, 2020 (https://blogs.lse.ac.uk/mec/2020/09/08/climate-change-and-the-rentier-states-of-the-gulf-cooperation-council/).

14. Ashraf Mishrif, "The GCC's Unsettled Policy for Economic Integration," *Muslim World* 111, no. 1 (2021): 70–95.

15. L. Alan Winters "What Can Arab Countries Learn from Europe? An Institutional Analysis," in *Arab Economic Integration: Between Hope and Reality*, edited by Ahmed Galal and Bernard Hoekman (Brookings), pp. 148–62.

Contributors

Adel Abdel Ghafar is fellow and director of the Foreign Policy and Security program at the Middle East Council on Global Affairs, and a nonresident fellow in the Foreign Policy program at the Brookings Institution in Washington, DC. He specializes in political economy and his research interests include state-society relations, socioeconomic development, and foreign policy in the Middle East and North Africa (MENA) region. Abdel Ghafar is the author and editor of several volumes and reports including: *Egyptians in Revolt: The Political Economy of Labor and Student Mobilizations 1919-2011* (2017); *A Stable Egypt for a Stable Region* (2018); *The European Union and North Africa: Prospects and Challenges* (2019); *China and North Africa: Between Economics, Politics and Security* (2021); and *The European Union and the Gulf Cooperation Council: Towards a New Path* (2021). He holds a PhD from the Australian National University.

Geneive Abdo is a fellow at the Wilson Center. She was most recently a visiting fellow at the Brookings Doha Center. Her current research focuses on the shifting political and religious alliances within Shi'a communities in the Middle East. She has worked at several Washington-based think tanks, including the Atlantic Council and the Stimson Center. She was a nonresident scholar at the Brookings Institution from 2013 to 2017. Among her vast publications, including monographs and works in scholarly journals, Abdo is the author of four books on the Middle East, including *The New Sectarianism: The Arab Uprisings and the Rebirth of the Shi'a-Sunni Divide* (2016). Her other books include a groundbreaking study of the Muslim Brotherhood's rise to power in Egypt. She has received many awards for her scholarship, including the prestigious John Simon Guggenheim fellowship. In her twenty-year career as a foreign correspondent, Abdo focused on coverage of the Middle East and the Muslim world. From 1998 to 2001, She was the Iran correspondent for the British newspaper *The Guardian* and a regular contributor to *The Economist* and the *International Herald Tribune*. She was the first American journalist to be based in Iran since the 1979 Islamic Revolution.

Noha Aboueldahab is assistant professor at Georgetown University in Qatar, where she teaches courses on public international law and on transitional justice. She is a nonresident fellow in the Foreign Policy program at the Brookings Institution and a nonresident fellow at the Middle East Council on Global Affairs. Aboueldahab co-chairs the American Society of International Law's Transitional Justice and Rule of Law interest group. She is an award-winning specialist in transitional justice and is the author of *Transitional Justice and the Prosecution of Political Leaders in the Arab Region* (2017). Aboueldahab has authored many publications, including contributions in the *International Criminal Law Review*. Her op-eds have been published by *Foreign Policy* magazine, Al Jazeera, and *The Globe and Mail*, among others. She serves on the editorial board of Hart Publishing's Studies in International and Comparative Criminal Law and is a peer reviewer for several academic journals and think tanks. Her forthcoming book examines how Arab diasporas have expanded the political, intellectual, and socio-legal spaces of transitional justice.

Yasmina Abouzzohour is a postdoctoral research fellow with the Harvard Middle East Initiative at the John F. Kennedy School of Government and a nonresident senior fellow at the Atlantic Council. She holds a PhD from the University of Oxford and a BA from Columbia University, both in political science. She specializes in persistence and transition in different types of authoritarian systems, focusing on the role of regime-opposition interrelations in shaping regimes' economic and political strategies during upheavals. Dr. Abouzzohour is completing a book on Arab monarchical survival in which she uses mixed methods to investigate the causal mechanisms that allow monarchs to contain different types of dissent. Her research has received accolades and support from the Carnegie Endowment for International Peace, the American Political Science Association, the Middle East Studies Association, the Project on Middle East Political Science, the American Institute for Maghrib Studies, the University of Oxford, Harvard University, Princeton University, Yale University, and Columbia University.

Irfan Aleem is a chief economist/technical advisor at the Saudi Ministry of Economy and Planning. He was previously a visiting fellow at the Brookings Doha Center, where he facilitated dialogue on economic issues facing Qatar and other regional economies in the wake of COVID-19. Between 2015 and 2018, Aleem has occupied various positions in the Qatari Ministry of Economy and Commerce and the Ministry of Finance, including chief economist and economic policy and researcher. Aleem is a macroeconomist with more than twenty years of experience in senior policy making and operational positions across the United Kingdom, the United States, the Middle East, East Asia, and Africa. He holds a PhD in economics from Oxford University.

Sara Bazoobandi is a Marie Curie Fellow at the GIGA Institute of Middle East Studies and an associate research fellow at the Italian Institute for International Political Studies (ISPI). She is also a nonresident senior fellow at the Atlantic Council. Prior to this, she was a senior lecturer in international political economy at Regent's University London and a visiting scholar at the Middle East Institute of the National University of Singapore. Bazoobandi has contributed to various global research projects on political, economic, and social affairs of the Middle East and North Africa (MENA). She was an associate fellow at the MENA program of the Royal Institute of International Affairs, Chatham House, and served as a member of the Global Agenda Council of the World Economic Forum on the Middle East and North Africa. She holds a PhD in Arab and Islamic studies from Exeter University; an MSc in economic development in emerging markets from the University of Reading; and speaks Persian, English, Arabic and German.

Robert P. Beschel Jr. is currently a nonresident senior fellow with the Middle East Council on Global Affairs, where his research interests concentrate on governance and public sector reform. He is leading the Center's work on the policy and institutional responses to the Covid-19 pandemic throughout the Middle East and North Africa region. Dr. Beschel also serves as a senior advisor for a number of leading management consulting firms and multilateral development banks. Dr. Beschel previously served as global lead of the World Bank's Center of Government Practice and lead public sector management specialist within the Bank's Middle East and North Africa region. He has written and worked extensively on economic and public sector reform issues in a diverse number of countries in the Middle East, East Asia, South Asia and Central and Eastern Europe. Dr. Beschel has a master's degree in public administration from Harvard University's John F. Kennedy School of Government and a master's degree and PhD in political science from Harvard's Government Department.

Aidyn Bibolov is a senior economist at the International Monetary Fund (IMF), where his specialty is the countries of the Gulf Cooperation Council. Prior to that, his positions at the IMF included resident representative and technical assistance mission chief; he also was a member of an IMF financial sector assessment program (FSAP) team. Before joining the IMF in 2008, Dr. Bibolov worked in banking and auditing, and taught at leading universities in Kazakhstan. He holds a diploma in economics from Pavlodar State University, an MBA from Binghamton University, and a PhD from Bocconi University.

Imco Brouwer is managing director of the Gulf Labour Markets, Migration, and Population (GLMM) programme. He has been affiliated with the Gulf Research Center since 2009. He was previously affiliated with the Robert Kennedy Center for Justice and Human Rights (RFK Center, Florence), the Arab Reform Initiative (ARI, Paris), and the European University Institute (EUI, Florence). His focus has been on international migration, human rights, democratization, higher education, and international cooperation in the Middle East, North Africa, and the Mediterranean area. His recent publications include: "Working and Living Conditions of Low-Income Migrant Workers in the Hospitality and Construction Sectors in Qatar," GLMM Research Report No. 1, 2019, and "Working and Living Conditions of Low-Income Migrant Workers in the Hospitality and Construction Sectors in the United Arab Emirates," GLMM, Research Report No. 2, 2019 (both with Philippe Fargues and Nasra M. Shah).

Tim Callen served as the International Monetary Fund (IMF) mission chief for Saudi Arabia and chief of the Gulf Cooperation Council (GCC) countries division from September 2012 to November 2021. In these roles, he was responsible for the IMF's published reports on Saudi Arabia and the GCC. Before joining the IMF in 1993, Callen previously worked at the Bank of England and the Reserve Bank of Australia in their economic departments; and at Hambros Bank, where he was responsible for bond and currency analysis for the G-7 countries. He holds a bachelor's degree in economics from the University of Essex and a master's degree in economics from the University of Warwick.

Kristian Coates Ulrichsen is a fellow for the Middle East at Rice University's Baker Institute for Public Policy in Houston, Texas. His research spans the history, political economy, and international relations of the Arab Gulf States as well as their changing position within the regional and global order. Coates Ulrichsen is the author of five books about the Gulf states, including *Insecure Gulf: The End of Certainty and the Transition to the Post-Oil Era* (2011), *The Gulf States in International Political Economy* (2015), and *Qatar and the Gulf Crisis* (2020); he is also the editor of three volumes of essays about the region. Coates Ulrichsen holds a PhD in history from the University of Cambridge. Prior to joining the Baker Institute in 2013, Coates Ulrichsen previously worked at the Gulf Center for Strategic Studies and the London School of Economics and Political Science.

Marvin Erfurth is interested in education and public policy in the broader context of human capital development, particularly regarding questions on higher education policy, governance, and the sector's relationships with other sectors and systems. Marvin completed his PhD in international and comparative education at the University of Muenster, with a dissertation exploring higher education policy and governance in the education hubs in Singapore and the United Arab Emirates. He worked at the University of Kassel and the University of Muenster in Germany, and has also taught at the University of Oslo in Norway before working as head of research at the Ras Al Khaimah/United Arab Emirates–based Al Qasimi Foundation for Policy Research. Since 2022, he has been working as a consultant advising German/European public sector organizations.

Sean Foley specializes in the contemporary history and politics of the Middle East and the wider Islamic world. He frequently visits Asia and the Middle East, follows events in both regions closely, and speaks Arabic and Bahasa Malaysian. He has published widely and has delivered public presentations to audiences around the world. He has also held Fulbright fellowships in Syria, Turkey, and Malaysia, and has lived and traveled extensively in Saudi Arabia.

Ibrahim Fraihat is an associate professor in international conflict resolution at the Doha Institute for Graduate Studies. He previously served as senior foreign policy fellow at the Brookings Institution, and taught conflict resolution at Georgetown University and George Washington University. His latest book publications include *Iran and Saudi Arabia: Taming a*

Chaotic Conflict (2020) and *Unfinished Revolutions: Yemen, Libya, and Tunisia after the Arab Spring* (2016). Dr. Fraihat has published extensively on Middle East politics, with articles appearing in the *New York Times, Foreign Affairs, Foreign Policy, Huffington Post,* Al Jazeera websites, and elsewhere. Fraihat received a doctorate in conflict analysis and resolution from George Mason University in 2006. He is the recipient of George Mason University's Distinguished Alumni Award (2014) for his achievements in the field of conflict resolution.

Courtney Freer is provost's postdoctoral fellow in Middle Eastern and South Asian Studies at Emory University in Atlanta. She previously served as an assistant professorial research fellow at the Middle East Centre at the London School of Economics and Political Science (LSE). She is also a nonresident fellow in the Foreign Policy program at the Brookings Institution, a visiting fellow at LSE, and a nonresident senior fellow at Gulf International Forum. Dr. Freer previously worked at the Brookings Doha Center in Qatar and the US-Saudi Arabian Business Council in Washington, DC. She holds a BA in Near Eastern studies from Princeton University, an MA in Middle Eastern studies from The George Washington University, and a DPhil in politics from the University of Oxford.

Matthew Gray is a professor at the School of International Liberal Studies, Waseda University, Tokyo, where his teaching and research specializes in the politics, political economy, and international relations of the contemporary Middle East, particularly the Arab states of the Gulf. He was previously at The Australian National University, Canberra, from 2005 to 2016; he has also been a visiting scholar at the School of Government and International Affairs at Durham University in 2011 and at the Institute for Advanced Studies on Asia at Tokyo University from 2015 to 2016. He is the author of four books on the region—*Conspiracy Theories in the Arab World: Sources and Politics* (2010); *Qatar: Politics and the Challenges of Development* (2013); *Global Security Watch—Saudi Arabia* (2014); and *The Economy of the Gulf States* (2019)—in addition to various journal articles and other pieces on Middle Eastern studies.

Samantha Gross is director of the Energy Security and Climate Initiative at the Brookings Institution and was a 2021 Brookings—Robert Bosch Foundation Transatlantic Initiative Fellow in Berlin. She focuses on the intersection of energy, environment, and policy, including climate policy and international cooperation, energy geopolitics, and the global transition toward a decarbonized economy. She has been a visiting fellow at the King Abdullah Petroleum Studies and Research Center, where she authored work on clean energy cooperation and post–Paris Agreement climate policy. She was director of the Office of International Climate and Clean Energy at the US Department of Energy, where she directed US activities under the Clean Energy Ministerial; she was also director of Integrated Research at IHS CERA. Ms. Gross holds a BS in chemical engineering from the University of Illinois, an MS in environmental engineering from Stanford University, and an MBA from the University of California at Berkeley.

Nader Habibi is the Henry J. Leir Professor of Practice in the Economics of the Middle East at Brandeis University's Crown Center for Middle East Studies. Before joining Brandeis University in June 2007, he served as managing director of economic forecasting and risk analysis for Middle East and North Africa in Global Insight Ltd. Mr. Habibi has worked in academic and research institutions in Iran, Turkey, and the United States since 1987. He earned his master's degree in systems engineering and his PhD in economics from Michigan State University. His most recent research projects are economic relations of Middle Eastern countries with China; analysis of the excess supply of college graduates in Middle Eastern countries; and impact of economic sanctions on Iranian economy. Habibi also served as director of Islamic and Middle East Studies at Brandeis University, from August 2014 to August 2019. Links to his publications are available at https://naderhabibi.blogspot.com/.

Steffen Hertog is an associate professor of comparative politics at the London School of Economics and Political Science. His research interests include Gulf politics, Middle East political economy, political violence, and radicalization. Over the last fifteen years, he has undertaken a wide range of public policy work in the Middle East and North Africa (MENA) region on issues including labor market and migration reform, and public sector governance and economic diversification, in conjunction with institutions like the World Bank, the ILO, the OECD, and ESCWA. His book about Saudi state-building, *Princes, Brokers, and Bureaucrats: Oil and State in Saudi Arabia*, was published in 2011. He is the co-author, with Diego Gambetta, of *Engineers of Jihad: the Curious Connection between Violent Extremism and Education* (2016). He has published in journals including *World Politics, British Journal of Political Science, Socio-Economic Review, Review of International Political*

Economy, Comparative Studies in Society and History, European Journal of Sociology, and *International Journal of Middle East Studies.*

Martin Hvidt is an associate professor at the Center for Contemporary Middle East Studies, University of Southern Denmark and a former professor at Zayed University, Dubai (2013–2016). He received his PhD from Odense University in 1995 and was bestowed the prestigious Dr. Phil degree in 2019 by the University of Southern Denmark based on a higher doctoral dissertation titled "Social and Economic Development in the Contemporary Arab Gulf States." His research focuses on the economic and social development of the Arab Gulf countries, mainly during the past fifty years, encompassing development models, diversification, knowledge economy and societal planning. Dr. Hvidt is the author of several books and many journal articles and book chapters.

Nader Kabbani is senior fellow, director of research, and director of the Governance and Development Program at the Middle East Council on Global Affairs. He is also a nonresident senior fellow with the Foreign Policy Program at the Brookings Institution in Washington, DC. A development researcher and practitioner with over twenty years of experience, Kabbani previously served as director of research and senior fellow with the Brookings Doha Center and director of policy and research at the Silatech Foundation in Qatar. Kabbani was the founding director of the Syrian Development Research Centre at the Syria Trust for Development. During his career, Kabbani held positions on the faculty of the American University of Beirut and on the research staff of the US Department of Agriculture and the California State Senate. Kabbani has served on the advisory boards of several nonprofit organizations and social enterprises and has published a diverse set of policy papers and academic articles. He has served as a consultant for several international organizations, including the World Bank, the International Labor Organization, and the United Nations Development Programme. Kabbani has a BA from Claremont McKenna College and a PhD in economics from the Johns Hopkins University.

Samer Kherfi is the head of department and an associate professor of economics at the American University of Sharjah in the United Arab Emirates. He teaches introductory economics, labor economics, and graduate econometrics. His current research focuses on education and labor-market issues in the Middle East. He has served as an economic and statistical consultant to a number of national and international organizations and is a member of several technical, administrative, and research review committees. His research appears in book chapters and academic journals such as the *Journal of Economic Education*, *Quarterly Review of Economics and Finance*, and *Journal of Economic Studies*. He earned his PhD in economics from Simon Fraser University, Canada.

Rami George Khouri is an internationally syndicated political columnist and book author, journalist-in-residence, and director of global engagement at the American University of Beirut, and a nonresident senior fellow at the Harvard Kennedy School. He has also worked as the executive editor of the Beirut-based *Daily Star* newspaper, the editor-in-chief of the *Jordan Times*, and was awarded the Pax Christi International Peace Prize for 2006. He teaches or lectures annually at the American University of Beirut and Northeastern University. He has been a fellow and visiting scholar at Harvard, Mount Holyoke, Princeton, Syracuse, Northeastern, Villanova, Oklahoma, and Stanford universities. He also serves on the joint advisory board of the Northwestern University journalism school in Doha, Qatar.

Rory Miller is a professor of government at Georgetown University in Qatar, where he also leads the Small States Research Program. His teaching and research focuses on small states and regional security; intelligence and national security; and theories of external intervention. Miller was previously the head of the Middle East and Mediterranean studies program at King's College London, and held visiting professorships at King's College London (2014 to 2017) and Trinity College Dublin (2020 to 2021). He is a fellow of the Royal Historical Society and serves on several advisory boards. He is founding co-editor of Intelligence and National Security in Africa and the Middle East, a Cambridge University Press book series.

Omar H. Rahman is a fellow at the Middle East Council on Global Affairs. He is also a writer and political analyst specializing in Middle East politics more broadly and American foreign policy in the region. Previously, Rahman was a visiting fellow at the Brookings Doha Center, where he researched and wrote about Israel-Palestine, the Arab Gulf, and the growing intersection between the two. Prior to this, Rahman was a research analyst at the Arab Gulf States Institute in Washington, where he focused on the political economy of the Gulf states. His writing on the region has been published in the *Washington Post, Foreign Policy, The Guardian, Rolling Stone, The National*

Interest, Lawfare, VICE, PBS NewsHour, Quartz, Al-Jazeera English, and *The National,* among other outlets. Rahman's other work includes peer-reviewed policy papers and academic articles, including a chapter in the upcoming edited volume *What Is Israel/Palestine?* (2022). He is currently working on a book about Palestinian defragmentation in the post-Oslo era.

Natasha Ridge is the founding executive director of the Sheikh Saud bin Saqr Al Qasimi Foundation for Policy Research. Prior to this appointment, she was the acting director of research at the Dubai School of Government. Natasha has over twenty years of experience in the international education sector, which includes work in Singapore and Australia. She holds a doctorate of education in international education policy from Columbia University, and a master's in international and community development from Deakin University. Natasha has more than thirty publications, including a book entitled *Education and the Reverse Gender Divide in the Gulf States: Embracing the Global, Ignoring the Local* and another entitled *Philanthropy in Education: Diverse Perspectives and Global Trends.*

Theodosia Rossi is a doctoral student at the University of Cambridge, where she researches the history of mental institutions and psychiatric discourses in khedival Egypt. Her research is funded by the Cambridge Trust and Centre of Islamic Studies. She is also completing a master's degree in Arabic language pedagogy at Middlebury College. She previously worked as a research assistant at the Brookings Institution and as a consultant to the United Nations Development Programme. She holds a master's degree in modern Middle Eastern studies from the University of Oxford and a bachelor's degree in political science from the University of Chicago.

Jean-François Seznec is a nonresident senior fellow at the Atlantic Council's Global Energy Center. He is also an adjunct professor at Johns Hopkins School of Advanced International Studies and at Georgetown University's McDonough School of Business and School of Foreign Service. He co-authored, with Samer Mosis, the book *The Financial Markets of the Arab Gulf: Power, Politics and Money* (2019). He has twenty-five years of experience in international banking and finance, of which ten years were spent in the Middle East, including six years in Bahrain as a banker. Seznec has a PhD, an MA, and an MPhil in political science from Yale University, and an MA in international affairs from Columbia University. He has a BA in international affairs from Washington College.

Perla Srour-Gandon is a policy advisor for the Secretariat of the Committee on Foreign Affairs at the European Parliament. She is responsible for relations with the Middle East and Gulf countries, Common Foreign and Security Policy matters, and climate/energy diplomacy. She was previously an international relations officer for the European Commission's Directorate-General for Energy, dealing with EU energy relations with the Middle East region. She also worked as a scientific officer for the European Commission's Directorate-General for Research and Innovation, with responsibility for several research projects on foresight, energy issues, and Middle East and North Africa (MENA) countries. She holds a magistère of international relations from the University Panthéon-Sorbonne and a diplôme d'etudes approfondies from the Institut National des Langues et Civilisations Orientales (Paris). She is also the author of several papers and articles on geopolitics, energy, and economic diversification in the MENA region appearing in specialized reviews and EU policy publications.

Zach Vertin is an American writer, foreign policy expert, and diplomat. He spent the last fifteen years working on international peace and conflict issues at the United Nations and in various countries including Africa, Asia, and in the Middle East. He currently serves in the Biden administration as senior advisor to the US ambassador to the United Nations. He is a lecturer at Princeton University's School of Public and International Affairs and was previously a visiting fellow at the Brookings Institution's Foreign Policy program and Brookings Doha Center, where he led a project on the changing geopolitics of the Red Sea. Vertin also previously served in the Obama administration and as a senior analyst for the International Crisis Group. He has written and provided commentary for a wide range of international media, and his 2019 book, *A Rope from the Sky: The Making & Unmaking of the World's Newest State*, chronicles the birth of South Sudan, its subsequent collapse, and a reckoning with the limits of American influence amid a changing global landscape.

Steven Wright is an associate professor of international relations and an associate dean at Hamad bin Khalifa University. He previously served as the associate dean and the head of the Department of International Affairs at Qatar University. His research expertise covers three main areas: the international relations and political economy of the Arab Gulf states; energy geopolitics; and US foreign policy toward the Gulf region. He has written widely in these areas, and his work has been published in multiple languages, including Arabic, Japanese, French, and Polish. He has held research fellowships at the London School of Economics, Exeter University, and Durham University. He has been an invited keynote speaker at a wide range of events hosted by multinational corporations as well as leading organizations such as the World Bank and the government of Japan. He earned a PhD in international relations from Durham University in 2005.

Karen E. Young is a senior fellow and founding director of the Program on Economics and Energy at the Middle East Institute. She was a resident scholar at the American Enterprise Institute. She has taught courses at George Washington University and at the Johns Hopkins School of Advanced International Studies. She regularly teaches at the US Department of State Foreign Service Institute. Her analysis has appeared in *Bloomberg Opinion*, *Foreign Affairs*, *Foreign Policy*, the *Financial Times*, the *New York Times*, the *Wall Street Journal*, and the *Washington Post*. Dr. Young has contributed numerous chapters to edited volumes, and is the author of *The Political Economy of Energy, Finance and Security in the United Arab Emirates: Between the Majilis and the Market* (2014). Her new book, *The Economic Statecraft of the Gulf Arab States: Deploying Aid, Investment and Development in the Middle East* will be published in 2022.

Tarik M. Yousef is senior fellow and director of the Middle East Council on Global Affairs. His research focuses on the political economy of policy reform in the Arab world. He has authored numerous articles and co-edited several volumes including *Young Generation Awakening: Economics, Society, and Policy on the Eve of the Arab Spring* (2016) and *Public Sector Reform in the Middle East and North Africa; Lessons of Experience for a Region in Transition* (2020) His policy experience includes working at the International Monetary Fund, the World Bank, and the United Nations. He has a PhD in economics from Harvard University.

Tian Zhang has been a research analyst for Saudi Arabia at the International Monetary Fund (IMF) since November 2018. In this role, she is responsible for data collection and analysis for the IMF's published reports on Saudi Arabia and the Gulf Cooperation Council. She previously worked at the Institute of International Finance, where she studied economic diversification in the Gulf Cooperation Council. She holds a master's degree in international economics from George Washington University.

Index

Note: Tables are indicated by a "t" following the page number and Figures are indicated by an "f" following the page number.

Printed in Great Britain
by Amazon

23628239R00179